Public Sector Accounting and Financial Control

The Chapman & Hall Series in Accounting and Finance

Consulting editors
John Perrin, Emeritus Professor of the University of Warwick and Price Waterhouse Fellow in Public Sector Accounting at the University of Exeter; Richard M.S. Wilson, Professor of Management and Accounting at the University of Keele; and L.C.L. Skerratt, Professor of Financial Accounting at the University of Manchester.

H.M. Coombs and D.E. Jenkins
Public Sector Financial Management

J.C. Drury
Management and Cost Accounting (3rd edn)
(Also available: **Students' Manual, Teachers' Manual, Spreadsheet Applications Manual** and a set of **OHP Masters**)

C.R. Emmanuel, D.T. Otley and K. Merchant
Accounting for Management Control (2nd edn)
(Also available: **Teachers' Guide**)

C.R. Emmanuel, D.T. Otley and K. Merchant (editors)
Readings in Accounting for Management Control

D. Henley, A. Likierman, J. Perrin, M. Evans, I. Lapsley and J. Whiteoak
Public Sector Accounting and Financial Control (4th edn)

R.C. Laughlin and R.H. Gray
Financial Accounting: method and meaning
(Also available: **Teachers' Guide**)

G.A. Lee
Modern Financial Accounting (4th edn)

T.A. Lee
Income and Value Measurement (3rd edn)

T.A. Lee
Company Financial Reporting (2nd edn)

T.A. Lee
Cash Flow Accounting

S.P. Lumby
Investment Appraisal and Financing Decisions (4th edn)
(Also available: **Students' Manual**)

A.G. Puxty and J.C. Dodds
Financial Management: method and meaning (2nd edn)
(Also available: **Teachers' Guide**)

J.M. Samuels, F.M. Wilkes and R.E. Brayshaw
Management of Company Finance (5th edn)
(Also available: **Students' Manual**)

B.C. Williams and B.J. Spaul
IT and Accounting: the impact of information technology

R.M.S. Wilson and Wai Fong Chua
Managerial Accounting: method and meaning (2nd edn)
(Also available: **Teachers' Guide**)

Public Sector Accounting and Financial Control

Fourth edition

D. HENLEY
Formerly Comptroller and Auditor General

A. LIKIERMAN
*Professor of Accounting and Financial Control
at the London Business School*

J. PERRIN
*Emeritus Professor, University of Warwick
Honorary Fellow of the University of Exeter*

M. EVANS
Head of Technical Division, CIPFA

I. LAPSLEY
*Professor of Accounting
University of Edinburgh*

J. WHITEOAK
*Group Director of Finance and Management Services
Cheshire County Council*

Published in cooperation with the Chartered Institute of
Public Finance and Accountancy

CHAPMAN & HALL
University and Professional Division
London · Glasgow · New York · Tokyo · Melbourne · Madras

Learning Resources
Centre

Published by Chapman & Hall, 2-6 Boundary Row, London SE1 8HN

Chapman & Hall, 2-6 Boundary Row, London SE1 8HN, UK

Blackie Academic & Professional, Wester Cleddens Road, Bishopbriggs, Glasgow G64 2NZ, UK

Chapman & Hall, 29 West 35th Street, New York NY10001, USA

Chapman & Hall Japan, Thomson Publishing Japan, Hirakawacho Nemoto Building, 6F, 1-7-11 Hirakawa-cho, Chiyoda-ku, Tokyo 102, Japan

Chapman & Hall Australia, Thomas Nelson Australia, 102 Dodds Street, South Melbourne, Victoria 3205, Australia

Chapman & Hall India, R. Seshadri, 32 Second Main Road, CIT East, Madras 600 035, India

First edition 1983
Reprinted 1983, 1985
Second edition 1986
Reprinted 1987
Third edition 1989
Reprinted 1989, 1990(twice)
Fourth edition 1992
Reprinted 1993

© 1983, 1986, 1989 D. Henley, C. Holtham, A Likierman and J. Perrin; 1992 D. Henley, A. Likierman, J. Perrin, M. Evans. I. Lapsley and J. Whiteoak

Typeset by 10/11.5pt Astor by Graphicraft Typesetters Ltd, Hong Kong
Printed in Great Britain by Clays Ltd, St Ives Plc.

ISBN 0 412 46380 6

Contents

Preface

The principal aim of this book remains the same as in previous editions – to help to improve financial management, control and accounting throughout the public sector by financial practitioners and those who are studying to join them. A second aim of the book is to assist students of public finance and administration, or of economics, management and political science more widely, to become aware of the variety and complexity of the financial and accounting arrangements existing in the public sector. Students of private sector accounting may benefit from understanding of the public sector, and from comparing the practices and problems of the two sectors.

In the brief three years since the third edition of this book there have been many changes in public sector accounting and finance. Central government has experienced the implementation and evolution of new structural and managerial financial and accounting initiatives. The nationalized industries have changed less, aside from being fewer in number. But local government has experienced major change, especially in its financing arrangements, and more especially in the consequences of the waxing and waning of the community charge. Perhaps the greatest pace of change has been in the National Health Service, with the introduction of new bases for resource allocation, capital asset accounting and charging, the internal market, NHS Trusts, and fund-holding budgets for some family doctors.

All the text in this fourth edition has been fully revised and updated, and more of it has been completely rewritten than in the last two editions – because of the pace of change, but also because three new contributors have joined the author team continuing from the previous edition: Martin Evans, Head of Technical Division, CIPFA; Irvine Lapsley, Professor of Accounting, University of Edinburgh; and John Whiteoak, Group Director, Finance and Management Services, Cheshire County Council.

Retained from the third edition are the range and order of chapters, and the updating and location of study questions, and of source references and bibliography, at the back of the book. The authors are grateful to the Chartered Association of Certified Accountants (ACCA) and to the Chartered Institute of Management Accountants (CIMA) for the use of selected past examination questions. They are grateful also to the Chartered Institute of Public Finance and Accountancy (CIPFA), both for the use of past examination questions and for wider support and technical information.

Foreword

Noel Hepworth, OBE, IPFA, DPA
*Director, Chartered Institute of Public Finance and
Accountancy*

Accountancy in the public sector is about financial management. Those
accountants who define their role either implicitly or explicitly in traditional terms as a keeper or inspector of accounts are not able to
provide the style of accountancy expertise which public sector financial
management now requires. Therefore accountants, if they are to be
successful, while they need an accounting technical background, also
require a thorough understanding of the political and economic
climate in which the public sector in general, and their part in particular, has to operate. But they also need to recognize that politics
is as much about relationships between institutions as between
political parties.

The public sector, though, is not a uniform organization. Parts of
it are very similar to and are subject to the same influences as commercial organizations, yet because they are part of the public sector,
the final sanction of bankruptcy does not exist. Other parts operate as
commercial organizations but in practice are in their own field monopolies and are consequently subject to constraints other than those of
the market-place to prevent exploitation of the consumer or to promote
value for money. Other parts of the public sector could in no way be
described as running commercial services, hence trading and profit
and loss accounts are entirely inappropriate ideas, but the problems
remain of how to contain costs, measure performance and promote
value for money.

Value for money is of underlying concern throughout the whole of
the public sector. It surfaces in the need for consistent planning, for
clarity in the statement of institutional or policy objectives, for the
adequate recording of events and for review of achieved performance
against objectives. Value for money is an expression of the economy,
the efficiency and the effectiveness with which the institutions of the
public sector operate.

The different parties involved in the management of public sector
institutions have different interests. Perhaps the most important difference of interest is between the politician and the professional
manager or administrator. The politician has a relatively short time

horizon, often no more distant than the date of the next election; the professional manager is concerned with the long-term success of his service or activity but he has to discharge his responsibilities under whichever political party controls the government or local authority. The difference is most marked over attitudes towards capital investment where consistency of decision and long lead times may be required but are not always forthcoming, for example investment in nuclear power generation. Again, political success in terms of potential electoral gain may be regarded from the professional manager's point of view as a failure. An example of this is a decision to manipulate the prices of the products of the nationalized industries for reasons which are unrelated to the interests of those industries, to optimal resource use, or even in the longer term to the interests of their customers. Divergence of interest may sometimes emerge between different parts of the public sector – for example, between the Treasury and other central government departments, between both and the nationalized industries, between central and local government, between the Department of Health and the regional health authorities. These differences of interest may lead to a concentration by one party on a definition of success to which the other may not subscribe. The Treasury may define success as causing spending departments and local authorities to keep within defined public expenditure plans, and the nationalized industries to keep within their external financing limits. Their paramount concern is the management of the economy and the control of total public spending. But central government also has a concern about the efficiency with which the public sector operates, and cash limits and external financing limits can be used in a crude generalized way to impose a resource squeeze upon the affected organization in an attempt to force out greater efficiency. In a sense this does create the opportunity for a coincidence of interest with the manager of the industry or local authority service. He has a direct interest in maximizing value for money in order to enable him to provide the most efficient and effective service in response to demand, but in practice this coincidence of interest may not emerge and in the face of constant pressure on public sector resources the relationship between central government and the other institutions of the public sector has tended to be one of greater or less friction.

Finance permeates most organizations because it is the measure of resource use and of priorities, but to provide a sensible message to management, finance needs to be related to work done or performance. The traditional attitude towards budget preparation and the provision of information to management has been a concern with cash. Obviously this is important because of the significance of cash flow management. In the private sector the developing position of the company treasurer (a post which exists also in some nationalized industries) recognizes this. But the accountant's role, particularly in the public sector, goes beyond that. The emphasis of central government controls upon the institutions of the public sector is certainly upon cash and the accountant needs to have the expertise to understand how far in the interests of his organization the rules governing the cash controls can be developed and defined. The accountant, though, needs to strive to establish a workable relationship between cash and organization performance because only the two combined give any real understanding of the efficiency with which the organization is operating. And that relationship needs to be established on a systematic basis, not limited to the result of *ad hoc* enquiries about which management may occasionally think.

In the trading part of the public sector, target rates of return can be established and performance compared with the target. But elsewhere the problem is more difficult to solve. In theory output measures should be developed as indicators of performance, but in practice such measures are difficult, indeed frequently impossible, to devise. The main source of information available to the accountant and manager is therefore about inputs – the number of employees, their pay levels, expenditure on textbooks and class materials, the number of hospital beds maintained; or at best 'intermediate outputs' – miles of motorway constructed, usage of vehicles, occupancy of hospital beds and so on. The financial manager in these circumstances needs a comparative yardstick to evaluate performance. That yardstick may be the performance of the same organization in a previous period or the performance of another organization.

Local authorities are particularly good at publishing comparative information at the most detailed level. Within the health service comparative information is also available, but not easily accessible to the public. The nationalized industries have developed a wide range of performance measures individually but there is no way of systematically comparing the discharge of similar functions between industries. To make comparative information more widely available for analysis would be particularly helpful to the public sector accountant in providing management with better performance indicators.

While the public sector accountant has the responsibility of developing systematic arrangements to assist management in comparing and improving the performance of the service or institution, the public sector auditor has, among other duties, the complementary role of examining whether management actually performs that task efficiently. In this way, the responsibility of the public sector auditor, apart from the auditor of the nationalized industries which are subject to the same type of audit as private companies, goes beyond the responsibility of auditors to companies in the private sector. Like them, the public sector auditor has to satisfy him- or herself that the accounts have been prepared in accordance with statutory and constitutional requirements and regulations, and that proper accounting practices have been observed in their compilation. But in addition to this there are other responsibilities, including those which in the local authority context take the form of ensuring that the accounts 'do not disclose any significant loss arising from waste, extravagance, inefficient financial administration, poor value for money, mistake or other cause'. That is a fairly wide, not to say daunting, remit.

The Chartered Institute of Public Finance and Accountancy has recognized these special responsibilities in its training arrangements for accountants in the public sector. It not only aims to provide basic technical skills but also emphasizes within its training scheme the need to develop financial management and audit skills, including analytical skills, within the context of the special requirements of the public sector including a knowledge of public sector finance, economics and institutional relationships.

This book is written for this style of accountant and auditor, and for others engaged in financial management in the public sector. The authors have examined the financial control mechanisms that affect the different institutions within the public sector at various levels, including those of policy formulation, policy control and intra-public sector institutional relationships.

Critics of the public sector tend to adopt a simplistic approach to the management of its institutions. They frequently fail to recognize the political element in management and to detach their own political judgements in making criticisms of the non-political managers in the public sector. The skill of the successful professional manager in the public sector is to be able to cooperate fully with the political policy maker but to retain that degree of independence which enables him to work just as closely with the present political policy-maker's opponent should that prove necessary in the future, and to retain the confidence of both. But to do that the manager has to have a thorough understanding of the environment in which he operates as well as the appropriate techniques. This is an authoritative up-to-date book, now in its fourth edition, which fills a significant gap and will help managers gain that understanding.

1

Introduction

Financial management and control issues in the public sector have become the focus of increasing attention in recent years. Cuts in public expenditure have been one cause. These have put pressure on public authorities to maintain services with less money (in real terms) and to do so they have had to improve their financial analysis so that action can be taken to improve efficiency and value for money. Another cause has been the call for improved measures of performance, as part of pressure for stronger accountability. This has brought accounting practices in public services under scrutiny. A third cause has been pressure within the accountancy profession to standardize accounting practices and to examine whether public sector practices should not be brought more into line with those in the private sector. Finally, on the heels of government interest in cutting expenditure and trying to improve performance and accountability in the public services, all the professional accountancy institutes have become more interested in public sector practice.

At the same time, many accountants in the public services have become more conscious of, and more concerned about, the differences of methodology and of philosophy which have separated their work from that of the other branches of the accountancy profession. This may have been the result of interests widened by the various (aborted) attempts to integrate the profession. It may also stem from cross-fertilization of thinking resulting from the increased mobility of accountants from different backgrounds. There were certainly moves into new branches of public service employment following the reorganization in the 1970s and 1980s of local authorities and the National Health Service. The moves to encourage the public sector to behave more like the private sector and privatization in the 1980s also helped to break down a number of barriers. These pressures have become more insistent and more political in recent years, as those who believe that the public sector was chronically inefficient moved to the centre of the political stage. Such people maintained with increasing vehemence that the only way to remedy the position was to transfer the provision of services where at all possible to the private sector, and that what remained in the public sector should follow private sector financial and management practices.

In general the public sector has not succeeded in mobilizing support for its own ways of doing things, and the political attacks at national level have been reinforced by calls at the local elected level for improved efficiency. All this has undoubtedly led to a lower morale in many public sector bodies, even though there are considerable misgivings about whether much of what is done in the private sector is in practice transferable. Accountants have not been immune to this fall in morale, though their status within the public sector may well have risen because of the increased importance attached to financial skills.

As a result of all these pressures and influences, there has been a growing self-consciousness among accountants in the public sector about following practices which are markedly different from those in the private sector or which do not receive the understanding and approval of fellow accountants and financial managers. There was a good deal of questioning, not only in the public sector but also throughout the accounting profession, about whether or not some public sector accounting practices were conceptually sound. The attempts in recent years to increase the degree of cooperation between separate professional institutes in the quest for improvement and greater standardization of accounting and financial practices have served to intensify this self-questioning. A more tangible manifestation of the need for an active public sector dimension to accounting rule-making has been the existence, since 1982, of the Public Sector Liaison Committee to advise on the application of accounting standards to the public sector. This was a standing sub-committee first of the Accounting Standards Committee, and since 1991 of the Accounting Standards Board. The result of their activities has not necessarily been complete consistency in public sector financial reporting, but at least there is greater clarity about the nature and problems arising from the inconsistencies. These issues are dealt with more fully in Chapter 2.

THE ISSUES

Some of the financial and accounting issues which have been the subject of public debate, for example external reporting and monitoring, are common to several parts of the public sector, and these are dealt with as such in this book. Some of these are conceptual issues, some practical. Some are related to external reporting and monitoring, others to internal financial control. But two general questions arise.

The first concerns how specific accounting and control problems should be tackled in a public sector context. Such problems arise because of the distinctive constitutional, economic and financial features of public sector bodies. These are bound to affect the way in which their operations are accounted for and controlled. Areas of special concern include, for example, the accounting treatment of capital equipment and the need to provide non-financial indicators to supplement financial data because of the non-profit basis of most parts of the public sector.

The second question, following naturally from the first, is how far should public sector practice relate to practice in the private sector and in what respects, if any, should it diverge? This question has been asked about most aspects of financial reporting, including the form of financial statements and the treatment of individual items in the accounts, such as capital asset valuation and depreciation. The question is also asked about internal financial and economic issues, such as the use of investment appraisal techniques and monitoring.

That such issues cannot be taken in isolation applies to almost all the main aspects of this book. For example, questions about the form of external financial statements cannot be separated from the nature and objectives of particular public sector operations and the fact that there are a variety of users for financial statements in the public sector, with different kinds of needs. Similarly, the relationship between auditing practices in the public and private sectors cannot be examined without looking at the different ways in which account-ability is exercised for public sector institutions compared to the purposes and forms of accountability of private concerns.

A number of other issues span the main chapters. In the area of financial reporting for example, there is the question of how far there should be uniformity, and how much flexibility ought to be allowed between similar types of institutions. Another recurrent theme is the issue of how accounting rules should be developed, while on the use of external financial information the nature and rights of different user groups are not always clear. As for internal financial control, the pressure on resources has in most cases given rise to a call for im-proved systems for monitoring, not only internally but also for exter-nal disclosure and performance review. Finally, on a more personal level, the role and status of accountants within their organizations and in relation to the accountancy profession as a whole continues to be a matter of concern to many public sector accountants.

PUBLIC SECTOR DIVERSITY

The public sector is both extremely diverse and, despite privatizations, extremely large. Even ignoring the large sums expended on transfer payments (such as pensions, welfare benefits and subsidies), the total expenditure of the public sector on employing people, goods and services in carrying out both trading and public service activities is enormous – over 30% of the gross domestic product. Figure 1.1 gives an idea of the relative size of net public sector expenditure analysed in four ways. It can be seen that local authority expenditure amounts to about a quarter of all public expenditure, and expenditure on health rather more than 10%. The nationalized industries, by contrast, make little overall demand on the public purse because, although the amounts they spend are large, they are trading entities and as such recoup their costs in whole or part from their customers. Figures 1.2 and 1.3 give the context for public expenditure growth over a period of 30 years and Table 1.1 shows the changes in the composition of expenditure in the 1980s.

While the scale of the public sector is essentially a matter of political choice, the financing of whatever size is chosen through a variety of combinations of taxes, rates, charges and prices is a matter of both politics and economics. In this book the financing of the public sector as a whole is taken as given. The concern is rather with the financial management and control of public sector activities, and with the accounting, financial control and audit practices whose underlying aims are to provide satisfactory accountability and promote the best service and value for money.

The private sector has managed to achieve a higher degree of standardization of financial, accounting and audit practices than has so far been achieved in the public sector. This is not surprising. There are some differences in accounting practices between, for example, industrial firms, retail firms and banks, but their common basic objectives relate to profitability, and managers, shareholders and employees of all three types of private sector organization have broadly the same information needs. They relate in particular to information on current profits and the stability and trend of profits (for guidance on valuation and risk) and, for lenders, further details on assets, liabilities and capital structures.

In contrast, the public sector has a considerable diversity of activities and aims. While nationalized industries operate commercially as trading entities, government departments, local authorities and health authorities do not exist to produce goods or services for sale, do not have shareholders, and are funded by compulsory levies – rates and taxes – or by borrowing on public credit. It is not therefore surprising that the results are presented in a different way. Another factor in explaining the diversity even within the public services sector is the factor of history. As an example, whereas local government has a long history of relatively autonomous development of its own distinctive accounting practices, the history of the National Health Service is much briefer and its accounting methods have been more closely

£ billion

By department etc.	By sector	By function	By economic category
Department of Social Security — 55.9		Social Security — 58.6	Pay and other current expenditure on goods and services — 104.4
Department of the Environment* — 28.8	Central government † — 161.7	Education and science — 27.5	
Ministry of Defence — 22.1		Health — 27.8	
Department of Health — 22.6		Defence — 22.1	Current grants to persons — 67.8
Scotland, Wales and Northern Ireland — 20.1		Law, order and protective services — 11.4	
Other departments — 37.1		Environmental services — 7.7	
Local authority self-financed expenditure — 14.5	Local authorities ‡ — 57.3	Other functions — 40.9	Net capital expenditure on assets — 11.6
Central government debt interest — 17.8		General government debt interest — 18.3	Subsidies, capital grants and lending — 12.1
Other § — 3.4	Other § — 3.4	Other § — 8.0	General government debt interest — 18.3
			Other § — 8.0

Planning total (excluding privatization proceeds)

General government expenditure (excluding privatization proceeds) £222.3 billion

Fig. 1.1 The planning total and general government expenditure: how it is planned and spent, 1990–1 (£ billion).

* Includes revenue support grant and non-domestic rate payments and certain transitional grants to local authorities in England. Comparable items are included in the figures for Scotland and Wales.
† Includes grants, subsidies and net lending to public corporations, including nationalized industries. It also includes central government debt interest (£17.8 billion).
‡ The total is made up of £42.7 billion financed by support from central government and £14.5 billion financed from local authorities own resources. It includes local authority debt interest (£5.2 billion).
§ Includes the national accounts adjustments. The differences in these figures reflect the different treatment of local authority debt interest and market and overseas borrowing of public corporations in the analyses of GGE by function and economic category.

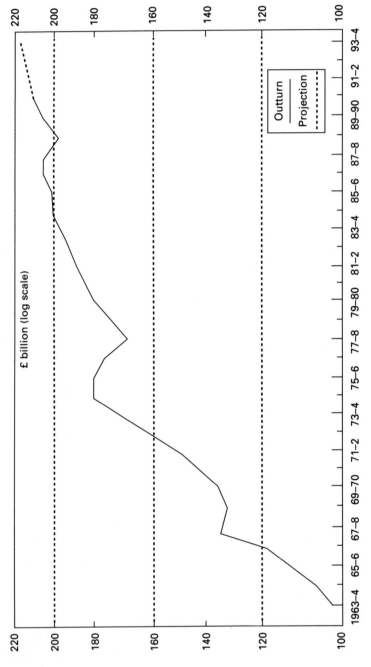

Fig. 1.2 General government expenditure (excluding privatization proceeds) in real terms 1963–4 to 1993–4. Cash figures are adjusted to 1989/90 price levels by excluding the effect of general inflation as measured by the GDP deflator adjusted to remove the distortion caused by the abolition of domestic rates. (Source: *Public Expenditure Analyses to 1993–94*, Cm. 1520, p. 5.)

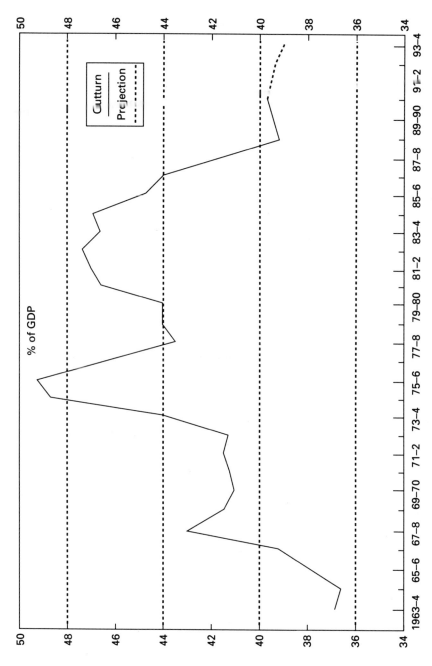

Fig. 1.3 General government expenditure (excluding privatization proceeds) 1963–4 to 1993–4. The figures and adjusted to remove the distortion caused by the abolition of domestic rates. (Source: *Public Expenditure Analyses to 1993–94*, Cm. 1520, p. 4.)

Table 1.1 Percentage distribution of total expenditure on services by function

	1980–1 outturn	1990–1 estimated outturn
Defence	12.2	11.3
Overseas services, including overseas aid	1.5	1.4
Agriculture, fisheries, food and forestry	1.8	1.5
Trade, industry, energy and employment	5.3	4.0
of which: Employment and training	2.1	1.6
Transport	4.7	4.1
Housing	6.2	2.9
Other environmental services	4.3	3.9
Law, order and protective services	4.3	5.8
Education and science	14.5	14.0
Arts and libraries	0.6	0.7
Health and personal social services	15.4	16.8
of which: Health	13.0	14.2
Social security	26.3	29.9
Miscellaneous expenditure*	3.1	3.7
Total	100.0	100.0

* Includes contributions to the European Communities and activities required for the general maintenance of government, such as tax collection, and the registration of population.
Source: *Public Expenditure Analysis to 1993–94*, Cm. 1520, p. 14.

directed by the monitoring and control requirements of central government.

For the future therefore it is still questionable how far and how fast it will be desirable and feasible to effect greater standardization of financial, accounting and reporting practices between the private and public sectors, and between different types of non-trading public sector bodies. Agreement on change between a number of interest groups would be needed. Many of these interest groups have their own reasons to oppose change and that change would then have to be reflected in extensive amendments to government regulations and perhaps legislation. For anyone seeking to understand the pros and cons of change, a clear understanding of the differences between public sector bodies and their financial practices is essential. This book sets out many of those differences in some detail.

THE AUTHORS' APPROACH

The diversity in financial, accounting and control practices in the various parts of the public sector is reflected in the use of authors who are experts in their own areas. Each author of this book takes responsibility for the coverage and views expressed in his own chapter(s). The authors claim no consensus on the detail of any standardized model of public sector accounting and finance in the future. They are deeply grateful to numerous contacts – too numerous to mention individually – within the several branches of the public sector, who have given much time to the reading of drafts and the framing of advice.

2

Financial reporting in
the public sector

Financial reporting in the public sector is a key element in the accountability of public sector bodies. This chapter deals with those elements of external reporting which cover financial matters, the rules for which vary greatly between different parts of the public sector. The objectives of public sector financial reports are first analysed, then the rules and potential users are categorized. After discussing what rights to financial information might mean in practice, the chapter goes on to provide an analysis of the differences between financial reports in the public and private sectors and a discussion of some current issues in financial reporting. The chapter concludes with details of what might be expected from a well-presented financial report.

INTRODUCTION

In the reporting of their activities, as in all other public sector accounting and control matters, the public sector cannot be treated as a single entity. It is true that there are **some** common factors in the financial reports of United Kingdom public sector bodies which mean that it is also possible to identify differences from private sector financial reports. But within the public sector there are a variety of organizational and functional arrangements which give rise to a similar variety of reporting arrangements. One is that not every public sector body has a formal requirement even to produce a published annual report (health authorities, for example) though many do anyway. So while there will be at least some exceptions to almost every generalization about financial reporting, this chapter is intended to give an overview of the financial aspects of published annual reports, not only the formal financial statements but also those aspects of the reports which deal with performance in financial terms. It therefore excludes those elements which are of a purely descriptive or policy nature, though the boundaries are often difficult to draw in practice.

The degree to which trading is involved is the key element in whether the financial reports follow private sector practice. At one end of the spectrum come those trading concerns which are very similar to private sector organizations. Nationalized industries, such as British Coal, come into this category. At the other end come those bodies where there is almost no trading element, such as health authorities and most central government departments. In between come a host of different types where there is a combination of trading and non-trading activity – local authorities, some central government agencies, etc.

But even trading organizations in the public sector cannot be compared in a straightforward way to those in the private sector. The very fact that they are in the public sector at all normally means that they are subject to non-commercial constraints and have objectives which are likely to conflict with purely commercial considerations. If they are monopolies they will be subject to political and other limitations on the exercise of their monopoly power. For example, the Civil Aviation Authority would not be expected to increase their charges to airlines to a level which exploited their position.

Even if trading organizations are not monopolies, they are likely to have restrictions on seeking to increase their revenues regardless of the wider social and economic implications. Thus there has been great moral pressure not only on central and local government but also on some nationalized industries to 'Buy British'. British Airways, when nationalized, was under pressure for many years to buy British planes and undertake certain non-commercial obligations such as flying some uneconomic routes for reasons of national prestige.

Finally, it is worth noting that categories do not always cross international boundaries. Thus in his 1978 report *Financial Accounting in Non-business Organisations*, Professor Robert Anthony divided United States non-profit organizations into two types:

1. 'Those whose financial resources are obtained entirely, or almost entirely, from revenues from the sale of goods and services';
2. 'Those who obtain a significant amount of financial resources from sources other than the sale of goods and services'.

The emphasis on privatization and revenue generation in the UK in the past few years has meant that the variety of 'types' has greatly increased and there is now a spectrum of many different kinds of organizations.

THE OBJECTIVES AND FUNCTIONS OF PUBLIC SECTOR FINANCIAL REPORTS

Despite the diversity of public sector organizations, there are some similarities between the broad objectives and functions of their financial statements, though all do not apply in all cases.

1. Compliance and stewardship:
   (a) to provide authorities and users with the assurance that there has been conformity with legal and other mandatory requirements in the organization's use of resources.
2. Accountability and retrospective reporting:
   (a) to monitor performance and evaluate management, providing a basis for looking at trends over time, achievement against published objectives and comparison with other similar organizations (if any);
   (b) to enable outsiders to have cost information on goods or services provided, and to enable them to assess efficiency and effectiveness in the use of the resources made available to the organization.
3. Planning and authorization information:
   (a) to provide the basis for planning future policy and activities;
   (b) to provide supporting information for further funds to be authorized.
4. Viability:
   (a) to help readers judge whether the organization can continue to provide goods or services in the future.
5. Public relations:
   (a) to give the organization the opportunity to put forward a statement of its achievements to influential users, employees and the public.
6. Source of facts and figures:
   (a) to provide information for the wide variety of interest groups who want to find out about the organization.

What is published varies greatly in the relative emphasis given to each of these objectives and functions but throughout the public sector the importance of public relations is steadily increasing. Indeed some published documents are effectively **only** exercises in public relations and the financial information plays a relatively minor role or is relegated to an additional, purely technical, document. On the other hand some public bodies are required to publish only accounts and do not publish any more information to expand on them. The position of some major central government documents, moreover, is different to that of other sectors, as Chapter 4 makes clear. These have a planning focus and some are used to support requests for public funds.

WHAT ARE THE RULES FOR FINANCIAL REPORTING?

There are four different types of rules for financial reporting by public sector organizations.

The law

Financial statements are governed by a legal framework, though the relevant legislation varies considerably from one part of the public sector to another. As examples, for local authorities in England and Wales, the 1980 Local Government Planning and Land Act gave powers to the Secretary of State to regulate the publication of information. For nationalized industries and bodies such as government trading funds, the relevant sections of the current Companies Acts are normally applied, with any necessary amendment or extension by any specific legislation by which a body has been set up or is governed.

Accounting standards

The SSAPs (Statements of Standard Accounting Practice) developed first by the Accounting Standards Committee (ASC) and now by the Accounting Standards Board (ASB) are framed in terms of private sector organizations. Technically the position is that they apply to 'all financial statements whose purpose is to give a true and fair view', a technical term not used in much of the public sector. The distinction in practice is less clear. Some SSAPs have obvious applications to public sector organizations, others do not. So SSAP 3, which deals with earnings per share, is clearly not relevant to organizations without share capital, while SSAP 2 (Disclosure of Accounting Policies) could potentially relate to every organization with financial statements. There are also grey areas where the position is less clear, notably where a public sector body is involved in trading, or where only part of an SSAP might be applicable.

There is a further difference between the public and private sectors in the application of SSAPs. In the private sector there is a constant tension between standard-setters and companies which have to abide by the standards. In the public sector such tension is far less, not least because of the lower expectations of public sector organizations about how much freedom is open to them. Nevertheless there may well be some tension between the government (effectively the Treasury in this field) and the public sector bodies that are under its wing. While the Treasury generally wishes to keep a sharp eye on developments and has made clear that it wishes to have the final say on their accounting practices to reflect the needs of financial control and public policy, some public bodies may be keen to have rules that mirror their particular requirements. Thus some may want to follow private sector practice, others to have special rules that reflect their own particular preoccupations.

In deciding the form of the accounts, the Treasury will not necessarily lay down the precise requirements for public sector organizations, indeed there are many occasions when it makes clear that it wishes them to follow best commercial practice. The requirements will normally follow the principles underlying what the ASB stipulates for the private sector, except where clearly inappropriate.

The ASB, like the ASC before it, set up a Public Sector Liaison Committee to deal with the public sector dimension of accounting standard setting. However, the approach of the ASB has been very different in one element of standard setting that was a feature of the ASC's regime. The ASC had a practice of providing a seal of approval for specific rules by 'franking' Statements of Recommended Accounting Practice (SORPs) which were developed by bodies representing parts of the public sector. Thus local authorities and universities were both covered by franked SORPs.

The ASB, however, neither franks nor issues SORPs. Instead, after recognizing the responsible body, which may be either in the private or public sector, and ensuring that the process has its prior approval, the ASB will issue a 'negative assurance statement'. This phrase (which apparently damns with faint praise, but has a clear technical meaning) is designed to confirm that there are no issues of principle which the Board considers unacceptable in current accounting practice, that the SORP is not in conflict with an existing or proposed accounting standard and has been prepared in accordance with the ASB's code of practice.

Accounting practice

This provides a framework for decisions about how items should be treated by those compiling the accounts. The basic structure of financial reports and the treatment of items which go into them have been developed over many years as part of accounting practice. For much of the public sector the framework is derived from accepted practice by professional accountants, though central government relies little on accepted practice and is bound much more by rules (see below).

Specific rules

In many cases there are rules laid down about how the whole of one part of the public sector, or indeed individual organizations within it, should lay out their financial statements. Within government, the sponsoring department for a public body will issue any directions or discuss codes of practice, though, as already noted, the Treasury will be highly influential behind the scenes. Thus while the nationalized industries have received directions on their accounts from the sponsoring departments, the Treasury determines many of the key aspects of each direction. Parliamentary committees may also be influential in asking for certain kinds of information to be included in published reports, though they can do no more than recommend.

It is also worth remembering that the organizational links of some public bodies are reflected in their accounts. Education and the police, for example, cannot be seen in isolation from local authority accounts.

USERS OF FINANCIAL REPORTS

When looking at many public sector financial statements it is not always clear who the intended readers are. Sometimes this may be a reflection of the multiplicity of audiences for these statements. At other times, those who compile the statements are evidently not clear themselves about their potential readership. This could include the following groups.

Elected members

Financial reports are very important in informing elected members, either as individuals or collectively, about the way in which the organization has fulfilled its functions. A distinction, however, needs to be made between Members of Parliament and elected members of local authorities. The reports provide both sets of elected members with information for assessing policy, judging efficiency and effectiveness, and providing the assurance that spending is within budget and has been on approved activities. But while Members of Parliament have no responsibility for the information (which they receive from the government), local authority members are themselves responsible for the information which is produced, though in practice there is little participation in the process of compilation.

Members of Parliament use examination of the reports of some public sector organizations, such as nationalized industries, as a point of entry for monitoring their activities. Other bodies will be under Parliamentary scrutiny only if there is a scandal.

The public as voters and/or taxpayers

Those who pay for the services provided, whether or not they are also consumers, will want to know how money is being spent on different types of activity. They will also want to evaluate performance, ensure that there is value for money in what is provided and that the interests of consumers are being served.

This group will also want information on the relationship between budget and actual spending and whether such spending was on approved activities. Where the performance of elected members is being judged, the statements may even be used to decide whether there are grounds for change.

The media can help to inform the public on developments and interpret the complexities of financial information for them. Although reporting is patchy and often sensationalized, at its best the media can play an important role in public perception of the relative importance of issues.

The customers or clients

Those who are the customers/clients (or equivalent) of the service provided by the public sector organization may well wish to know how the service is organized and its prospects for the future. Financial matters may also be of interest – students, for example, may want to know more about the distribution of resources within a university or local authority tenants about the position of the housing budget. However, the financial reports are less likely to be used by individuals than by pressure groups and representative organizations (such as community health councils in the Health Service) looking after the interests of groups of consumers or clients. Such organizations will generally need to interpret complex financial information to those who are less financially aware.

Employees

This is not a group with homogenous interests and the preoccupations of different members (even among the management) are likely to vary considerably. Thus top management do not normally have to rely on what is available through external financial reports, but middle and junior management may well find published reports useful in putting their own efforts in perspective and published reports have often been used to help internal communication in this way. The process of compiling the report will also provide a focus for top management having to agree on how policies are presented and explained to all user groups. Those who are not members of the management group or, more commonly, their representatives, will be interested in the prospects for security of employment and wage settlements.

Customers and suppliers

Those buying from, or selling to, the public body will be interested in the organization's plans and position. Customers will be specifically interested in the future security of their supplies, suppliers in the financial strength of their customers.

Government

A number of government bodies are likely to be interested in the financial reports of other public sector bodies. Each of the major parts of the public sector will have a 'sponsor' department with specific responsibilities – the Department of the Environment for local authorities, the Department of Health for health authorities, etc. Individual public sector organizations also have sponsor departments and each major government department will have a larger number of bodies reporting to it. Two taken at random are:

1. the British Council reports to the Foreign and Commonwealth Office;
2. the BBC reports to the Department of National Heritage.

   The sponsor departments will almost always be aware of, or be given, the financial results before publication but will not necessarily know about all other parts of the report. Government departments other than the sponsor may well be interested in aspects of the work of a public sector body. Thus a good deal of the work of the British Council is of considerable interest to the Department of Education and Science, and because of its responsibility for tourism, the relevant section of the Department of Employment will be interested in English Heritage.

In addition to these groups, a further six groups have interests in certain circumstances.

Competitors

Organizations in competitive markets will want to know as much as possible about their public sector competitors. For example, Her Majesty's Stationery Office is in competition with other suppliers of similar goods. For obvious reasons public sector bodies in this position will want to disclose as little as possible about their competitive position other than what is required by relevant statutory and professional reporting requirements.

Regulators

A regulator may have a direct interest in a financial report, for example the Office of Electricity Regulation will want to see the results of the two nationalized industries in the same sector – Nuclear Electric and Scottish Electric. There may well also be an interest for another body because of the importance for the competitive environment of a regulated industry. Thus the Post Office is in competition with BT and is therefore of interest to the Office of Telecommunications.

Lenders

The financial position of those organizations which borrow money from non-government sources will be of great interest to those that have lent them money, assuming the loan is not guaranteed by the government itself. What they require includes updated information on plans and prospects as well as commitments for the long and short term, though in practice the historic basis of the accounts means that they provide only very limited information for this purpose.

Donors or sponsors

A number of institutions which rely on funding by donors, such as universities for research, use their annual financial reports to inform benefactors of progress and to acknowledge publicly the support which they have been given.

Investors or business partners

Where ventures have been set up in association with partners in the private sector, the partners or investors will obviously be interested in the financial position of the organization as a whole.

Other pressure groups

In some cases – environmental groups in relation to the activities of some government departments, for example – the financial reports will provide important information, such as the relative priorities attached to different aspects of their work.

RIGHTS AND USER NEEDS IN FINANCIAL INFORMATION

The user groups listed above would claim a variety of rights to the financial information in which they are interested. What is the basis of the rights which they claim? There are three kinds of assertions which are made to justify requirements for disclosure by public bodies.

First, there are statements implying user rights, without spelling out the basis of those rights. Such statements often reflect the influence of private sector reporting. The most influential examples of such statements have come from the United States, including the 1973 report from the American Institute of Certified Public Accountants known as the Trueblood Report. The report stated that it was 'fundamental and pervasive' that 'the basic objective of financial statements is to provide information useful for making economic decisions'.

Next there are statements of needs implying rights. Such statements refer to user needs as justifying claims by users to have information. In the United Kingdom, *The Corporate Report* declared that statements 'should seek to satisfy, as far as possible, the information needs of users' and the Trueblood Report claimed that in the United States, 'financial statements of not-for-profit organizations should provide information which serves users' needs'. More recently, both the influential study from the Institute of Chartered Accountants in Scotland, *Making Corporate Reports Valuable*, and the ASB in its work on standards have stressed the importance of user needs and there is widespread agreement that they are the key to providing the basis of improvements in financial reporting. However there are problems in identifying and reconciling such needs. The problems in identifying them are set out at the end of this section. In relation to reconciling needs, the late Professor Stamp (1980) concluded in a study for the Canadian Institute of Chartered Accountants that:

> There is no doubt that users' needs are different. Research is necessary to establish not only how wide the differences are but to monitor changes in user needs.

So it may be that some needs are difficult to define and reconcile. If members of the public ask how much is being spent on the Secret Service, are they seeking to destabilize society or exercising democratic rights? Do the same considerations apply to nuclear power, rubbish collection or landing rights?

Finally there are statements conferring user rights. *The Corporate Report* stated that:

> we define users of corporate reports as having a reasonable right to information concerning the reporting entity. We consider that such rights arise from the public accountability of the entity

whether or not supported by legally enforceable powers to demand information.

It would be difficult to disagree with such sentiments, but here again there are questions about what is meant by 'reasonable' and how the conflicts between the claims of different users can be reconciled with each other. An indication of how it is likely to be done in practice came from Macve (1981) in a study primarily concerned with the private sector when he concluded that:

> Recognition of the variety of user needs and of conflicts between different interests and different rights leads to the view that reaching agreement on the form and content of financial statements is as much a political process, a search for compromise between different parties, as it is a search for the methods which are technically best.

But while there are philosophical aspects to the nature of user rights, there are also highly practical ones in relation to user needs. The key to successful reporting may be identifying potential users and their needs, but how are the users (or potential users) to be identified? If they can be identified, how can users find out what they need? It may not be difficult to find out what the specialists who will be reading the report – perhaps as part of their job – want, but it is not at all easy to find out what a more general audience needs. Even for the specialists, and certainly for a more general audience, it will be easier to criticize what is provided than to define what they might need instead. And if they do know what they need, how are they to signal those needs to the preparers, since there are normally limited opportunities to do so. Finally, even if those needs are articulated, how are they to be reconciled? The practicalities of this aspect of financial reporting have not yet been satisfactorily answered either for the private or the public sectors. Until they are, the political process set out by Macve is likely to apply to the reconciliation of needs as well as rights.

DIFFERENCES FROM THE PRIVATE SECTOR

Some differences between public and private sector accounts have already been mentioned. This section can only be a brief analysis of the other such differences because while certain aspects of reporting – notably accountability and the stewardship of public funds – have a number of features across the public sector, the subject in detail is a complex and many-faceted one. It is thus difficult to make many generalizations without having to qualify them and any analysis of differences such as those in Table 2.1 need to be made for each part of the public sector.

Table 2.1 Some differences and similarities between government departmental reports and annual reports

Some differences

Government Departmental Reports	Private Sector Annual Reports
Financial and political focus	Financial focus
Performance measured both financially and non-financially	Performance measured largely financially
Parliamentary and wider public accountability	Accountability to shareholders and lenders
Focus on disaggregate picture	Focus on organization as a whole
Forward-looking in detail	Cannot be forward-looking in detail (commercial confidentiality)
Reporting rules determined by Treasury	Reporting rules determined by law, accounting standards, the Stock Exchange (for quoted companies) and accounting practice
Figures checked by Treasury	Figures (and some facts) audited by independent auditors
Cash accounting	Accrual accounting

Similarities

Source document

Public relations role

Source: A. Likierman and A. Taylor, *Government's New Departmental Reports*, CACA, 1990.

The differences are in purpose, scope and method of performance measurement, as well as other factors, including the nature of audit (see Chapter 9). Thus it is true that there is no 'bottom line' profit measure for most, but not all, of the public sector, which helps to explain the great variety of performance measures used, including non-financial measures which reflect social as well as economic considerations.

The fact that most public sector organizations are not subject to competition accounts in part for the greater degree of disclosure which is possible compared to the private sector. This extends to the disclosure of plans, often in great detail as, for example, in the government's Supply Estimates. Another key factor influencing the difference between public and private sector accounts is the fact that the vast majority of public sector organizations cannot 'go broke'. Except in very special circumstances, the government would be expected to step in to support the public sector, something which is clearly crucial for lenders and suppliers.

The emphasis on plans reflects the need for elected members of public sector bodies to be able to have the information to vote on the spending priorities for the coming year. This aspect of the difference from the private sector is a manifestation of an even more significant factor than the lack of competition in influencing the financial statements which is common to all public sector bodies – ultimate accountability to an elected body. Responsibility of this kind is quite different to the position of private sector organizations' responsibility to their shareholders. (Those tempted to think that elected bodies are rather like public sector shareholders should think whether the public, or their representatives, can sell their 'shares' in a public body.) Public accountability also means that the scope of the audit is normally wider in the public than in the private sector.

The importance of assessing plans has a further implication for the difference between private and public sector organizations in the way in which performance is measured. While the focus in the private sector is on trends and on comparisons with other, similar, organizations, the emphasis in the public sector is much more on achievement of objectives and on performance against budget, as the illustration in Table 2.2 from the report of Westminster City Council illustrates. Not that published statements are always as helpful as Table 2.2 to readers in allowing them to make these comparisons. Often readers have to compare statements from different years to do so.

As the basis of their accounting, public sector organizations are broadly split between those which use cash accounting and those which use accrual accounts in a way similar to the private sector, though the division between the two is becoming increasingly blurred. Thus while there has been an enhancement of the importance of cash in the private sector by the Accounting Standards Board, the arrival of Balance Sheets in the Health Service is illustrated in Table 2.3 by the South Glamorgan Health Authority. Furthermore, for reasons outlined in Chapter 7, some parts of the public sector have maintained an attempt to account for changing prices after most of the private sector has given up. Table 2.4 gives an illustration for British Rail. However many parts of the public sector remain unambiguously in cash terms, as illustrated by the Foreign and Commonwealth Office in Table 2.5.

Despite the differences in the nature of the organizations, much of the terminology used in accounts is very similar between public and private sector organizations. The similarity is misleading in some cases, however, and can give rise to confusion. For example, the term 'loan' is used to cover the long-term government financing of nationalized industries which in practice is their permanent capital. In the private sector much of the permanent capital is provided by equity capital, with loans having precise repayment requirements, although refinancing is common. Care therefore needs to be taken before it can be assumed that the meaning is transferable from private to public sector or vice versa.

Finally, it is worth considering whether public sector financial reports are in some way intrinsically worse than those of the private sector. The fact that this accusation is often levied against them may be due to a number of possible factors – the cash basis of some accounts; the reports being tarred with the image of allegedly poorly-run organizations; the influence of government and other public authorities; perhaps even the frustration of readers accustomed to a private sector format. Those who believe that private sector accounts are superior need to bear two factors in mind. First, that there are no immutable accounting or other financial reporting rules which apply irrespective of the nature and purposes of the organization whose activities and results are being displayed or the objectives of presentation. Second, that cash accounts, despite their crudeness, have a degree of transparency that accrual accounts cannot give and that many private sector financial reports do not seek to offer.

ISSUES IN FINANCIAL REPORTING

Considering general agreement on the importance of satisfying user needs, remarkably little information is available for almost any part of the public sector on how far any user groups actually use the accounts. From the producer's point of view this makes it difficult to identify precise suggestions for improvement. From the reader's viewpoint the lack of communication means that it may well be difficult for those who might be interested to know that is happening unless public bodies make it clear where the information is to be found and keep the cost of acquiring the information within reasonable limits. The documents themselves must then be sufficiently user-friendly to allow the interested reader to acquire the information. The dilemma here is to know how far to go in meeting the needs of a wider audience without having the evidence that such an audience exists. There are those who say that it is unrealistic to assume that public sector reports will be read outside a very narrow circle. Others assert that, with encouragement, a wider audience will develop. The evidence in this area is unclear and work is needed to give public sector bodies a better basis for their decisions.

The identification of user needs is also crucial to decisions about almost every aspect of how to present a financial report. Thus whether

Main reasons for differences between revised estimates and outturn 1989/90

	£000
Increased contributions from parking places reserve account	3506 –
Additional income from fees and charges – trade refuse	482 –
Increased interest earnings	1668 –
Additional expenditure – salaries	630 +
– Social Services – agency payments etc.	535 +
– highways – city and principal roads	735 +
– capital financing costs	424 +
– premises costs including repairs and maintenance	330 +
– equipment costs	273 +
Increased provision for irrecoverable debts	1400 +
Reduced income – housing and other rents	878 +
– off-street parking – car parks	666 +
Other net variations	114 +
	329 +

Source: *Westminster City Council Annual Report 1989/90*, p. 3.

Table 2.2 Performance against plan (Westminster City Council)

Comparison of estimates and outturn 1989/90

Committee	1989/90 Original estimate £000	1989/90 Revised estimate £000	1989/90 Actual expenditure £000	Variation between revised estimate and actual expenditure £000
Education	11 756	14 065	14 412	347 +
Environment and Licensing Subcommittee	27 935	28 339	27 726	613 –
Housing	10 402	12 060	12 589	529 +
Planning and development	8286	4622	4962	340 +
Policy and resources	7833 Cr	4412 Cr	3475 Cr	937 +
Social Services	38 518	41 290	40 079	1211 –
Contingency sum	5685	–	–	–
	94 749	95 964	96 293	329 +

The original estimates of each Committee's net expenditure were mainly based on pay and price levels in November 1988 and a contingency sum, controlled by the Policy and Resources Committee, was provided to meet subsequent pay and price increases and unforeseen items. The revised estimates were determined in early 1990 and included allocations from the contingency sum already approved.

Table 2.3 Accrual accounting – the Health Service. (South Glamorgan Health Authority)

	£000	£000	£000
1. Fixed assets			
Land		69 832	
Buildings		138 679	
Engineering services		41 745	
Plant and equipment		35 235	285 491
2. Working capital			
(a) Current assets			
Stock	3583		
Debtors	4375	7958	
(b) Current liabilities			
Cash overdrawn	98		
Creditors	6924	(7022)	936
3. Net assets			286 427
Represented by			
4. General reserve			
(a) Underspending 1989/90	312		
(b) Specific funds carried			
forward to 1990/91	2248	2560	
5. Accumulated funds provided by central government in prior years		283 867	
6. Liabilities			286 427

Notes to accounts
1. Fixed assets. Following the asset identification and valuation exercise undertaken in conjunction with Touche Ross Management Consultants and the District Valuers Department, the Authority's assets have been valued at £285m. This substantial investment covers land, building, engineering support service, i.e. boilers, and equipment across the whole of the Authority.
2. Working capital represents the net amount of current assets, i.e. the value of stock held and debtors (people who owe the Authority money), and current liabilities (people who are owed money by the Authority).
3. The total amount represents the aggregate value of the Authority's 'worth' as at 31 March 1990.
4. The assets are represented by the Authority's commitment to certain aspects including the underspendings brought forward and the earmarked funds which will need to be spent in 1990/91 on specific items.
5. The accumulated fund represents the prior resources spent by the Authority on behalf of central government.
6. The total liabilities therefore represent the Authority's indebtedness to the government.

Source: *Annual Report and Accounts 1989/90*, p. 58.

Table 2.4 Current cost accounts in a nationalized industry (British Rail)

	Year to 31 March 1991	Year to 31 March 1990
	£m	£m
Turnover	**3776.8**	3485.0
Historical cost operating loss before interest	**(38.7)**	(22.6)
Current cost operating adjustments (Note 1)	**(109.8)**	(130.1)
Current cost operating loss	**(148.5)**	(152.7)
Interest and similar charges	**(54.4)**	(23.8)
Current cost loss on ordinary activities	**(202.9)**	(176.5)
Extraordinary profit (Note 2)	**63.4**	291.2
Group current cost (loss)/profit for the year	**(139.5)**	114.7
Appropriation of (loss)/profit for the year		
Transfer to reserves	**79.8**	310.9
Deficit after transfer to reserves	**(219.3)**	(196.2)
	(139.5)	114.7

Source: British Rail, *Annual Report and Accounts 1990/91*, p. 47.

it is worth producing a more expensive document than the basic information required by law, government directive or any other set of rules depends on whether the cost is justified in terms of making the document of more use. Glossy pictures may be very helpful in this respect to help a general audience or they may be irrelevant if the document is read only by professional analysts.

There is also the issue of the gloss getting in the way of the substance, as the Treasury and Civil Service Select Committee, in their report on the Next Steps Initiative, pointed out:

> there is a potential conflict between the Annual Report's main function, which should be to give a clear picture of the agency's performance in the previous year and the[se] wider 'public relations' uses to which the report may be put (7th Report, 1990–1).

With public sector bodies under continuing pressure to justify themselves, the decision on how to resolve the conflict will tend to be one

Table 2.5 Cash accounts – central government

Foreign and Commonwealth Office

£ million	1985-6 outturn	1986-7 outturn	1987-8 outturn	1988-9 outturn	1989-90 outturn	1990-1 estimated outturn	1991-2 plans	1992-3 plans*	1993-4 plans*
Diplomatic Wing									
Central government's own expenditure									
Voted in Estimates									
Overseas representation	360	404	439	449	514	552	634	700	720
Other external relations	104	91	93	114	163	169	141	140	150
External broadcasting and monitoring	94	101	99	119	123	143	156	160	170
British Council	50	53	57	58	63	78	90	80	90
Total Diplomatic Wing	608	649	687	739	864	942	1021	1090	1130
Overseas Development Administration									
Central government expenditure									
Voted in Estimates									
External assistance programme									
Overseas aid for developing countries†	1009	1092	1124	1274	1364	1458	1503	1600	1660
Economic assistance to Eastern Europe and the USSR					64	19	65	60	60
Global environmental assistance							5	–	–
Overseas superannuation	89	93	95	136	103	109	120	120	130
Crown Agents				16					
Total Voted in Estimates	1097	1185	1219	1426	1530	1587	1693	1790	1850

Other (non-Voted)									
Overseas aid for developing countries‡	142	118	102	129	139	161	218	190	200
Commonwealth Development Corporation§	5	-7	-30	-14					
Crown Agents§	-1	-1	-1						
Total other (non-Voted)	147	110	71	115	139	160	218	190	200
Total central government expenditure	1245	1295	1290	1541	1669	1747	1911	1980	2050
Of which:									
Central government's own expenditure	1211	1271	1291	1507	1620	1695	1869	1950	2020
Public corporations (excluding nationalized industries)	34	24	-1	34	49	52	42	30	30
Of which:									
Commonwealth Development Corporation	35	25		32	50	52	42	30	30
Crown Agents	-1	-1	-1	2					
Total Overseas Development Administration	1245	1295	1290	1541	1669	1747	1911	1980	2050
Of which:									
External assistance programmes	1156	1202	1196	1405	1566	1638	1791	1860	1920
Of which:									
Overseas aid for developing countries	1151	1209	1226	1403	1503	1619	1721	1790	1860
Total Foreign and Commonwealth Office	1853	1944	1978	2280	2533	2690	2932	3070	3180

* Figures for 1992–3 and 1993–4 are rounded to the nearest £10 million.
† Includes net lending to the Commonwealth Development Corporation.
‡ Mainly amounts attributed to the Aid Programme for EC budgetary spending on aid as follows:
§ 141 116 101 129 138 176 215 190 200
§ Net lending from the National Loans Fund.

Source: *1991 Department Report*, Cm. 1502, p. 2.

of politics, not accounting. In practice the needs of those who produce the reports are usually dominant. Since the public relations aspects of financial reports are therefore becoming increasingly important for management, the expense of improved presentation may well be argued to be justified, not only as a sign of professionalism but also in order to influence those who deal with the organization. Against this are those who argue that excessive gloss is wasteful and is more about persuasion than information.

The amount of public pressure for improved information is generally small. Individuals who are electors or voters rely on their representatives to elicit and interpret the information on their behalf. Yet representative groups vary greatly in knowledge and activity. They are highly active in some areas (road transport) and virtually dormant in others (psychotherapy). Nor are individual representatives better placed, with few having any financial training and many being uninterested in financial matters.

A further factor which militates against greater accessibility is that there is little incentive for those who produce financial reports to make them more accessible. While there is general public agreement that financial reports should be as intelligible as possible, improved reader understanding is sometimes felt to be a disadvantage, giving rise to time-consuming questioning from what are felt to be hostile and ill-informed readers. Giving such people the necessary ammunition to criticize the organization would be seen as giving a hostage to fortune. This view is reinforced by the importance to many in the public sector of maintaining an element of ambiguity in how public sector organizations are assessed. Such ambiguity blurs outcomes so that elected members and officials feel less vulnerable to criticism. Yet the dangers in such a strategy include the two potentially dangerous vicious circles shown in Fig. 2.1.

Many of the issues in reporting in the private sector apply equally to the public sector. Creative accounting – slanting figures to show an organization in a favourable light – has been a feature of both in the past few years. In the public sector, some of the more prominent manifestations have included the netting off of receipts against expenses, sale and lease-back arrangements, write-offs to capital or revenue, the use of reserve accounting, deferring or accelerating payments and even barter. While each of these examples is within the rules, the intention of using them as part of creative accounting is to respond to pressures rather than to reflect the underlying economic realities of the relevant transactions. As in the private sector, those who engage in creative accounting will not admit (at least in public) to doing so and motive is in practice very difficult to prove. It is also very difficult to disentangle creative accounting from many of the inherent features of accounting measurement. One of these is the

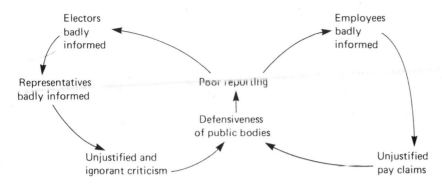

Fig. 2.1 Two vicious circles arising from poor reporting.

annual cycle, which means that some limited scope is available to charge items to one year rather than another. Another is the need for prediction in accrual accounting, which gives scope for matters of judgement. There is also the precise definition of certain items, for example as net or gross, or whether they are part of 'normal' operations or not.

The scope for creative accounting differs greatly from one part of the public sector to another. It is greatest where there is trading, accrual accounting and ambiguity in the rules. It is least with cash accounting and clear rules. It is possible at all because some flexibility generally has to be allowed to cover varying circumstances in financial reporting. With commercial-style accounts there are further pressures which reflect the much greater creative accounting possibilities of the private sector. These may increase in the next few years with the pressures to move from cash to accrual accounting in the public sector although the ASB has made it clear that it will seek to restrict the scope for such manoeuvring.

Meanwhile a number of underlying issues of financial reporting are of particular interest. For example, the question of whether capital assets should be valued and depreciated has been raised in the context of central government, health authorities and local government in recent years on the grounds that the value of what is invested each year, the value of capital tied up and the rate of using up that capital should all be known. Among the arguments used against changes from current practice are that the division between capital and current expenditure is too difficult to draw, that the valuation process is too complex and that the purpose of valuation is unclear unless the assets have alternative uses. This is a complex area and one which is discussed in other chapters for different parts of the public sector.

A more general issue which has been the cause of considerable concern in the past few years is the basis on which rules for financial reporting are set. It is well known that the private sector's problems in this area are bad enough, with difficulties in the process of agreeing standards. With a higher degree of control over the form of accounts, enforcing compliance in the public sector is easier than in the private sector but the standard-setting process itself is not wholly straight-forward. There is a lack of clarity about whether some standards should apply to public sector bodies and some ambiguity about the role of the government in setting standards. The nature of the ambi-guity is illustrated by the fact that there is government representation on the Accounting Standards Board with observer rather than member status.

A different aspect of rule-making is the issue of whether there should be greater standardization of financial reports. It is understandable that readers should have a reasonable expectation that they will find similar information in the financial reports of different bodies in the same sector, and indeed be able to make comparisons on the basis of such information. It is also reasonable that the way the information is compiled and presented should not be at the mercy of the manage-ment of each organization. On the other hand there are variations in the circumstances of different bodies in the same sector and there is room for doubt about the best way of presenting information because many rules are by no means well established. So it could be argued that it would be wrong to stifle all initiatives for clearer, though less uniform, accounting.

Finally the question of whether, and if so, how far, public sector bodies should follow private sector practice in reporting, is often a matter of controversy which goes beyond the purely accounting issues which have already been outlined in the previous section.

THE WELL-PRESENTED FINANCIAL REPORT

This section takes as given that there has been some identification of users, some assessment of their needs and that one at least of the audiences includes non-specialists. Because of the potential variation in audiences and the different circumstances of each sector the comments below are not intended to be comprehensive. They are intended only to help those seeking to compile reports or to assess an existing one and as a supplement to this section, two excellent gen-eral sources of information on the presentation of financial reports (and indeed annual reports generally) are *Annual Reports: a Practical Guide* published by CIPFA and the comments in the Institute's jour-nal *Public Finance and Accountancy* which reported the annual Public Sector Accounts Award, organized by CIPFA until 1990.

Basis of compilation

As an essential starting point, reports have to conform with the relevant legal and professional requirements rules. But once these basic requirements have been satisfied, the single most important factor for any report is that it should be relevant to the needs of users. As has already been made clear, it may not be easy to identify the users and means of doing so could include invitations to comment (which might include reply-paid cards) or more systematic market research. But even without clear knowledge of the users, assumptions have to be made in any case about their existing background interests and knowledge, including knowledge of, or access to, other information. It is far better that these are explicit, agreed among those compiling the report and if possible that the assumptions are set out in the report. Cheshire County Council shows how this can be done in a way that is also friendly (Figs 2.2a and 2.2b). Assuming that the target users have been identified, the report has to be cost effective in reaching them, bearing in mind particularly that if price is based on cost, extra gloss will add to the price and may therefore place a barrier to purchase.

On content, the report must not be blatantly biased (or simply an extended defence of the record of the management) and should enable the reader to clearly separate fact from opinion. It must also be neutral between the interests of different user groups. In addition to the specific requirements set out below, there should also be enough supporting information to give user groups the context within which to put the information (such as the structure of the organization and its funding arrangements) and details of where further information can be found.

Usefulness

It should be possible to:

1. identify the current activity level of the organization, recent changes in activity (both financial and non-financial) and the prospects for the future;
2. identify income from all sources, including a split between income received from grants and income from trading and other sources;
3. understand the split between expenditure on the organization's main activities;
4. assess, in appropriate cases, whether the organization is maintaining its assets;

INTRODUCTION

The purpose of this report is to account for the County Council's income and expenditure and general stewardship of its affairs for the financial year ended 31 March 1990. Whilst the emphasis is on finance, the report also gives more general information about the County Council and the services it provides.

This report is aimed primarily at the people of Cheshire, who are both providers of funds and users of services. It also provides a valuable source of information to all those with an interest in the County Council's activities.

The County Council's budget for 1989-90 was the last to be prepared under the domestic rating system. The rate precept of 248p in the pound was set after much consideration of the impact on ratepayers and the changing needs of services, with emphasis being placed on the protection and improvement of front-line services such as Education, Social Services and Police.

A great deal of work was undertaken in 1989-90 planning for the implementation of the Local Management of Schools and Colleges schemes, which are effective from April 1990. Social Services dealt with, and will continue to deal with, a wide range of issues stemming from both legislation and increasing demands on services, in particular the move from residential care to community based services, whilst the Police Force gave specific attention to combating burglaries in the home, vehicle-related crime and crime against the elderly.

More details of significant activities and developments are given on the individual service pages of this report, together with information on service responsibilities, spending and comparisons with other authorities. Other sections of the report give broader information on the County Council as a whole, and the formal statement of accounts appears on pages 38 to 52.

The County Council is always looking for ways to improve the quality of its reporting and would value your views. If you have any comments or require further information, please refer to the contact points listed at the back of the report.

Fig. 2.2a Cheshire County Council. (Source: *Financial Report and Accounts 1989/90.*)

FOREWORD BY THE CHAIRMAN OF THE COUNTY COUNCIL

It gives me great pleasure to present to you Cheshire County Council's Financial Report and Accounts for 1989-90.

The purpose of the County Council is to help and support the people of Cheshire by identifying their needs and speaking for them. In doing this, the Council provides a range of services aimed at improving the quality of life of all Cheshire residents. The County Council also promotes Cheshire as an attractive location for business and industry.

To enable you to judge how effective we have been, this document provides an account of the Council's finances and how they have been used. It is available to anyone at public libraries and copies are available on request from the County Finance Officer at County Hall, Chester. In addition to this document, an Annual Report is published in newspaper format and circulated to homes and businesses throughout Cheshire. The two documents complement each other and aim to keep Cheshire residents informed on the activities of the County Council.

Whilst continuing to provide services as efficiently as possible, the County Council is also responding positively to the many new challenges it is facing, to ensure that it is in a position to meet the needs of the Cheshire community in the years to come.

Pamela Hayward

Mrs P W HAYWARD
*Chairman of Cheshire County Council 1990-91
and elected Councillor for Groves
and Whitby, Ellesmere Port*

Fig. 2.2b Cheshire County Council. (Source: *Financial Report and Accounts 1989/90.*)

5. establish variances from budget or target;
6. understand links between financial and other objectives (including statutory objectives) and whether these are being met;
7. establish trends and performance over time;
8. make comparisons with other comparable bodies or services;
9. establish indebtedness;
10. establish, in appropriate cases, whether the organization is solvent, viable and able to meet its commitments.

It should be possible to do all these from information which is at an appropriate level of detail to meet the needs of stated user groups.

Accessibility

A common complaint among those who compile public sector financial reports is that they are not read. While minimal response and low sales might seem to justify such comments, it is often difficult for compilers to understand that few people even know that their reports exist or, if the documents are distributed automatically, that readers need help in understanding them. Potential readers of a report should be helped in this way after being made aware of its existence and offered the information at a reasonable price.

So as a minimum, financial reports should be understandable, available and affordable to those interested and willing to make a reasonable effort to understand them. A number of steps can be taken to help the process. For example, a report should:

1. minimize jargon and acronyms, but not be patronizing;
2. have a logical structure and layout;
3. have a summary of key points;
4. have the relevant amount of detail for user groups (regular pruning helps);
5. mix text, illustrations and numbers appropriately for the users;
6. not be unduly distorted by public relations considerations;
7. be clear about the nature, cost and progress of major projects;
8. be clear about the impact of changing price levels.

Presentation is a particularly important aspect of accessibility. Despite the significant advances in the presentation of many financial reports in the past few years, there is still a great deal of room for improvement in the printed matter. The considerations to be taken into account will vary greatly between reports, but among those worth bearing in mind are the need for:

1. good balance between figures, text and photos/charts;
2. clear textual explanation of figures.

Figures 2.3 and 2.4 show examples of how information can be clearly presented. They are taken from the annual reports of Cambridgeshire County Council and Strathclyde Regional Council – two organizations which have won CIPFA awards. Some bodies have used less conventional means – Humberside County Council adding a cassette tape to its information pack recently. Others have two-tier financial reporting, with a simplified version for non-specialists and the full report for those with expertise. Simplified financial reports, usually included as part of a simplified annual report, are cheaper to produce and may well be suitable for large numbers of employees. The principles of good reporting apply with equal force to simplified reports, however, not least because they will be regarded with considerable suspicion and have little value for communication if they are seen as propaganda sheets for the management.

SUMMARY

This chapter has illustrated the varied nature of public sector financial reports covering financial matters. It has shown how the multiplicity of objectives of such reports reflects the variety of bodies and different kinds of users. Nor can private sector practice simply be transferred to a public sector context – the nature of accountability is different and affects not only the formal differences of structure and rules but also the way the reports are used. Despite real problems in identifying users, improvements in financial reporting are possible in both content and presentation.

FURTHER READING

There are many kinds of sources on aspects of public sector financial reporting. At a conceptual level, there is little work specifically on the public sector in the UK. Each part of the public sector has some literature on the practical aspects of financial reporting and details of the latest developments are available from the relevant professional organizations and their journals. Good practice in presentation is set out in *Annual Reports: a Practical Guide* published by CIPFA.

Introduction

The performance of Cambridgeshire may be compared in many different ways, none of them perfect. The method chosen here is to compare statistics for Cambridgeshire with those of three neighbouring authorities that are broadly similar to Cambridgeshire and with an average for the 39 English Shire Counties (which includes Cambridgeshire and the three neighbouring counties).

The statistics shown represent the more important indicators recommended by the Code of Practice on Local Authority Annual Reports. It should be noted that whereas figures in the other sections of this publication mainly relate to the financial year 1983–84, the statistics in this section are based on information for the year ended 31st March 1983 (1982–83) unless otherwise indicated.

The statistics by themselves cannot explain variations in local policies, practices and circumstances, which are an inherent feature of local services. Nor can they fully measure comparative levels of efficiency or service provision. However they can provide a starting point for more detailed enquiries.

Comparisons with other Local Authorities

Some statistics are expressed in terms of 'per head' which means that the total figure for Cambridgeshire has been divided by the June 1982 population (598,600). Similarly, for the 'per 1000 population' statistic the total has been divided by 598.6.

	Cambridge-shire	Lincoln-shire	Norfolk	Suffolk	Shire Counties' Average
Population (as at June 1982)	**598,600**	551,800	704,900	611,200	736,487
Area (Hectares)	**340,892**	591,481	536,774	379,663	312,476
Population Density (per Hectare)	**1.76**	0.93	1.31	1.61	2.36

Fig. 2.3 Example of comparative information (Cambridge County Council). (Source: *Report and Accounts 1983/84.*)

General Net Cost of all Services (£ per head of population)

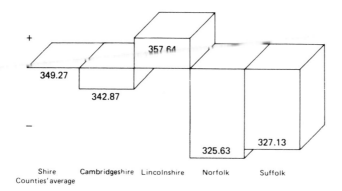

349.27   342.87   357.64   325.63   327.13

Shire
Counties' average   Cambridgeshire   Lincolnshire   Norfolk   Suffolk

General Rate Precept for 1982–83(p)

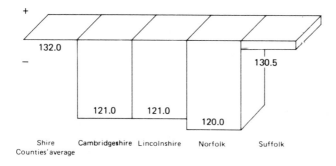

132.0   121.0   121.0   120.0   130.5

Shire
Counties' average   Cambridgeshire   Lincolnshire   Norfolk   Suffolk

General Proportion of Net Expenditure met from Government Grant (%)

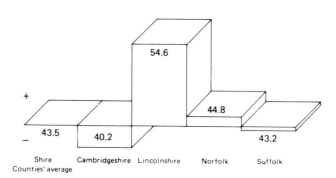

43.5   40.2   54.6   44.8   43.2

Shire
Counties' average   Cambridgeshire   Lincolnshire   Norfolk   Suffolk

Education

The Education Service is by far the largest of all Shire Counties' services. The number of schools required is related to the population size, its distribution and the size of each particular County.

	Cambridge-shire	Lincoln-shire	Norfolk	Suffolk
Number of Schools	**357**	432	513	381
Number of Pupils	**98,702**	90,791	108,837	96,912

Education Net Cost (£ per head of population)

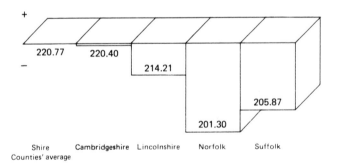

Shire Counties' average	Cambridgeshire	Lincolnshire	Norfolk	Suffolk
220.77	220.40	214.21	201.30	205.87

Education Proportion of Children aged under 5 years in Education (%)

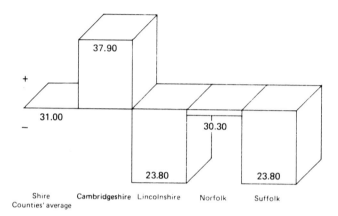

Education Net Cost of Non-Advanced Further Education (£ per head of population)

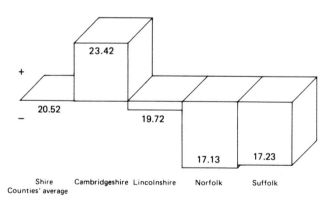

POLICE & FIRE COMMITTEE

in four areas while discussions continued regarding police input to the "Safer Cities" initiative, focusing on Castlemilk and Easterhouse.

Although the overall crime rate increased slightly (0.8%), the incidence of serious crimes involving personal violence reduced by 3.7%. The inordinate rise in thefts from motor vehicles continued. This will be addressed by crime prevention advice and within the limits of available manpower, resources will continue to be allocated to alleviate the problem.

Road Safety
Liaison between traffic and divisional personnel was improved leading to a more productive exchange of information on road safety. New opportunities were sought to expound broadly based road safety advice; this was reinforced by Traffic Groups conveying more specific advice to those considered most at risk, while maintaining traditional avenues of contact.

As a result of concern expressed by the public, special measures were taken to deal with aspects of bad driving which place the community at risk. It was encouraging to note that despite an increase of 3.6% in the number of recorded road accidents during 1988, the number of fatalities and serious injuries decreased by 0.5% and 0.3% respectively. The Force supported the national campaign against drinking and driving. New and more accurate roadside breath-testing equipment was introduced and produced a saving in man-hours coupled to an increased availability of road patrol officers.

Contingency Planning
Review of existing plans was paralleled with assessment of the need for new plans to cover wider contingencies. The value of anticipatory training exercises to develop expertise in a variety of skills including the handling of major incidents was well proven following the Lockerbie disaster in December 1988 when, subsequent to a request for aid from the Chief Constable of Dumfries and

Police Officers Patrolling, Garthamlock, Glasgow

Galloway Constabulary, 500 officers from the Force were deployed to assist, along with specialist equipment.

Media
Excellent liaison continued to exist between the police and the press. This provided invaluable opportunities to publicise a variety of issues of concern or interest to the community. In the broader sense favourable relationships continued with all branches of the media.

Personnel
Personnel issues were addressed through regular divisional personnel panels, appropriate rotation of duties and review of training programmes particularly for probationer Constables. Specific briefing sessions provided opportunities for enhancing communication and where appropriate local specialists were invited to participate. The Working Group on Stress met on several occasions during the year to keep pace with new developments and consider the implications for Force Policy.

BUDGET PERFORMANCE

The year end position reflected a net underspend of £0.542 million, the major elements of which where:—

1 An overspend within employee costs of £1.266 million due to:—
   (a) Overtime costs were overspent by £0.894 million due mainly to the secondment of police officers to the Lockerbie Air Disaster, for which there was a recovery of £1.878 million through the mutual aid scheme.
   (b) Staff Costs relating to Police Agency Services were overspent by £0.373 million but this is offset by the over-recovery in General Income.
   (c) Pension costs were overspent by £0.658 million due to a greater number of officers retiring than had been anticipated.
2 Property, supplies and transport costs were underspent by £0.213 million. The underspend in property costs of £0.392 million was due mainly to expenditure on rates and repairs and maintenance being lower than anticipated together with the underspend of £0.146 million on transport and plant partially offset by the overspend of £0.324 million on supplies and services.
3 Loan charges were underspent by £0.052 million due to the interest rates being lower than anticipated.
4 Other expenditure was underspent by £0.348 million mainly due to the expenditure on police common services being lower than anticipated together with savings in administration costs.

5 (a) General Income was over-recovered by £1.603 million due to the recovery through the mutual aid scheme mentioned at (1a) above and the over-recovery in general Income from Police Agency Services mentioned at (1b) above.
   (b) Specific government grant was underrecovered by £0.408 million due to the net underspend.

SERVICE DELIVERY

	1987/88	1988/89
Total crimes made known to the Police (Groups 1-5)	257,722	259,666
Road Accidents Investigated	28,625	29,652
Incidents and Reports from the Public	886,552	903,921
Responses to Alarm Activations	114,965	123,852
Processions and Demonstrations Policed	1,348	1,335
Senior Football Matches Policed	346	396
Number of Fires Investigated	4,656	4,393
Persons Reported Missing from Home	9,143	8,500
Sudden Deaths Investigated	4,868	4,929
Items of Found Property Received	44,316	46,668
Number of Crime Prevention Surveys carried out	1,013	736
Number of Crime Prevention Panels	54	54
Net annual expenditure per head of population	£76.09	£79.60
Full-time equivalent staff per 1,000 population	3.90	3.92

WHAT THE SERVICES COST

1987/88 Actual £000		1988/89 Budget £000	1988/89 Actual £000
86,104	Police	90,808	90,257
3,203	School Crossing Patrols	3,418	3,410
3	Emergencies Planning—Police	—	17
89,310		94,226	93,684

WHAT IT WAS SPENT ON

1987/88 Actual £000		1988/89 Budget £000	1988/89 Actual £000
169,720	Employees	178,090	179,356
11,429	Property, Supplies and Transport	12,100	11,887
4,942	Loan Charges	5,663	5,611
6,965	Other Expenditure	7,231	6,883
193,056		203,084	203,737
17,500	General Income	17,719	19,322
86,246	Specific Government Grant	91,139	90,731
103,746		108,858	110,053
89,310	Net Expenditure met from Rates and Rate Support Grant	94,226	93,684

MANPOWER NUMBERS

1987/88 Actual		1988/89 Budget	1988/89 Actual
6,784	Police Officers	6,772	6,770
1,748	Police Cadets, Traffic Wardens and Civilians	1,764	1,712
1,483	School Crossing Patrollers	1,483	1,487
10,015		10,019	9,969

Fig. 2.4 A service encapsulated – Strathclyde Regional Council. (Source: *Annual Report and Financial Statement 1988/89*, p. 41.)

3

Management accounting
in the public sector

This chapter examines management accounting in the public sector. It does so, not only by examining existing practices, but also by seeking to place the actual and potential use of a variety of management accounting techniques in the distinctive context of the public sector. The new emphasis on **management** in the public sector is outlined, as is the particular difficulty of establishing criteria by which management accounting techniques can be applied successfully in the public sector. Also, in examining management accounting practices, a slightly broader view of management accounting is taken which emphasizes the importance of strategic planning to public sector organizations.

MANAGEMENT ACCOUNTING IN A CHANGING ENVIRONMENT

The topic of **management** accounting may seem, at first sight, to be at odds with the nature of much of the public sector. For many years, the public services in the UK have been **administered** rather than **managed**. That is, the senior officials were charged with the responsibility of delivering services in accordance with statutory obligations and the governments interpretation of these (by way of central government departments issuing detailed guidance, 'circulars'). While public services continue to have statutory obligations there is a new dynamic within the public sector with (a) the explicit introduction of **management** (not only in terms of formal designation but also in terms of expectations regarding changes in the behaviour of senior public sector officials and in the use of management language and terminology) and (b) the introduction of pseudo or quasi-markets in the delivery of public services.

The first of these can be seen from the introduction of general managers in the NHS (Griffiths, 1983), accountable management in central government, and the new style direct service organizations (DSOs) in local authorities. The second aspect of this fundamental change – the introduction of markets and competitive behaviour – can be seen from the new internal market in health care; the proposed market in community care; notions of bidding for student numbers in higher education in contractual relationships between financiers (the UFC) and service providers (the Universities). A further aspect of this creation of markets (or, more accurately, 'notional' or 'quasi'-markets) for public services where these have never existed before is that of longstanding pressure on all public services to undertake compulsory competitive tendering for a whole variety of services across the public sector which had not faced a market test. This includes, for example, tendering for laundry and domestic services by the hospital service, and tendering for local authority refuse collection.

In this situation of continuing, fundamental change, the potential for, and existing demand for, management accounting information is, at least on the face of it, quite considerable. Instead of a situation where administrators execute predetermined policies and plans, much of the new market dynamic is aimed at the devolution of budgets, control and decision-making to lower levels of management, in which a managerial, problem-solving, innovative, objective-setting regime is expected to flourish. This should intensify the demand for management accounting information, as managers explore the actual/possible/probable cost consequences of their actions and examine the revenue implications of alternative plans for the public service for which they are responsible. This chapter explores how a variety of management accounting techniques might/do fulfil this role, by examining their actual importance (extent of use), potential importance and particular relevance to the management of public services. This discussion focuses not only on the technical merits (or otherwise) of such techniques but also their transferability across the public sector, the appropriateness of importing some of these techniques from the private sector and the actual and potential implementation problems in different parts of the public sector.

A PUBLIC SECTOR MANAGEMENT ACCOUNTING MODEL

In selecting management accounting techniques for use in public service, it is important to take account of the **context** in which such information is provided and used. In this regard, a useful typology of successful management accounting in public and not-for-profit activities has been constructed by Hofstede (1981). In Hofstede's view, conventional management accounting techniques often fail in the public sector because management (and accountants) are not sensitive to the differing needs of different levels of management and of different activities within such organizations.

The model is summarized in Table 3.1.

Hofstede has established four criteria by which management processes and activities can be classified for purposes of management control. The first of these relates to the nature of the organization's objectives. If these are **unambiguous**, a series of conventional management control techniques may be utilized. If not, the logical process for control is political control, i.e. it is dependent on power structures and negotiation processes which recognize the need to address conflicting values and the distribution of scarce resources.

In Hofstede's terms, this type of control may be in use at top management level while more rational/mechanistic control procedures may be used in the same organization for lower levels. The factors which give rise to ambiguities in objectives, according to this model, are conflicting values within the organization, a lack of knowledge of means–end relationships, and environmental turbulence. These factors are in evidence in UK public service organizations, in which there are professional cadres with contrasting ethos in a variety of services (although this is perhaps most marked at the hospital doctor – health care manager interface); patterns of service delivery which do not equate with the more explicit manufacturing model of converting raw materials to finished products; and a situation in which there have been numerous, successive changes in the operating environment (for example, the recent changes in systems of local government taxation; the new internal market in health care). Indeed, UK public service organizations are often characterized as having conflicting and ambiguous aims and objectives, which are stated generally in terms of providing an often vague and ill-defined level of service. For example, British Rail has had a statutory objective of providing railway services with 'due regard to efficiency, economy and safety of operation' (Transport Act 1962) and to provide a railway passenger service which is comparable to that provided in 1974 (Railways Act 1974), although what this means in operational terms is not explicit.

The second criterion in Hofstede's model is that of an ability to measure 'outputs'. The difficulty of output measurement in public services is well known. For example, what is the 'output' from the provision of nursery facilities for children under five? How can this be compared, meaningfully, to the 'outputs' of other public services, such as the provision of sheltered accommodation for the elderly or road maintenance? Clearly, in local government, there are a variety of services and, in the absence of a market for these, in which the 'willingness to pay' criterion allows comparisons to be made across different parts of its services, there will be major difficulties of output measurement for managers of these services, with a tendency to concentrate on the costs of input, with, at best, surrogate measures of

Table 3.1 Accounting in the public sector and not-for-profit activities: Hofstede's typology of control

	1. Routine	2. Expert	3. Trial and error	4. Intuitive	5. Judgemental	6. Political
A. Type of Information/ Process						
B. Level of Management	Lower		Middle		Upper	
C. Characteristics of Activity						
1. Objectives Unambiguous	X	X	X	X	X	\
2. Outputs Measurable	X	X	X	X	\	–
3. Effects of Intervention Known	X	X	\	\	–	–
4. Repetitive	X	\	X	\	–	–

Note: X denotes a positive response to the characteristic of activity; \ indicates a negative response.

Source: Compiled from Hofstede (1981) Management control of public and not-for-profit activities, *Accounting Organisations and Society*, vol. 6, no. 3, pp. 193–211.

the 'worth' of output (for example, in the above illustrations, numbers of children provided for, and the proportion of the local population seeking such provision which this represents). Similar observations can be made regarding other public services, such as health care. It might be considered that the introduction of the internal market in health care, and, indeed, similar structures for community care will ease this particular difficulty. However, it should be recognized that these new quasi-markets are just beginning – the indications are that these 'markets' may continue to operate with block grant-type arrangements or, at best, cost per case arrangements, which are not genuine prices set in a free market. These observations have implications, not only for the context in which such information is generated and used but also in its construction, as discussed in the following section. In terms of Hofstede's model, where the objectives of a public service organization (or a part of one) are unambiguous, but its outputs are not measurable, the form of control exercised is that of **judgemental** control. In this situation there may be one supreme judge (e.g. a General Manager of a health authority) or a coalition of judges (e.g. elected lay members comprising a subcommittee of a local authority). This has implications for how management accountants construct, present and interpret information for key decision-makers. In this context, management accounting is not simply a set of techniques with obvious applications.

There are two further criteria which complete Hofstede's model: (1) whether the effects of managerial intervention will be known and (2) whether activities are repetitive. The first of these is a circumstance which is not unique to the public sector, but may be writ large in such organizations. There are a number of factors which may confound or frustrate managerial interventions in public service organizations. At one level, for example, the means–end relationships between resources utilized and quality of services delivered is not explicit. The manager in the public service organization is unlikely to receive the signals from the market-place of increasing or decreasing revenues. Also, within organizations, distinctive methods of operation by specific tightly knit groups which have their own values and behaviour patterns (in effect, subcultures within organizations) may confound directives which stem from a managerial or financial imperative. Examples of such groups in public services might include social workers, nurses, doctors. The final criterion in Hofstede's model is that of the presence/absence of repetitive behaviour. If there is repetitive behaviour there will be a learning curve effect which will make such activities more malleable from a managerial and accounting perspective.

In circumstances where objectives are unambiguous and outputs measurable, but the effects of managerial intervention are not known and activities are not repetitive, Hofstede maintains that management of such activities and/or organizations is an **art** rather than a science. Under these circumstances, this model recommends an **intuitive** style of management or leadership. From a management accounting point of view, rational analysis of costing and financial data may not be regarded in the same light as in more controlled, stable conditions. Where the effects of management intervention are not known, but activities are repetitive, Hofstede sees this situation as one in which trial and error will determine corporate and managerial behaviour. This could be seen as a circumstance in which greater reliance could be placed on management accounting information by key decision-makers. Where there are positive responses to all of the criteria, except that activities are not repetitive, Hofstede sees the dominant managerial model as that of reliance on an **expert**. In this context, a critical factor in determining the use and importance attached to management accounting information may be the expert's professional origins (see above comments on subcultures within public service organizations).

Finally, Hofstede's typology envisages a situation in which objectives are unambiguous, outputs are measurable, the effects of management intervention are known and activities are repetitive. In this circumstance, decision-making, planning and control are **routine** activities. This is the well-ordered situation in which conventional management accounting techniques might achieve a good fit of the organization's needs for management information. The critical question for management accountants in public service organizations is whether this **is** the typical situation which they **assume** that they are addressing in implementing management accounting systems and generating accounting reports. Clearly, if Hofstede's typology holds true, such accounting information may not be achieving its aim.

In the next sections, a variety of management tools are examined for which there is an actual or potential role for management accountants in public service organizations. The topics addressed are:

1. strategic planning;
2. capital investment;
3. budgeting;
4. costing and short-term decision-making.

These are considered, in turn, below.

STRATEGIC PLANNING

The concept of organizational strategy may seem central to the continuing success of any organization, public or private. That is, without both a clear mission and pathway to achieve this, organizations would be drifting and reacting to external events, as they occur. However, in the public sector, the history of long-term planning of this type is one of comparative failure. In this regard there is a clear message for practising management accountants to become involved, to ensure that costing and financial data is drawn upon, as appropriate, in the compilation of such plans. The original impetus for strategic planning can be seen in the context of a particular central government philosophy, viz. central planning by controlling the 'commanding heights' of the economy (i.e. in the 1960s and 1970s). The Hofstede analysis cited above is pertinent here, as the advocacy of such planning was at a time when central government planning was allied to significant central government intervention in such matters as the pricing and investment policies of state industries, all of which served to confuse or make ambiguous already vague objectives.

The failure of such planning systems can be seen from the experiences of different parts of the public sector. In local authorities, the use of corporate plans (a forerunner of strategic plans) and structure plans (which were directed at the physical developments within a given local authority, taking account of such matters as national and regional policies) proved to be a failure. Corporate planning was couched in the language of growth and appeared ill-suited to a conversion to the era of retrenchment in the 1980s; structure planning was slow in completion, exhaustive in its detailed content and exhibited little ability to respond to change (Caulfield and Schultz, 1989). This undermining of long-term planning in local authorities was concurrent with a system of strategic planning being implemented in the NHS which also proved to be a failure. This failure was largely because of its cumbersome, unwieldy nature.

The planning system in use at that time was static and deterministic. Furthermore, it was conceived in terms of longer term (five years or more) **strategic** plans with shorter term **operational** plans, which addressed detailed planning issues within the next three years. These systems tended not to be articulated well, and there was a reliance on planning mechanisms which did not generate fully costed options. This view of the NHS is mirrored in the findings of the Berry *et al.* (1985) study of the then National Coal Board (NCB), in which **physical** planning and **financial** planning were distinct processes which did not form a coherent picture of the NCB's overall plans. In the words of Berry *et al.* these two information systems were competing, 'loosely coupled' systems rather than forming an integrated approach to planning. Indeed, the Berry *et al.* study indicated that this schism was quite deliberate, on the part of the groups within the NCB who had different values. On the one hand, those with an engineering background identified with and used physical planning whereas the financial services/managerial interests conceived of plans in financial terms. The resultant ambiguity confirms the ideas in Hofstede's model cited above and underlines the need to place strategic planning in its organizational context, otherwise the accounting input to such plans may become part of a formal process which does not recognize or relate to the realities of organizational management.

However, despite such negative experiences, there has been a renewed interest in the ideas of strategic planning in the public sector (see, for example, Caulfield and Schultz, 1989). It is recognized by such proponents of strategic planning that, even in an era of limited central planning by government, there is merit in strategic planning. Indeed, this forms a backcloth against which capital investment decisions can be made, as discussed further in the following section.

The basic process of strategic planning is well established:

1. identify the long-term objectives of the organization;
2. evaluate the means of attaining these objectives; and
3. match existing, available resources, and additional resources required, to 1. and 2. above.

However, as noted above, it is important that, not only is there an appropriate management accounting input at these different stages to cost the various alternatives under consideration, but that such exercises recognize difficulties over ambiguities of objectives and potential for competing interest groups to evolve their own versions/ interpretation of plans, and the need to involve such groups in the construction of such plans. The alternative is to perpetrate the difficulties of strategic planning systems mentioned above, in which there is no adequate integration of financial and physical planning, in its widest form.

CAPITAL INVESTMENT

Many public services are labour-intensive. However, the management of such services are also involved in decisions over significant capital outlays. This aspect of management accounting in the public sector is also affected by the criteria in Hofstede's model: particularly (a) the presence/absence of ambiguity in objectives and (b) difficulties over output measurement. These issues are considered in the following discussion, which examines, in turn:

1. basic techniques of investment appraisal;
2. refinements to the techniques in (a) above;
3. the particular problem of output measurement, and the potential roles of cost–benefit analysis and options appraisal in addressing this.

Basic techniques of investment appraisal

HM Treasury guidance (HM Treasury, 1982) recommends that public service organizations should use discounted cash flow techniques in undertaking investment appraisals. Indeed, there is evidence of increasing use of such techniques in the public sector (Lapsley, 1986a, b; Ferguson and Lapsley, 1988). However, it is also evident that (a) such techniques are not used with all appraisals, (b) often they are used in combination with other techniques and (c) frequently such organizations use accounting techniques as investment criteria which do not take account of the time value of money (or make adequate refinements for inflation, risk and uncertainty). A notable example of this is **revenue account analysis**, in which the effects of a capital project proposal are assessed by reference to its potential impact on revenue account, usually in the first full year of operation. Thus a project coming on stream in 19xx would increase the overall operating revenues of a public service organization with revenue-raising powers (such as a local authority) and its costs in 19xx would increase by any additional labour, material, financing and other associated costs caused by its implementation. In a public service organization, such as the NHS, which has no substantive revenue-raising powers, the focus would be on the revenue cost consequence of capital schemes. (This was once formal guidance issued by central government to health authorities, which has since been superseded, as discussed further, below). This approach is biased against strategic projects and supports projects which show up favourably based on short-term financial considerations. The use of this technique can be seen as being akin to 'income smoothing', in which organizations strive to project a favourable financial performance by manipulation of accounting numbers. It is also, of course, more straightforward than the more time-consuming appraisal using discounted cash flows from long-term projections.

Refinements to basic techniques

The mere adoption of discounted cash flow techniques of itself is not without complications. There are a number of issues which have to be addressed and which are of particular concern to large public services, such as local authorities and health authorities. One particular problem is that of **output measurement**, i.e. in the absence of prices for the services delivered there is no numerator or stream of cash inflows from revenues, comparable to private sector organizations. This matter is addressed further in the next section. Other issues which need to be considered by management accountants in public services are:

1. which **discount rate** should be used?
2. how should **inflation** be taken into account?
3. how should **risks** and **uncertainties** (if any) be taken into account?
4. how should the particular problem of **capital rationing** be dealt with?

Each of these is considered below.

Discount rate

In the typical private sector organization, which is financed from a mixture of long-term sources of capital, it is possible to construct a weighted average cost of capital, which can be used as a cost of capital for discounting future streams of net cash flows. However, in the public sector, long-term finance is likely to be borrowings only. This would give a measure of cost of capital for certain parts of the public sector, such as local authorities. However, for those public sector organizations, such as the directly managed units in the NHS, which are financed by block grant allocations from central government, which are funded from general taxation, there is a need for a proxy for the cost of capital. Under these circumstances, the public sector equivalent, the opportunity cost of capital (or 'test discount rate') is available. The rationale behind this discount rate is that it represents the typical rate of return which might be earned on a low-risk marginal project in the private sector. In other words, if the public sector organizations cannot achieve this return, they are, in effect, displacing investment which could be undertaken more profitably in the private sector and should, therefore, reject such proposals.

Currently the test discount rate or required rate of return (RRR) is 8%. However, one drawback of this mechanism is the inevitable failure of governments to match the sensitivity of the capital markets in generating current measures of the cost of capital. In this regard, the discount rate should not be seen as a precise alternative to the private sector's cost of capital.

Inflation

For those public service organizations which use the test discount rate, the issue of how to deal with inflation is straightforward. This discount rate is deemed to be a real rate by HM Treasury and the cash flows to be discounted should be expressed at constant prices. This is, in fact, the typical practice of public service organizations using the test discount rate (Lapsley, 1986a). An exception to the use of constant prices is where adjustments are necessary for relative price effects. This is where the prices of one specific cost move at a significantly different rate from the general rate of inflation. There is some evidence that such adjustments for relative price movements are made by public corporations, particularly for energy costs (Lapsley, 1986b). However, the same survey showed that, for those public service organizations which do not employ discounting techniques, in capital investment appraisals **either** adjustments for changes in the general rate of inflation are incorporated in estimates of accounting data **or** inflation tends to be ignored.

Risk and uncertainty

Sometimes it has been suggested that public sector organizations face a 'risk-free' environment with relatively more stable operating conditions than private sector firms (see, for example, AAA, 1973). However, the reality of the capital investment decision in public sector organizations is that they do face major risks, and uncertainties. These range from **financial** considerations (availability of capital and revenue funds, changes in capital cost and interest rates), **operational** considerations (slippage in construction deadlines, contractor viability, uncertainty of demand) to **wider** issues (changes in government policy and in the nature of services provided). There are a number of well-known possible techniques which might be adopted to assess the impact of risk and uncertainty on a project proposal, for example, simulation, decision trees, sensitivity analysis. However, there is evidence that, in general, less sophisticated, and more questionable practices are adopted by public sector organizations (Lapsley, 1986a, b). Thus while a limited number of health authorities and local authorities reported the use of sensitivity analysis in the above study, the majority either (i) ignored risk altogether, (ii) made 'informal' assessments of risk, (iii) 'over programmed' (i.e. built in budgetary slack), (iv) varied the payback period or (v) increased the discount rate. Practices (i), (ii), and (iii) are expedient; treatments (iv) and (v), which formerly were part of formal guidance, are now recognized to be crude. In part, this lack of sophistication in the treatment of risk and uncertainty may be a reflection of the reluctance of some public sector organizations to adopt discounted cash flow techniques. The selection of appraisal techniques such as revenue account analysis exacerbates this, as not only is the initial appraisal rather crude but also aspects such as risk and uncertainty (and, indeed, inflation) are also treated in a rather crude fashion.

Capital rationing

Where any organization faces constraints on the amount of funding available for capital expenditure it is in a situation of capital rationing. In this circumstance, there are more project possibilities than there are funds available and an internal opportunity cost rate is required to rank projects. Where the capital rationing is for a single period, the benefit/cost ratio, which is the ratio between the discounted sum of the benefits and the costs of the project, will provide a ranking. Where multi-period capital rationing exists, a linear programming model will give a ranking of projects by generating an internal opportunity cost rate ('shadow price'). The problem of capital rationing in the private sector is often self-imposed, i.e. the top management of an organization may decide upon a budget limit for its capital expenditure. In this situation (of 'soft' capital rationing) the linear programming model will give a ranking of projects by generating an internal opportunity cost rate ('shadow price'). Where the capital rationing is hard, the linear programming model is internally inconsistent in that it needs an internal opportunity cost rate ('shadow price') to rank project possibilities, but it also needs an initial discount rate (which is not available in hard capital rationing) to generate an initial set of discounted cash flows, prior to ranking. However, for public sector organizations, the opportunity cost of capital (test discount rate) is available. There is evidence (Lapsley, 1986a, b) that little use is made of such techniques in investment appraisal by public sector organizations. However, the devices mentioned above as means of dealing with risk and uncertainty, such as 'over-programming', might also be seen as informal means of dealing with capital rationing.

The output measurement problem

Much of the above difficulties of adoption or adaptation of basic techniques and refinements to those for public sector organizations might be traced to the issue of output measurement identified in the discussion of Hofstede's model above. The classic response to this difficulty is the use of cost–benefit analysis, as devised by welfare economists. This approach to capital investment addresses the particular difficulty of 'spillovers' or external effects (i.e. those events which are not subject to, or part of, trading in markets), as they affect both costs and benefits. Examples in transport include time savings from the easing of traffic congestion, and noise pollution. The use of cost–benefit analysis entails (1) the identification of externalities, (2) the quantification of these and (3) their valuation. In practice, in its fullest form, this approach has not been used widely within the public sector. It has been confined to the appraisal of exceptionally large projects. It tends to be undertaken by central government (in, for example, major transport infrastructure decisions) rather than by the operational branches of the public sector. Indeed, central government guidance to operational activities, such as nationalized industries, has been **not** to use this approach, particularly because of its inherent subjectivity.

There are a number of methods of tackling this difficulty of output

Table 3.2 Points system for ranking project proposals: an illustration

Criterion	Option	1	2	3	4	5
Revenue		1	1	3	3	4
Capital		3	3	3	1	1
Access		3	1	2	3	3
Flexibility		1	1	2	3	4
Care group considerations		1	1	4	0	1
Land required		2	4	3	4	4

Notes:
1. In the present illustration, a five-point scale is utilized, with each point indicating the merits of each of the criteria, with 0 at 'zero', 1 is 'poor', 2 is 'acceptable', 3 is 'good', 4 is 'excellent'.
2. In practice, each option would be briefly described, rather than simply numbered.

Source: I. Lapsley (1986b) Investment appraisal in public service organisations, *Management Accounting*, pp. 28–31.

measurement under the general label of **cost-effectiveness** studies, i.e. those in which monetary values are assigned only to costs, but benefits are measured in non-monetary terms. This section looks at two approaches – one specific and one more general. These are not mutually exclusive. The specific technique examined here is that of the **points scoring system**. In this system, the management or the capital project team (usually multi-disciplinary) identifies key attributes of the project under consideration and seeks to rank these in terms of their potential importance. An illustrative example of how this might be carried out is shown in Table 3.2. This is a severely condensed version of the characteristics of possible project proposals. In this example, option 3 scores most highly on most of the criteria. This serves to illustrate how informed decision-makers can seek to (a) weigh different characteristics of capital proposals and (b) make explicit what these judgements are. A more fundamental approach to tackling the difficult questions of measuring the output of public services, and, indeed, of making explicit the objectives of such organizations (two of Hofstede's fundamental criteria, as discussed above) is that of using **options appraisal**. This particular approach to investment appraisal has been recommended to the operational branches of the NHS by the relevant central government departments (DHSS, 1982; SHHD, 1986). It recognizes both the need to employ discounting techniques and the difficulties of measuring benefits in monetary terms. While it has been recommended heavily for the NHS, this approach could be applied throughout the public sector where both the output measurement problem and ambiguity of objectives exist. The framework within which options appraisal is recommended to operate is that of strategic planning (see above). This addresses the issue of stating the organization's objectives. There are then a distinct series of stages to be followed in an iterative process, in implementing options appraisal. This can be summarized as follows (for a more detailed breakdown, see Fig. 3.1):

1. define objective;
2. identify options for achieving 1.;
3. quantify (value, where possible) the costs and benefits of these options;
4. examine options and refine and/or reduce the number of options;
5. decide on the most appropriate option.

In this regard, it is interesting to note that the 'search process' of identifying possible project proposals is one which is fairly well developed within the public sector. Indeed, there is evidence that such organizations may have been forced to address the difficulties of both output measurement and grappling with ambiguous objectives by conducting fairly extensive search processes to ensure that their initial set of project possibilities are the best possible (see Lapsley, 1986a, b; Ferguson and Lapsley, 1988). This context would make the more general adoption of options appraisal most fruitful.

BUDGETING

In many ways, the annual budget is **the** central component of management accounting in public sector organizations. In part, this is a reflection of the environment in which public service organizations operate, with an emphasis on the short-term, particularly the fiscal year. In this scenario, the annual budget becomes the dominant management tool for planning, coordinating, organizing and controlling activities. This multi-faceted role is a difficult one to fulfil and the implementation of the budget in public sector organizations is often a source of controversy. An interesting example of this can be found in a case study of budgets as they affect police authorities (Colville, 1989). However, it is outside the scope of this chapter to explore all of the ramifications of budget setting and implementation in public sector organizations. The following discussion focuses not only on actual practices but also on recommendations for 'best practice' and the possible reasons for their failure or non-adoption. It examines the role of the annual budget across three dimensions:

1. the budget: long-range plan interface;
2. the budget: management control interface;
3. the budget: central government interface.

It will be shown below that Hofstede's typology of characteristics influencing management control is also pertinent to the other dimensions of budgetary activity listed above. Each of these is considered.

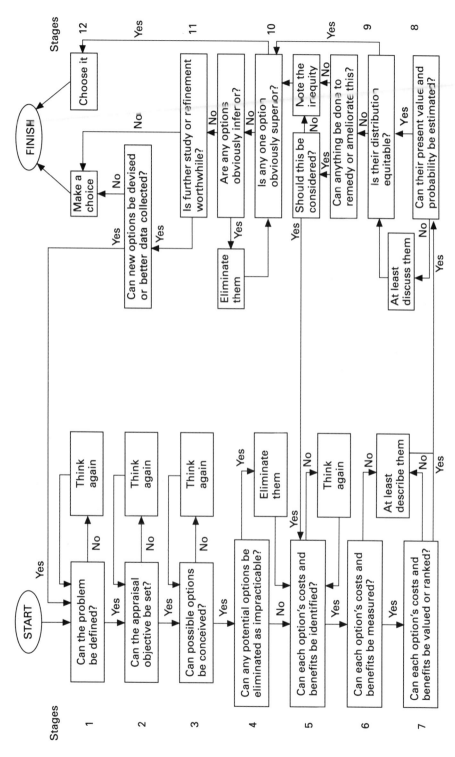

Fig. 3.1 Stages of option appraisal. (Source: Henderson, 1984.)

The budget: long-range plan interface

If strategic or long-range planning is to be meaningful, it should articulate with the organization's short-term plan, i.e. its budget. In the absence of such a relationship, the strategic plan may become remote and ineffectual and the annual budget may become a matter of expediency and short-term objectives. One of the most obvious means by which such an articulation of these different aspects of planning might be achieved is that of a planning, programming, budgeting system (PPBS). However, PPBS has become a much vaunted but little used management tool. This section (a) briefly describes what PPBS is, (b) suggests why it has not been a success and (c) reaffirms the need to link short and longer term planning devices.

PPBS is noted for its success in the US Department of Defence in the 1960s and 1970s. However, it has also been the subject of frequent criticism, particularly the lack of subsequent successful implementations, and its virtual abandonment by US central government departments. The manner and difficulties of its implementation are discussed below, but something of the nature of such difficulties can be gleaned from what PPBS is, or purports to be. In the first instance, a fully comprehensive PPBS could require a well-developed cost–benefit analysis or cost-effectiveness appraisal system to take account of expected/planned changes in activities. Secondly, the PPBS system focuses on **programmes** of activities. For example, within a local authority programmes might focus on particular client groups, such as the elderly. To articulate fully with longer term planning, annual budgets should also be based on specific programmes (their costs/revenues and the nature of the activities involved).

However, despite the essentially simple nature of the **concept** of PPBS, its implementation problems have inhibited its widespread acceptance. The first difficulty with PPBS is that its focus on programme budgeting contrasts sharply with the conventional structure of public sector organizations' annual budgets which tend to follow a line-by-line basis. For example, the typical public sector budget will have amounts of expenditure for all categories (budget heads) of expenditure, such as payroll, administration. A second difficulty is that, while it is recognized that formal organization charts do not accurately reflect the realities of organizational life, particularly because of the informal activities of members of the organization, they do give a **version** of how the typical public sector organization operates. In practice, this version of organizational relationships is closer to reality than the concept of a hierarchy of responsibilities based on programme budgeting. A final aspect of the difficulties of implementing PPBS was its over-reliance on sophisticated, unfamiliar jargon; excessive form-filling; and information overload (see Caulfield and Schultz, 1989, p. 12).

Nevertheless, while the PPBS approach cannot claim to have been a success in UK public sector organizations and may not be fully realized unless, at least, such organizations adopt a management and budgeting structure based on responsibilities for specific programmes of activities, there is a clear need for management accountants to identify relevant costs which are meaningful for operational management or risk strategic planning being too remote and detached from those managers charged with delivering their services.

The budget: management control interface

The role of the budget as a control device in public sector organizations is examined here from two perspectives: (a) what might have been (the use of zero-based budgets) and (b) what is currently being attempted (resource management systems). It will be shown that the concepts outlined above in the discussion of Hofstede's work are of particular relevance here.

Zero-based budgets

The story of zero-based budgets (ZBB) within the UK public sector is similar to that of PPBS. The concept of ZBB is credited with first being introduced into the private sector by Peter Phyrr of Texas Instruments in the USA (Phyrr, 1970). The underlying concept is very straightforward, as illustrated in Fig. 3.2. It revolves around the idea that, too frequently, budgets are merely rolled forward with little modification other than marginal changes for inflation and growth. This budgetary process – incremental budgeting – leads ultimately to a loss of management control, as the organization's priorities and patterns of activity may change, but the resource allocation process may become embedded in historical patterns of expenditure, with only minor, marginal, or cosmetic changes. The proposed alternative of ZBB is radically different. Its basic premise is that **all** activities should be challenged and justified before the organization should commit resources to any of its departments or units.

However, the original concept of ZBB rests on a distinct structure which is rather more complex than the fundamental ideas expressed above. This can be summarized as follows:

1. identify **decision units**;
2. establish **decision packages**;
3. **rank** all decision packages;
4. **allocate** resources to decision units.

The **decision unit** is any distinct part of the organization for which it is meaningful to establish data on resources utilization. The **decision**

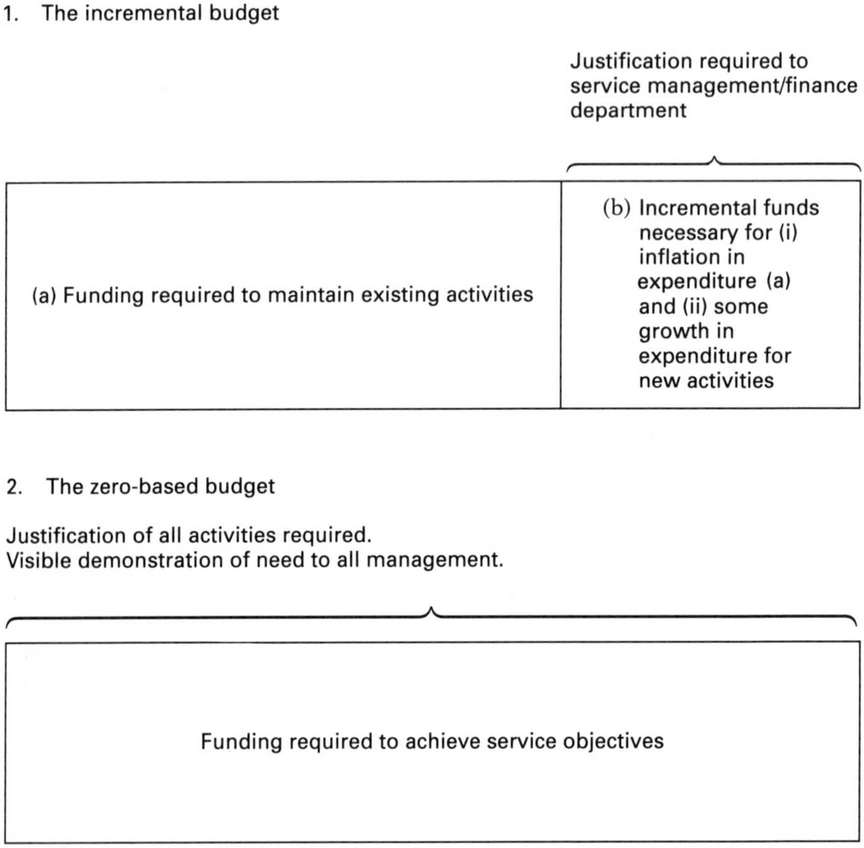

1.   The incremental budget

Justification required to
service management/finance
department

(a) Funding required to maintain existing activities	(b) Incremental funds necessary for (i) inflation in expenditure (a) and (ii) some growth in expenditure for new activities

2.   The zero-based budget

Justification of all activities required.
Visible demonstration of need to all management.

Funding required to achieve service objectives

Fig. 3.2 Incremental and zero-based budgets compared.

package represents a bid for resources by such units. It entails a full specification of all such requirements. This may be difficult enough, particularly if such units cut across well-established organizational boundaries/relationships. However, major difficulties may arise at the third stage where the issues of ambiguity of objectives and difficulty of output measurement may make the trading off of the various decision packages a hazardous business. Indeed, an early study of ZBB implementations noted that, despite some successful applications, there were considerable tensions aroused by this procedure in public sector organizations (Wright, 1979, p. 182). Also, *ad hoc* evidence gathered by this writer in contacts with public sector organizations over the past 12 years suggests that considerable time and effort of skilled, scarce finance manpower are required to make ZBB a success and, indeed, this might best be regarded as a technique which might be undertaken in (say) a three year cycle, rather than as an annual event.

Resource management

While ZBB has had limited application in the UK, there is currently an attempt to encourage the implementation of budgetary control systems which are broader than conventional ones, in the sense that their focus is not merely on narrow financial considerations, but also extends to non-financial, activity and performance data. This development can be seen as a mechanism by which members of organizations, who have had a significant influence on the consumption of resources, without formal budgetary responsibilities are brought under management control. This development is most marked in the NHS. For a detailed statement of this development (and its precursors) in the NHS, see Perrin (1988). It is outside the scope of this chapter to explore the details of such schemes. However, it is interesting to note that the official Department of Health evaluation of resource management in the NHS is sceptical on whether the benefits of such initiatives exceed their costs (Packwood *et al.*, 1991).

The budget: central government interface

There are a number of aspects to the relationship between the individual public service organization's budget construction and central government. However, this section is devoted to the critical question of how cash-limited public sector organizations manage the cash limits imposed upon them by central government. The budgetary control systems in such organizations will be constructed typically on the basis of income and expenditure (modified accrual) accounting numbers, with some going further than this by utilizing commitment-based accounting systems. However, in parallel to this, finance departments of such organizations must ensure that their overall cash limit is not breached. An illustration of the annual cycle of expenditure control to cash limits is shown in Fig. 3.3. The typical process by which finance departments may manage their cash position includes the delaying or freezing of vacancies, the build up (or run down) of stocks, the acceleration of (or delays in) payments to creditors. Clearly, this is a critical aspect of the overall financial management of public sector organizations.

COSTING AND SHORT RUN DECISION-MAKING

For many years, the matter of costing for short run decision-making – the pricing of services, decisions on scarce resources, the buying in of services v. internal provision – have not been a major part of the activities of public sector management accountants. A major excep-

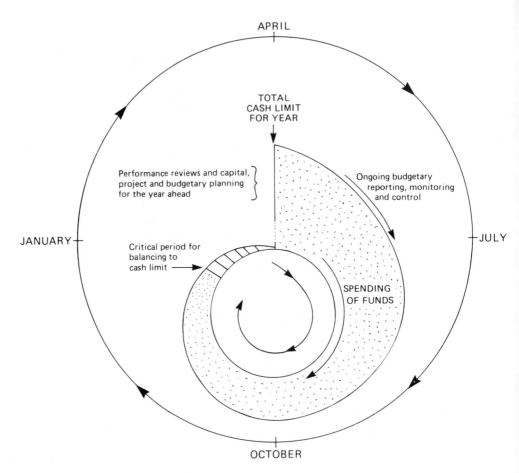

APRIL

TOTAL
CASH LIMIT
FOR YEAR

Performance reviews and capital,
project and budgetary planning
for the year ahead

Ongoing budgetary
reporting, monitoring
and control

JANUARY

JULY

Critical period for
balancing to
cash limit

SPENDING
OF FUNDS

OCTOBER

Fig. 3.3 Annual cycle of control to cash limits.

tion to this is the somewhat convoluted and tortuous guidance given
to the nationalized industries on costing for pricing in the 1960s and
1970s. Basically, this advice recommended that these industries should
adopt versions of marginal costing as the basis of their pricing policies.
However, the interventions of successive governments undermined
these policies. At present, the major aspects of short-term decision-
making which need to be addressed by management accountants in
the public sector are:

1. competitive tendering;
2. charging for services.

The first of these can, of course, be regarded as a longer term decision
extending over a number of years, in the manner of an options appraisal. However, where the public sector organization is considering

entering into short-term contractual arrangements for the provision of in-house services, it is important that:

1. both alternatives are costed accurately;
2. quality of service considerations are given adequate weight in any such decisions;
3. proper controls (penalty schemes, monitoring) are established to ensure that value for money is achieved where services are contracted out.

As for the **charging** of services, this is a major uncertainty in the current climate of recently established notional or quasi-markets in public services. Where public service organizations have focused on meeting cash limits (see above) and remaining within budget by monitoring aggregate levels of expenditure, there is not a need to cost accurately the individual components of service provided to establish suitable charges for services provided. This will represent a major departure for any such organizations and critical issues which need to be considered include:

1. the elements of costs to be included in charges;
2. the appropriateness of overhead recovery schemes;
3. the extent to which cross-subsidization of services may exist;
4. the impact of charging schemes on the overall financial position.

It remains to be seen how successful or otherwise public service organizations are at adapting to this new (operating, financing and accounting) environment.

SUMMARY

The public sector has always posed challenges to management accountants. This even more so today, with the rapid pace of change, not only in terms of the more sophisticated needs of potential users of management accounting information (as evidenced by new style management arrangements throughout the public sector) but also because of structural changes in the environment, notably the introduction of notional or 'quasi-markets' for public services. These developments underline the need for prompt, relevant, management accounting information. It has been shown above that, for critical decisions in public sector organizations, the selection of management accounting techniques is not straightforward. For example, in both capital investment and budgeting decisions, there are a variety of possible techniques available to management accountants. However it has been suggested here that, for management accountants in the public sector, their role and the selection of accounting techniques to be used cannot be reduced to technical considerations alone. A major factor of concern which influences the successful adoption or use of management accounting techniques in the public sector is the context in which the organization operates, notably the extent to which it has unambiguous objectives and a measurable output. Where these circumstances do not prevail there is a danger that accounting techniques will be used in a routine fashion with dysfunctional consequences. The recognition that not only are there technical difficulties but also contextual ones in the selection and use of management accounting techniques has been a major theme of this chapter and sensitivity to such issues will be the hallmark of the successful public sector management accountant of the 1990s.

FURTHER READING

Further reading on public sector management accounting of a practical nature can be found in *Public Finance and Accountancy*. Regular articles of interest can also be found in both *Public Money & Management* and *Financial Accountability and Management*. There are also occasional articles on public management accounting sector topics in *Management Accounting Research* and in *Accounting, Organisations & Society*.

4

Central government

The planning and control of public expenditure is an essential element in the government's financial and social policy. This chapter explains how public expenditure is planned, controlled and monitored by central government and how that relates to the role of Parliament. It describes the system of central government accounts and the development of financial management within government departments.

THE MEANING OF PUBLIC EXPENDITURE

In the United Kingdom the public sector comprises central and local government and the public corporations, including the nationalized industries. Broadly speaking, public expenditure is the total in cash terms of central and local government spending, plus financial transfers from the former to the public corporations. Central and local government expenditure together form 'general government expenditure' (GGE), which is a definition also widely used in Europe. It is this total which is the focus of policy for determining the size and composition of public spending, but the government seeks to achieve its objectives by exercising direct control on the narrower 'planning total', redefined in 1988, which comprises only direct government expenditure, support grants to local authorities, the external financing requirements of the nationalized industries, and the reserve. Table 4.1 shows the main figures for the expenditure plans for three years ahead (1991–2 to 1993–4) and how the planning total is related to GGE. A large part of local authority expenditure is financed by grants from central government – in effect from the taxpayer – so these amounts are netted out when calculating general government expenditure. But they are included in the funds for which central government has to apply to Parliament through the 'Supply' procedure explained below.

Table 4.1 Public expenditure plans

	£ billion 1989–90 Outturn	1990–1 Estimated outturn	1991–2 Plans	1992–3 Plans	1993–4 Plans
Central government expenditure	**127.5**	**140.6**	**152.1**	**161.6**	**167.9**
Of which:					
Department of Social Security	46.9	51.8	58.2	62.6	66.7
Department of Health and OPCS	19.9	22.5	24.9	26.3	27.5
Ministry of Defence	20.8	22.1	22.8	23.4	23.4
Scotland	4.4	4.9	5.8	6.0	6.2
Wales	1.9	2.2	2.5	2.6	2.7
Northern Ireland	5.7	5.9	6.4	6.8	7.1
Other departments	27.9	31.9	31.5	33.9	34.3
Overseas contributions to cost of Gulf conflict		−0.7			
Central government support for local authorities	**38.4**	**42.6**	**52.5**	**55.7**	**56.6**
Of which:					
revenue/rate support grant	13.0	13.1	13.6		
non-domestic rate payments	11.4	12.1	14.3	49.9	50.7
current specific grants	9.7	12.2	18.9		
capital grants	0.9	1.1	1.5	1.5	1.5
credit approvals	3.4	4.0	4.3	4.3	4.4
Financing requirements of nationalized industries	**1.1**	**2.5**	**2.3**	**2.1**	**2.0**
Privatization proceeds	**−4.2**	**−5.3**	**−5.5**	**−5.5**	**−5.5**
Reserve			**3.5**	**7.0**	**10.5**
Planning total	**162.9**	**180.4**	**205.0**	**221.0**	**231.5**
Local authority self-financed expenditure	14.5	14.7	9.1	9.5	11.5
Central government debt interest	17.8	17.6	16.7	17	17.5
Other adjustments	4.2	3.4	3.9	5	5.5
General government expenditure	**199.4**	**216.0**	**234.8**	**252**	**266**

Source: *Financial Statement and Budget Report 1991*, HCP 300. All tables and the figure in this chapter are reproduced with the permission of the Controller of HMSO.

As Fig. 1.1 (p. 5) showed, public expenditure can be examined in various ways, for example:

1. by department (ministry) – Department of Health, Ministry of Defence, Department of Trade and Industry, and so on;
2. by function – health, social security, employment, housing, transport;
3. by economic category – direct calls by government on labour and other resources, transfer payments to individuals or companies.

The departmental and functional categories may largely coincide, for example in defence, where all the functional responsibilities fall to one ministry. In other cases several departments may be involved in the provision of a functional service, for example law and order, where not only does the Scottish department share responsibility with the Home Office but also there is a major local authority component as well. For nearly 30 years it has been accepted policy to consider the total demand of public expenditure programmes in relation to the nation's taxable capacity, including taxes locally imposed, and in relation to national resources. Figs 1.2 (p. 6) and 1.3 (p. 7) and Table 1.1 (p. 8) show the growth of public expenditure over a 30-year period and its broad functional distribution.

THE PUBLIC EXPENDITURE SURVEY SYSTEM

There have been major changes in the way in which public expenditure is planned, controlled and presented in the last decade or so and changes are still in progress. Their significance is best appreciated in the light of a brief review of the public expenditure survey system.

The system originated with the report in 1961 of the Committee chaired by Sir Edwin Plowden: *The Planning and Control of Public Expenditure*. The central recommendations were that 'regular surveys should be made of public expenditure as a whole, over a period of years ahead, and in relation to prospective resources; decisions involving substantial future expenditure should be taken in the light of these surveys'. This system has formed the basis of successive governments' approaches ever since, though the techniques have been progressively developed, and policy on the scope and purposes of public expenditure has changed markedly from time to time.

The main features of the system were as follows:

1. a factual forward costing of 'existing policies' governing expenditure was made annually by a committee of senior officials – the Public Expenditure Survey Committee – with proposals for further spending by departments identified separately.
2. this was done at 'constant prices', which led to severe problems of estimating and budgetary control.

3. although the estimates – for up to four years ahead – covered the whole of public expenditure, important parts of it, notably local authorities' current expenditure, were not subject to direct control by central government.

The survey completed, ministers had to take decisions. The Chancellor of the Exchequer put forward his own proposals for levels of public expenditure in relation to his judgement of their validity and of the prospects for the economy. The way in which this judgement was made, and the methodology used, varied over the years. The following alternative methods have been used in the past.

1. The expected growth rate of the national output (gross domestic product) was compared with the estimated growth of public expenditure, generally with the object of avoiding the latter exceeding the former.
2. An assessment was made of the demands of 'prior claims' on the national output – the resources required for productive investment and the balance of payments – and a view was taken of the desirable division of the remainder, itself the bulk of the total, between public expenditure and private consumption. This work centred on the 'medium-term economic assessment' and was related to the use of resources in the economy rather than to financial objectives.
3. Linked to 2., attention was concentrated on the implications for personal and company taxation of public expenditure plans, to see if prospective tax levels appeared acceptable or not.

When ministers had taken decisions about the totals of public spending in the years ahead and its distribution among the departmental programmes, the annual Public Expenditure White Paper was prepared and presented to Parliament. This was done every year from the late 1960s, until the major changes in the presentation of public expenditure described below were made in the late 1980s.

The survey system had the great merits of bringing together, for ministerial consideration, the whole of the spending plans which had to be financed by publicly imposed rates, taxes or charges, or by public borrowing, and doing so, not just for a year ahead, but for several years. Thus future costs could in principle be foreseen and taken into account. In practice, the successive costings even of unchanged policies showed large increases from one survey to the next, and additional spending decisions continued to be taken throughout the year, on a scale which could not be met from the contingency reserve established for that purpose. It was therefore necessary both to reform the technique of expenditure planning and control and to strengthen the system of ministerial decision-taking based upon it.

THE CASH LIMITS SYSTEM

The major problem of technique in public expenditure control to emerge in the mid-1970s was the absence of an effective cash budgeting system. Some programmes were necessarily planned and controlled in cash terms, for example the large social security schemes and other types of transfer payments. Local authorities' spending was determined by their own cash budgets for the year ahead. The allocations to individual health authorities, from within the total health programme, were also made in cash terms. In addition, cash controls were superimposed on some other types of government expenditure when exceptionally high cost inflation made this essential, for example building and construction in 1973. But the greater part of central government spending was planned in volume, resource, or 'real terms', through the use of constant prices in each survey. There was no general use of cash budgets to set spending limits in advance of current prices: pay and price rises were provided for as they occurred. The Parliamentary procedures did ostensibly provide for full cash control: departments were not allowed to overspend their original Estimates without submitting a Supplementary Estimate. But in practice Parliament had no option but to grant the extra funds, so that the formal control was illusory.

Control in resource or real terms had some advantages. It enabled departments to staff, build, equip and supply the projects and services that had been authorized without risking shortfalls and disruption due to their cash provision falling short of actual inflation. But if all wage and price increases were 'for free' so far as departmental managers were concerned, there was little incentive to keep cash costs within bounds and the discipline of firm cash allocations was absent. More seriously, the government had no means of knowing, within wide margins, how much money would actually be spent at a time when financial policy was moving strongly towards monetary controls.

The working out of the cash limit system in 1974/75 was designed to remedy these problems and it remains a crucial element in the current system of control. It has the following essential features.

1. Cash limits are set for as many central government programmes as possible for the next financial year.
2. They are set in terms of current prices, with an allowance for inflation.
3. The cash limits are regarded as firm, not to be increased save in highly exceptional circumstances, and then only with Treasury permission.
4. Consideration is given to extending cash limit control to as many further programmes and services as possible. The main exclusions

are services which are 'demand-determined', such as social security benefits, where the sums paid out follow automatically from
the numbers of qualified recipients and the levels at which benefits
are set from time to time by policy decisions.

Cash limits could not be applied to the current expenditure of individual local authorities without extensive machinery for approving
the plans of over 450 authorities. It was therefore originally decided
to apply a cash limit to the rate support grant (block grant) made
available by central government. (The present system of control of
local authority expenditure is explained in Chapter 6.) Cash limits
were clearly not appropriate to the expenditure of the nationalized
industries and other public corporations, but their borrowing is controlled by external financing limits (see Chapter 7).

At the same time as the cash limit system was being worked out in
1974/75, a new central financial information system was developed by
the Treasury, in consultation with the spending departments, to provide early and accurate information about current central government
spending in relation to both the vote provision and the Public Expenditure White Paper figures. The course of actual expenditure was
analysed on a monthly basis. This analysis was compared with the
expected 'profiles' of expenditure for the year as a whole, since the
rate of spending might not be uniform either throughout the year or
by different types of service. Any necessary corrective action could
thus be considered in good time. It was clearly essential that for cash
limits to be monitored and enforced, an effective financial reporting
system of this kind should be in operation.

Cash limits are essentially the same as the cash budgetary arrangements in force in many other countries. But they are closely related
to the broader public expenditure survey system, some of whose
limitations they were designed to remedy; and they were not imposed
where they could not have been enforced. The main developments in
the cash limit system have included the following:

1. extension of cash limits to some services not originally covered,
   for example, certain forms of assistance to industry where as a
   policy decision an overall limit was imposed to override the
   'demand-determined' criterion;
2. cash limits covering Supply expenditure have been aligned with
   Votes in the Parliamentary Estimates, thus facilitating the reconciliation between the parliamentary and governmental control
   systems.

In 1982/83, a major change was made by the government in the
basis of the public expenditure survey itself and its relation to cash
limits. Previous to this date the cash limits had been grafted on to the
volume system of planning public expenditure; no change had been

made in the constant price or real terms basis of the survey. From 1983 the survey itself was conducted in cash terms. The previous year's cash figures for the various services over the survey period were the starting point. Any increases, also in cash terms, for inflation or policy changes had to be justified,

THE PRESENT SYSTEM OF EXPENDITURE CONTROL

Building on the foundations and developments summarized above current policies for managing public expenditure show distinctive features which derive from the government's economic, financial and social objectives. The survey system itself has spanned many governments with widely differing views of the role of the state and the priorities to be accorded to different spending programmes. In recent years, for example, funds for certain types of government assistance to industry and for publicly provided housing have been severely reduced, while spending on industrial training and law and order services has been substantially increased. But the methodology of control can be applied in the interests of efficient management to any level of total spending and to any variations, large or small, in its composition or objectives.

It is of interest that the decision to introduce cash limits was taken by the Labour government of 1974–9. The aims of tighter spending control and improved financial discipline were given priority over the guaranteed achievement of departmental projects in resource terms. It is highly improbable that any government, whatever its view of the state's role in the provision of services, would revert to the former system of planning and control in resource or real terms. It would be possible to apply the present system of cash budgeting with more flexibility if full delivery of certain projects or programmes within a given time scale was held to take priority over the maintenance of spending allocations in money terms. But a slippery slope, leading in some circumstances to a nasty looking precipice, awaits ministers who weaken methods of public expenditure control instead of applying them efficiently in the furtherance of their chosen policies.

It is useful to have the present government's objectives for the economy in mind in setting out the current approach to control. They are to reduce inflation, and to promote improvement of the industrial and commercial performance of the economy. The chosen means, in so far as they impact on public expenditure, are to restrain its rate of growth below the growth of the economy as a whole so that taxes can be reduced and public sector borrowing minimized. It is believed that the public sector, generally speaking, uses resources inefficiently.

The same machinery for planning and control could be used to serve quite different objectives. A previous Conservative government (1970–4) spent large sums in the attempt to stimulate employment and exports. A future government might take a different view of the effect of taxation on incentives and the growth of national income, and thus alter the guidelines for the planning of public expenditure. It is possible that the primacy accorded to monetary objectives could lose favour. But the public expenditure management system as it has evolved – and as it will no doubt continue to do so – can be applied to widely differing political requirements.

The public expenditure cycle

In the spring of each year ministers give general guidance about the way the survey is to be conducted, including the kind of information they will require in taking their decisions and any changes in their priorities. Thus in 1990 the survey reviewed plans for 'years 1 and 2', i.e. 1991–2 and 1992–3, and formulated plans for the first time for 'year 3', i.e. 1993–4. The cash figures for the first two years will be those in the previous survey, as modified by any subsequent decisions. For the third year they will, on current policies, be those in year 2 increased by a specific percentage, related to but not necessarily identical with forecast inflation rates. This procedure cuts out the earlier sometimes protracted argument about the estimated future costs of 'existing policies'. It also carries the implication that if inflation turns out to be higher than expected, the additional costs will have to be met from within the allotted cash provision.

Existing policies nevertheless exist, and their periodic review is an essential component of any coherent policy for public expenditure. Major reviews have recently included the National Health Service and education systems. But such major studies cannot sensibly be run as part of the public expenditure survey itself, into whose machinery the financial effects of the new policy decisions will be fed.

Any new bids resulting from new policy initiatives, and the latest estimates for demand-led programmes, e.g. social security benefits, will be examined between the Treasury and spending departments as part of the survey process. When costings are complete, by early summer, the Chief Secretary puts to the Cabinet an assessment of the position and personal proposals for the planning totals for the next three years. Ministers then decide what total spending can be afforded in the light of the prospects for revenue and expenditure shown in the medium-term financial strategy, published earlier as part of the Budget. Whatever future policies on monetary control or other approaches to economic stability may be, it is unlikely that public expenditure decisions would be taken without consideration of their effects on the economy as a whole.

Further ministerial decisions are necessary during the summer or early autumn to agree:

1. the level of local authority current expenditure on which the government will base their support grants for local authorities for the coming year;
2. the departmental spending programmes;
3. the external financing limits for the nationalized industries.

All these decisions are required for the preparation of the Autumn Statement (see below). The decisions concerning 2. in particular can involve strong argument between the Treasury and spending ministers. If bilateral discussions between the Chief Secretary to the Treasury and spending ministers cannot settle departmental allocations, it is the practice for the issues to be discussed in the 'Star Chamber', a small group of senior ministers without large departmental programmes of their own, in an effort to reach acceptable solutions, sometimes with a modest further allocation of funds from the Treasury. The last resort, avoided if possible, is reference to the full Cabinet.

PUBLIC EXPENDITURE PUBLICATIONS

For 20 years, from the late 1960s to the late 1980s, the government's expenditure plans were presented to Parliament and the public in the Public Expenditure White Paper, a document whose increasing size and sophistication did not deter criticism that it gave insufficient information to enable those plans to be properly assessed and judged, and that what was given was presented in indigestible form. For good measure, it was also considered self-evident that the publication of expenditure plans some months in advance of the annual budget meant that the government failed to relate their spending and revenue policies.

Be that as it may, in 1988 the government responded to suggestions from the Public Accounts Committee and the Treasury and Civil Service Committee for a new structure of expenditure documents, with the following proposals (Cm 375).

1. The Autumn Statement would include as much as practicable of the key material from Chapter 1 of the White Paper.
2. Volume II of the White Paper, which gave the individual departments' plans, would be split into separate volumes, to be published before Budget day, in conjunction with the Parliamentary Supply Estimates which they would help to clarify.
3. The remaining material in volume I – the so-called additional analyses – took more time to produce and could be made available in various ways in the spring.

From 1990 these proposals were implemented with a new array of publications, whose main features and objectives can be summarized as follows.

1. *The Autumn Statement*, presented by the Chancellor to Parliament in November, now includes, in addition to a discussion of economic prospects for the coming year and notes on national insurance contributions and a tax revenue 'ready reckoner', the main figures and features of the government's spending plans for the next three years following the conclusion of the public expenditure survey. This information includes a range of analyses, statistical time series, and comparisons covering all the main components of public expenditure and their interrelationships. It also broadly describes the aims of each departmental programme, for example:

   (a) Agriculture, Fisheries and Food: 'The Department's main aims are to seek improvement to the European Community's Common Agricultural Policy and to create the conditions in which efficient agriculture, fisheries and food industries can flourish, to protect the public, to enhance the environment and to prevent flooding.'

   (b) Transport: 'The Department's aims are to provide a safe, cost-effective and environmentally friendly road and public transport system.'

   (c) Education and Science: 'The Government's aims are to raise standards of achievement at all levels of ability, to increase parental choice, and to widen access to higher and further education and make them more responsive to the needs of the economy.'

   These statements are obviously at a high level of generality. Nevertheless, they are a start; other governments would no doubt give similar broad indications of their differing policy objectives; and they are substantially expanded and refined in the departmental reports (see below) into specific activities which are increasingly susceptible to performance assessment.

2. *Public Expenditure Analyses: Statistical Supplement to the Autumn Statement*. This supplement is presented to Parliament by the Chancellor in February. It provides much greater detail and extensive analysis of the public expenditure figures in the Autumn Statement, including a summary of the detailed plans in the departmental reports. Among much other material there are figures and trends for public sector asset creation, sales and purchases of land and buildings, and public sector manpower; not limited to central government but covering the local authorities, the nationalized industries and public corporations as well. In recognition of the familiar point that some of the objectives of government policies can be more suitably achieved through the tax system than by

grants to individuals or companies there are estimates of the cost of all the reliefs, allowances and exemptions available to direct taxpayers. The Autumn Statement and the Statistical Supplement supersede Part 1 of the Public Expenditure White Paper.

3. *Departmental Reports*. Separate departmental reports took over, expanded, and glossified – in the best sense – the material formerly in Part II of the White Paper. They give full details of each department's expenditure plans as outlined in the Autumn Statement, and are published about three months later – normally in February. They explain the operation and objectives of all the activities for which the department is responsible; how those activities link with public spending by the local authorities on the same or related programmes; and they describe the operations of any nationalized industries or public corporations for which it is the sponsor. Again therefore the integrated public sector framework is used.

The reports are presented jointly by the departmental minister and the Chief Secretary to the Treasury, under arrangements set out in Cm 918, *Financial Reporting to Parliament*. The Treasury requires certain core material to be included, notably a table of the department's cash plans over a nine-year period which must be consistent with the information given in the Autumn Statement and the supplementary analyses. For the rest there is discussion between the department and the Treasury about the content, the extent and nature of which is still in an evolutionary stage, but the intention is 'to allow departments more flexibility in the format and content of the presentation of their expenditure plans' and the indications are that most departments will wish to take full advantage of this delegation. There will be strong incentives, not least the political one, to present their aims, activities and performance in the most convincing style. Several departments have invited public comment on their reports, offering personalized points of contact for the purpose; and bibliographies are becoming a matter of course. There is likely to be a progressive advance in the explanation of public services, their costs, financing and results. It will be largely up to the parliamentary select committees and outside commentators to assess this progress and to suggest further improvements to meet user needs.

One further important document is the Financial Statement and Budget Report – the *Red Book*. This has been published for several years as a supplement to the Chancellor's Budget statement and concentrates on the Budget measures in relation to the economic prospects and the government's monetary policy. But it also reproduces the main public expenditure figures and provides an opportunity to incorporate any changes since the earlier documents were published. Finally, receipts and expenditure are brought together in a comprehensive picture of the public sector finances for the current and coming year, taking account of the Budget measures and leading up to estimates of the public sector borrowing requirement or debt repayment.

Local authorities

Central government is responsible for spending over 70% of the public expenditure total. Local authorities are responsible for spending most of the remainder.

Local authorities are elected bodies accountable to their own electorates, not to Parliament, for their policies and administration. But Parliament determines their powers and responsibilities as the sovereign legislature. That role is currently exercised mainly in the following ways.

1. Services provided by local authorities are authorized by statute, e.g. education and housing Acts, which lay down, in considerable detail, what is to be or may be provided and how services are to be administered.
2. Legislation also provides for the way in which local authority expenditure is to be financed, including arrangements for central government contributions by way of block grants or specific grants, and the financial relations between central and local government generally.
3. Parliament holds accountable to itself the government departments responsible for national policy on locally provided services, e.g. education, housing, personal social services, roads and transport, and, in the case of the Department of the Environment, policy on relations generally between the central and local authorities. This accountability is usually pursued through the select committees which may examine ministers and officials on the exercise of their responsibilities under the governing statutes.

In this constitutional situation, expenditure by local authorities is treated for many purposes as part of public expenditure as a whole. Cm 441 states: 'In the UK the Government formulates policies which may be implemented by either central or local government', and: 'It is total public spending which is the main expenditure aggregate and of importance in the macro economic context.' The definition of 'general government expenditure' will continue to reflect this analysis, and figures for it will continue to be given in public presentations and policy statements. The definition of the public expenditure planning total, which includes only the expenditure which is under the direct control of the government, including the grants to local authorities, is designed to clarify responsibilities. But it is not intended to weaken control over public expenditure as a whole. Quoting again from Cm

441: '...if the Government felt that this expenditure was growing too rapidly...(they) would need to consider whether to take action to moderate the growth of spending within the planning total, whether its own spending or grants to local authorities'. The intention clearly is to bring pressure to bear on local authorities by their own electorates if increases in 'their' spending, with a squeeze on subventions from central government, forces them to raise locally imposed charges to a politically difficult degree.

While these objectives are clear, it is not in fact usually possible to relate the respective responsibilities of central and local government for the policy underlying an expenditure programme to the split in its financing. In some areas – education is the outstanding current illustration – central government is centralizing policy, and thus heavily influencing expenditure, even in areas formerly left to local decision. And as the figures in Cm 441 make clear, 'local authority self-financed expenditure' is a comparatively small proportion of the total programme.

Nationalized industries and other public corporations

The remaining nationalized industries and several other public corporations, for example the Scottish and Welsh Development Agencies, have the following distinguishing characteristics.

1. They are established by Act of Parliament which lays down their constitution, powers, responsibilities and relations with the government.
2. Subject to 4. below, their boards are not directly answerable to Parliament, but are subject to the control of their sponsoring ministers as provided for in legislation, those ministers in turn being accountable to Parliament for the discharge of their statutory duties in respect of the industries.
3. As a corollary of this constitutional position the industries are fully backed by the Exchequer and have no independent credit standing of their own.
4. Their annual reports and accounts are required to be laid before Parliament, which brings them formally within the purview of the Public Accounts Committee. But by parliamentary agreement they are investigated by the select committee which shadows the government department sponsoring the industry. Note that this right to question boards and to report on their operations depends on convention and not on the statutes establishing the industries.
5. Though by agreement with other select committees the Public Accounts Committee has in general not examined the industries, the committee has shown an increasing interest in the sponsor

departments' actions in relation to their industries and has issued reports in this area.

The nationalized industries and some of the other public corporations are trading bodies which operate in the market like private corporations. Others, for example the Royal Mint, trade with the private sector but have obligations also to the government. Yet others are not essentially trading bodies at all but discharge a variety of public responsibilities, for example the Bank of England, the BBC, the General Practice Finance Corporation. The main element in the public expenditure total deriving from this sector is the external financing of the nationalized industries and some other corporations, that is the total of the finance they need which is not provided from their own operations, whether by way of grant, subsidy or loan, and whether met by the government or from private sources. By controlling these external financing limits the government influences commercial policies and management. The industries are dealt with in full in Chapter 7.

THE ROLE OF PARLIAMENT

It is the government which formulates plans for public expenditure and manages their execution. It is Parliament which exercises formal control over the spending of public funds, as over the raising of public revenue. This section summarizes how this is done and relates the parliamentary process to the governmental planning and control systems.

The Supply procedure

Parliament exercises constitutional control over the annual expenditure of government departments and certain closely related bodies, for example the research councils and national museums, by what is known as 'Supply' procedure. Every department prepares its Estimates for expenditure in the coming financial year and is required to agree them with the Treasury. The Treasury submits the approved Estimates in November to the House of Commons, thus meeting the long-established constitutional practice by which the Crown (the government) demands money from Parliament. Three 'Estimate Days' are allotted in the House of Commons timetable each session for debating the Estimates, usually on the basis of reports from the relevant select committees (see below). Statutory authority for the supply of funds to meet the expenditure set out in the Estimates, or Votes, is given in the Consolidated Fund (Appropriation) Act, passed before the summer recess.

The Supply procedure also has to meet further requirements. Government departments need authority to start spending money from the first day of the financial year, whereas the Appropriation Act will not be passed until some months later. Parliament is therefore asked to provide it by a system of 'Votes on Account', usually presented in November and amounting to about 45% of the amount authorized to date in the current financial year. Statutory authority for these advances is given in a winter Consolidated Fund Act. Second, departments are permitted to present Revised Estimates before the Appropriation Act is passed, but this normally occurs only where reduced financial provision is sought, or to take account of transfers of departmental functions. Third, the government may need to ask Parliament for additional money during the year, necessitating the presentation of Supplementary Estimates at various times, and authorization in a Consolidated Fund Act. Fourth, it is sometimes essential, in ministers' judgement, for urgent additional expenditure to be incurred in advance of provision by Parliament. The Contingencies Fund, established by Parliament, exists for this purpose, but money advanced from it under strict criteria applied by the Treasury must be repaid when the sums have been subsequently voted.

In 1991–2 the separate Estimates or Votes totalled 163 grouped into 20 classes. Table 4.2, reproduced from the government's *Summary and Guide to the Supply Estimates*, shows this classification and the amounts provided in 1991–2. It will be seen that the classification aligns completely with the departmental presentation in the Public Expenditure White Paper, though the figures differ for reasons explained below.

Each Vote contains the following information about the services for which it provides.

1. An introductory note describes the expenditure, indicates whether the Vote is treated as a cash limit (see below), and compares the provision sought with the provision and/or likely outturn in the previous year.
2. Part I gives a brief formal description of the services to be financed (known as the 'ambit' of the Vote), the net sum required, the department which will account for the Vote, and the amount allocated in the Vote on Account. The ambit is important because it describes and limits the purposes for which the expenditure can legally be incurred.
3. Part II analyses the provision by sector, section and subhead, matching the descriptions in the corresponding departmental reports. The provision sought is compared with actual expenditure in the last completed year and total provision in the current year (actuals will not be known at this stage), and for the Vote as a whole the forecast outturn for the current year is also shown.

Table 4.2 Supply Estimates by class,* 1989–90 to 1991–2

Class	1989–90 Outturn	1990–1 Original provision	1990–1 Total provision	1990–1 Forecast outturn	1991–2 Provision
			£ billion		
I Ministry of Defence	20.8	21.2	22.2	22.1	22.9
II Foreign and Commonwealth Office	2.4	2.5	2.6	2.6	2.8
III Ministry of Agriculture, Fisheries and Food	0.6	0.7	0.9	0.8	0.8
IV Trade and Industry	2.1	2.1	2.2	2.1	1.8
V Energy	5.0	2.2	3.3	3.1	1.4
VI Department of Employment	3.2	3.2	3.3	3.1	2.9
VII Department of Transport	3.0	3.7	4.0	4.0	4.3
VIII Department of the Environment	15.1	28.2	28.8	28.6	33.3
IX Home Office (including Charity Commission)	5.4	6.1	6.4	6.4	6.8
X Lord Chancellor's and Law Officers' Departments	1.1	1.2	1.4	1.4	1.5
XI Department of Education and Science	5.8	6.7	6.8	6.8	7.6
XII Office of Arts and Libraries	0.4	0.5	0.5	0.5	0.6
XIII Department of Health and Office of Population Censuses and Surveys	16.6	18.9	19.4	19.3	21.7
XIV Department of Social Security	23.1	22.9	25.8	25.7	28.3
XV Scotland	7.8	7.6	8.4	8.3	8.7
XVI Wales	3.3	4.2	4.3	4.2	4.7
XVII Northern Ireland	1.8	1.7	1.8	1.8	1.9
XVIII Chancellor of the Exchequer's Departments	4.2	4.5	4.6	4.6	4.7
XIX Cabinet Office, Privy Council Office and Parliament†	0.3	0.4	0.4	0.4	0.4
Total	**122.1**	**138.5**	**146.9**	**145.6**	**156.7**

* Class XX is excluded as no funds are sought for payments to the European Communities in 1991–2 main Estimates nor were any required in 1989–90 or 1990–1.
† Includes House of Commons: Administration (Class XIXA) and the National Audit Office (Class XIXB).

Source: *Summary and Guide to the Supply Estimates,* 1991, Cm 1454.

Expenditure must be accounted for by subheads: savings on one subhead may be applied, with Treasury sanction, to meet excesses on another – a process known as 'virement'. Part II also shows those receipts which may be 'appropriated in aid' of the Vote, i.e. used to meet some of the gross expenditure. Any receipts above the amounts so specified must be surrendered to the Exchequer (Consolidated Fund) as 'extra receipts'.

4. Part III shows particulars of receipts which are expected to be received but will be paid into the Consolidated Fund and not 'appropriated in aid'.

5. Additional information about the expenditure on the Vote is given in appended tables, e.g. details of long-term projects and works services, and apportionment of running costs and staff numbers to various departmental functions.

The Estimates are entirely on a cash basis, as is the public expenditure system. The sums authorized to be spent are those which 'come in course of payment' during the year, i.e. where the liability to pay has matured and the instrument of payment has been issued. The strict application of annuality to government expenditure, whereby money voted for one year must all be surrendered to the Exchequer if unspent, has long been criticized as the cause of inefficient planning, particularly of capital projects, and end year spending sprees to use up unspent funds. The principle applies not only to the Supply procedure of Parliament but also to the government's public expenditure control system. In 1983 an end year flexibility scheme was introduced enabling departments to carry forward to the following year up to 5% of their capital provision, later extended to include major maintenance projects, subject to certain conditions. Full annual parliamentary control was still maintained by the need to revote any money so carried forward in the next year's Estimates. In 1988 the scheme was further extended to cover up to 5% of departmental running costs, subject to Treasury acceptance of the relevant management plans; though such costs, mainly for pay and accommodation, are clearly not subject to the kind of slippage which can affect capital projects. The Treasury continues to maintain that, in general, annual control of expenditure is vital for economic management; it has been calculated that the flexibility scheme has led to expenditure on departmental programmes being higher by about £200 million a year than it would have been in its absence. But the benefit in improved management can be secured with no loss of overall control if account is taken of the fact that spending may now be rather closer to the planning totals.

While the Appropriation Act gives annual authority for expenditure which conforms to the ambit and structure of the votes, Parliament expects government to seek specific statutory powers for continuing services. For example, the extensive system of social security benefits and the various forms of agricultural and industrial assistance are authorized by special legislation, which governs the preparation of the relevant annual Estimates.

Moreover, the fact that money has been made available in the Estimates and the Appropriation Act does not necessarily give departments the right to spend within those limits: they must also seek Treasury approval for individual projects not covered by their own delegated powers, though in the case of major departments such delegations will be large. Any new policy proposals which involve expenditure – and there are few which do not – must be discussed with the Treasury before ministerial approval is sought. The Treasury's views on such proposals will take full account of their likely cost, current and future, in relation to the forward planning and control of public expenditure as a whole.

The Supply Estimates, public expenditure plans and cash limits

The Supply Estimates cover expenditure only by central government. Public expenditure includes spending by local authorities and the external finance of public corporations. Some funds provided to government through the Supply Estimates are transfers within the public sector, notably the large grants to local government, and are therefore netted out in calculating the public expenditure (GGE) totals. The important distinction between GGE and the expenditure planning total has been explained above.

Some funds spent by central government come from sources other than the annual Parliamentary Votes. The most important are contributory national insurance benefits, such as pensions, which are met from the National Insurance Fund, and 'Consolidated Fund services', such as payments to the European Communities and the salaries of judges and the Comptroller and Auditor General, which it would not be appropriate to submit to annual parliamentary authorization. Cash limits are aligned with the Estimates, each of which is, or is not, subject to cash limit control. Some non-voted expenditure, including certain capital expenditure by local authorities, is subject to cash limits although not voted in the Estimates. There are a number of other differences between the coverage of the three main control systems.

All this needs detailed numerical reconciliation, but with the substantial progress which has been made in aligning the interlocking systems the main features can be fairly simply illustrated and their rationale understood. This is done in the Treasury's *Summary and Guide to the Supply Estimates* (Cm 1454, 1991), from which the chart in Fig. 4.1 is taken. It should, however, be noted that the layout

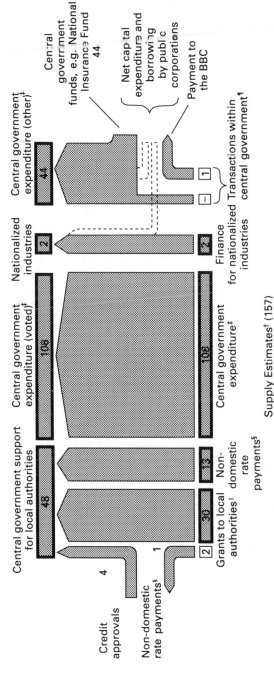

Fig. 4.1 Relationship between the public expenditure planning total and Supply Estimates, 1991–2. (Source: *Summary and Guide to the Supply Estimates*, 1991, Cm 1454.)

* The figures are taken from Table 3.8 of the Statistical Supplement to the 1990 Autumn Statement. The Reserve (£3.5 billion) and privatization proceeds (−£5.5 billion) are excluded.

† Expenditure which is counted within the public expenditure planning total is shown in the boxes marked with heavy lines.

‡ Includes the financing requirements of public corporations (excluding nationalized industries).

§ Non-domestic rate payments in Scotland are, unlike England and Wales, not covered by Supply Estimates.

‖ In addition to grants within the planning total, this includes financing grants which are not counted in the planning total to avoid double counting with credit approvals.

¶ This covers transfers within central government, for example, the transfer of money to the Northern Ireland Consolidated Fund, the National Health Service allocation from National Insurance Contributions and a payment to the BBC in respect of TV licence revenue.

Figure 4.1 shows, for 1991–2, the relationship between the planning total and Supply Estimates. Taking the different flows, in turn:

1. **Central government support for local authorities**: within the total support of £49 billion, some £30 billion is made up of grants, £14 billion comes from non-domestic rate payments (£13 billion for England and Wales within Supply Estimates and £1 billion for Scotland not covered by Supply Estimates) and £4 billion is accounted for by credit approvals. The total figure is higher than that published in the Statistical Supplement to the 1990 Autumn Statement because it includes the additional provision for the Community Charge Reduction Scheme announced in January. The expenditure which local authorities finance for themselves, for example through the community charge or from capital receipts, is not counted in the planning total.

2. **Central government expenditure (voted)**: the Supply Estimates include most of the direct expenditure (£108 billion) by central government departments. In addition to departments' running costs, this includes expenditure on programmes, such as defence, the National Health Service and that part of social security expenditure which is not financed from the National Insurance Fund. It also covers part of the financing requirements of public corporations (excluding nationalized industries). When voted the funds are drawn from the Consolidated Fund. This expenditure is all within the planning total.

3. **Nationalized industries:** the planning total includes the external finance of nationalized industries. Part of this external finance, some £2 billion of grants, subsidies and voted lending, is included in Estimates.

4. **Other central government**: comprising expenditure not directly provided for in Supply Estimates. The £44 billion in the planning total is financed from other central government non-voted funds such as the National Insurance Fund or directly from the Consolidated Fund (e.g. payments to the European Community).

---

and information in the Supply Estimates may well change, and should be monitored from year to year.

Cash limits are the closest form of budgetary control which can realistically be imposed. Where they are imposed the intention is to avoid if at all possible any increase in spending during the year, so that unexpected demands or increases in cost are expected to be absorbed or offset. Where, however, expenditure is 'demand-led', so that once policy is decided there is no option but to provide the necessary funds, it would be pointless to declare a cash limit because it could not be enforced. Of the total of Supply Estimates about two-thirds (three-quarters if social security is excluded) where cash limited in 1991–2. The principle is well illustrated by two of the largest services. The defence budget, at just under £23 billion, was wholly cash limited; social security (DHSS), at over £28 billion, was cash limited only to the extent of £1.3 billion.

A final point needs to be added to the discussion of the parliamentary aspects of expenditure control. All public expenditure must be authorized by statute. But neither the Chancellor's Autumn Statement nor the cash limits receive formal parliamentary authority. They are presented for Parliament's information as executive acts by the government. Parliament gives the necessary authority:

1. by legislating to provide for defined services, e.g. assistance to industry and agriculture, provision of housing, health and education, or the establishment of permanent funds;
2. by providing funds each year through the Supply procedure for most of central government spending, including the block grant and other financial support to local government;
3. by authorizing certain permanent charges directly on the Consolidated Fund.

Select committees

These traditional, somewhat complex arrangements whereby Parliament, assisted by the Comptroller and Auditor General (see Chapter 9), controls departmental spending and its allocation to particular services are constitutionally important but have little substantive impact on the government's plans. The enormous growth in the size and range of governmental expenditure since the main features of these procedures were instituted in the nineteenth century has made it impossible for the House of Commons to make any effective examination of it or exercise any appreciable influence on its composition or development. Increasing attention has therefore been given in recent years to the activities of Select Committees of the House in this role. The numbers and terms of reference of these committees, normally consisting of 11–15 members reflecting the party composition of the House of Commons, has varied, but the present system includes:

1. the Public Accounts Committee, originally established in 1861, with a continuous but developing interest in the examination of departmental and other accounts laid before Parliament, and the related conduct of financial management (see Chapter 9);
2. a number of departmentally related committees, established in 1979, charged with 'shadowing' the policies and operations of the main government departments and scrutinizing their Estimates, e.g.

defence, trade and industry, transport, energy, health and social services;

3. as a special example of group 2., the central Treasury and Civil Service Committee which oversees the operations of the Treasury in expenditure control and its conduct of economic and monetary policy, as well as the central control and management of the Civil Service;

4. the Liaison Committee, consisting of the chairmen of select committees, which coordinates their activities.

All these committees select the subjects they will examine within their terms of reference, take written and oral evidence, usually from senior officials but occasionally from ministers, and make public reports. Their recommendations are backed by no formal powers, but are considered on their merits by the government. Some such system is the only way of involving Members of Parliament in a detailed and informed way with the departmental conduct of expenditure and the underlying policies. The Select Committee on Procedure carried out the first parliamentary enquiry into the working of the select committee system in 1989–90.

FINANCING OF PUBLIC EXPENDITURE

This book is not concerned with the theory or practice of taxation, but mention must be made of the ways in which the government and other public authorities raise revenue or borrow to meet their expenditure. They are as follows:

1. central government taxes, imposed or changed under the authority of the annual Finance Act, following the Budget;

2. local authority charges or taxes, formerly the rates, currently the community charge, to be superseded by the proposed council tax on property;

3. charges for goods or services sold by the nationalized industries, other public corporations or bodies, and central and local government. Sizeable trading activities are carried out by central government, for example in the Stationery Office and the Royal Mint, and by local government, for example bus services. Moreover, both central and local government and the National Health Service raise a wide variety of charges for goods or services provided to the public, ranging from council house rents to prescription charges and passport fees;

4. sales of surplus assets, for example land or buildings, equipment or stores;

5. borrowing on the private capital or money markets, or, in the case of most governmental agencies, from the central government itself.

In addition, the large sums received on privatization of publicly owned undertakings reduce the government's borrowing requirement.

Central government capital expenditure is financed through Votes whatever its economic category, but that part of capital investment by the nationalized industries which cannot be financed from their own internal resources is mostly financed by borrowing. The government may incur deficits on its own spending/revenue balance, and the local authorities also borrow to finance much of their capital spending. The public sector borrowing requirement (PSBR) is the total of these components. It is increased by higher revenue deficits and larger externally financed capital investment programmes. It can be reduced by lower spending, higher taxation, higher nationalized industry prices, and sales of public sector assets, ultimately to the point where borrowing gives way to net repayment of public debt. The size and management of the PSBR have been a major concern of government policy in recent years.

The central government's statutory power to borrow, in the National Loans Act 1968, sets no upper limit to the total which may be borrowed, nor specifies the manner or terms of borrowing. These are matters on which the Treasury and the Bank of England – 'the authorities' – will consult, with final decisions as always in the hands of ministers.

Although Parliament does not at present set any overall limits on government borrowing, it does impose periodic limits on borrowing by each of the nationalized industries and certain public corporations, usually estimated to meet their external capital financing needs for three to four years ahead. All lending to the industries, apart from some short-term bank finance, to other public corporations and the local authorities is centralized through the National Loans Fund in the interests of monetary management.

ACCOUNTING FOR PUBLIC EXPENDITURE

It remains to describe how public expenditure is accounted for, as distinct from controlled. There is no general accounting system for the public sector as a whole: its component parts are too diverse, both constitutionally and operationally, for that. Local government has its own accounting system, fully described in Chapter 6. The nationalized industries and those public corporations that are predominantly commercial in character such as the Scottish and Welsh Development Agencies produce their accounts in full commercial form. They also provide more information in their annual reports than do commercial enterprises in the private sector, to meet the requirements of public and parliamentary accountability. A summary of central government arrangements follows.

The annual Appropriation Accounts of government departments

and closely related bodies follow the form of the Estimates – the Votes and subheads – and show: how much cash has been spent against the amounts provided by Parliament; the composition of short-falls and, occasionally, excesses: receipts appropriated in aid of the Votes or surrendered to the Exchequer; and supporting information, including statements of losses, special payments and so on. They are audited by the Comptroller and Auditor General and presented to Parliament, where they may form the basis of examination by the Public Accounts Committee. An example from the Department of the Environment is given in Table 4.3.

For many years those departments that carried on commercial or industrial activities were required to produce, in addition to the relevant Vote accounts, trading accounts to exhibit the results of those activities in commercial form. Those activities which remain in the public sector have now been established as trading funds under the Government Trading Funds Act 1973, as amended by the Government Trading Act 1990 which provides a wider enabling power to establish trading funds. There are at present (1990) five funds: Her Majesty's Stationery Office, the Royal Mint, the Central Office of Information, the Buying Agency (the former Crown Suppliers having been abolished), and the Vehicle Inspectorate; and Companies House and the Patent Office are due to become trading funds in 1991. Their financing has ceased to depend on the cash vote system under which unspent balances have to be surrendered at the year end to the Exchequer. They are suitably capitalized and expected to be run, subject to over-riding government requirements, on commercial lines, and they may be given financial objectives in relation to their earnings. Their accounts are accordingly produced in full commercial form, though they continue, as departmental bodies accountable to ministers, to be audited by the Comptroller and Auditor General. The HMSO's Operating Account for 1989–90 is reproduced in Table 4.4.

The government maintains the central funds through which money is dispensed for the various services and loans made to nationalized industries and other Exchequer-financed bodies. The Consolidated Fund is the government's main account at the Bank of England, receiving revenue from taxes and other receipts and providing cash for most government expenditure.

The National Loans Fund, set up by the National Loans Fund Act 1968, handles all government borrowing, payment of debt interest and most domestic lending transactions. Both these are under Treasury control.

The National Insurance Fund, under the control of the Secretary of State for Health, receives the contributions from employees, employers and the self-employed, and a contribution from the government. It pays out the corresponding benefits, about half of which are pensions. Payments from the fund are included in the public expenditure

Table 4.3 Royal palaces, royal parks, historic buildings, ancient monuments and the national heritage: Class X, Vote 4, 1989–90

Summary of Outturn, and the Account of the sum expended, in the year ended 31 March 1990, compared with the sum granted, for expenditure by the Department of the Environment on royal palaces etc. (including administration), royal parks, etc. (including administration), historic buildings, ancient monuments and certain public buildings, the national heritage, on grants in aid and other grants, on payments to the Inland Revenue covering assets accepted in lieu of tax, on an international subscription and on the resurvey of listed buildings

SUMMARY OF OUTTURN

Section	Estimated			Actual		
	Gross Expenditure	*Appropriations in Aid*	*Net Expenditure*	*Gross Expenditure*	*Appropriations in Aid*	*Net Expenditure*
	£000	*£000*	*£000*	*£000*	*£000*	*£000*
Royal palaces, royal parks and board of trustees for the armouries						
ABC	35 215	12 912	22 303	34 066	14 708	19 358
Historic buildings, ancient monuments and the national heritage						
D	81 749	185	81 564	81 452	179	81 273
Total	116 964	13 097	103 867	115 518	14 887	100 631*

* This figure is £1 790 000 less than the net total of expenditure on the Appropriation Account being the difference between the Appropriations in Aid realized (£14 887 000) and those authorized to be applied (£13 097 000).

Table 4.3 Continued

ACCOUNT

Service	Grant	Expenditure	Expenditure compared with grant	
			Less than granted	More than granted
	£000	£000	£000	£000
Section A				
Occupied royal palaces and other historic buildings				
A1 Capital expenditure – purchase of furniture and equipment, etc.	603	532	71	–
A2 Board of Trustees of the Armouries: grant in aid	3400	3485	–	85
A3 Accommodation at Buckingham Palace, Windsor Castle, etc.: grant in aid	75	75	–	–
A4* Capital expenditure – refurbishment of Albert Memorial	750	134	616	–
A5 Current expenditure	1233	1722	–	489
A6 Running costs	220	182	38	–
Section B				
Historic royal palaces (including Hampton Court gardens, home park and Tower of London gardens)				
B1† Capital expenditure	5790	4972	818	–
B2 Current expenditure	5938	5744	194	–
B3 Running costs	5691	5361	330	–
Section C				
Royal parks (excluding Hampton Court gardens, home park and Tower of London gardens)				
C1 Capital expenditure – purchase of furniture and equipment, etc.	404	594	–	190
C2 Current expenditure	3200	3300	–	100
C3 Running costs	7911	7965	–	54

Section D

Historic buildings, ancient monuments and the national heritage

	£000	£000	
D1 Historic Buildings and Monuments Commission for England:			
grant in aid	72 899	72 899	—
D2 Redundant Churches Fund	1600	1600	—
D3 The National Heritage Memorial Fund: grant in aid	1500	1500	—
D4 Assets accepted in lieu of tax	1000	1000	—
D5 Royal Commission on Historical Monuments	4605	4397	208
D6 Miscellaneous	145	56	89

Gross total

	£000	Estimated £000	Applied £000	
Original	116 534			
Supplementary	430	116 964	115 518	2364 918

Deduct

	Estimated £000	Applied £000
Z Appropriations in Aid	13 097	13 097

Net total

	£000	Estimated £000	Applied £000	
Original	103 437			
Supplementary	430	103 867	102 421	Surplus 1446

Actual surplus to be surrendered   £1 446 093.23

* A4 Reduced expenditure due to slippage in letting contract for exploratory work and in preliminary planning.
† B1 Slippage of planned expenditure due to delay in the launch of the Historic Royal Palaces Agency.

Source: *Volume of Appropriation Accounts 1990.*

Table 4.4 HMSO Trading Fund: operating account for the year ended 31 December 1990

	Notes	1990 £000	£000	1989 £000	£000
Turnover		388 600		360 752	
Change in stocks of:					
finished goods		2086		973	
work in progress		(5633)		4905	
Government grants	3	2526		3044	
Other operating income		1428		1148	
			389 007		370 822
Raw materials and					
consumables		47 092		44 899	
Other external charges		238 292		232 910	
Staff costs	6	57 944		51 978	
Depreciation	4	4492		4133	
Other operating charges		33 475		30 989	
			381 295		364 909
Operating surplus	2/4		7712		5913
Net interest receivable					
(payable)	7		(319)		1301
			7393		7214
Exceptional item	5		562		–
Surplus on ordinary activities			6831		7214
Interest payable on long-term					
loans	8		3079		4107
Retained surplus for the year	19(c)		3752		3107

Source: *HMSO Report and Accounts*; Crown copyright.

totals, together with the rest of the large social security programme provided through Votes, including the non-contributory benefits such as child benefit.

These three government accounts, though showing the origin and use of very large sums, are simple in structure: see, for example, the National Insurance Fund for 1989–90 given in Table 4.5.

The Redundancy Fund, under the Secretary of State for Employment, finances claims from employers for certain payments made to redundant employees. There are a number of other 'White Paper accounts', so-called because they are published in that form, showing the annual outcome, on an appropriate accounting basis, of services financed

Table 4.5 National Insurance Fund: account for the year ended 31 March 1990 prepared in accordance with section 133 of the Social Security Act 1975 Receipts and Payments

	£000	1989–90 £000	1988–9 £000
Receipts			
Contributions	30 756 362		
Less Employers' recoveries in respect of SSP	1 044 000		
Less Employers' recoveries in respect of SMP	307 000		
		29 405 362	27 393 783
Consolidated Fund Supplement		–	1 653 000
Income from investments		1 040 377	777 502
Other receipts		1018	1072
		30 446 757	29 825 357
Less			
Payments			
Benefits		27 000 207	25 396 625
Personal Pensions		2 434 461	288 505
Transfers to Northern Ireland		210 000	185 000
Administration		856 536	865 786
Other payments		7222	8253
		30 508 426	26 744 169
Excess of payments over receipts		61 669	–
Excess of receipts over payments		–	3 081 188
Statement of Balances			
Balance at beginning of year		10 368 808	7 287 620
Less			
Excess of payments over receipts		61 669	–
Add			
Excess of receipts over payments		–	3 081 188
Balance at end of year		10 307 139	10 368 808

Source: HCP 617; Crown copyright.

by statutory funds but managed separately from the departments' own direct expenditure.

There are no accounts, properly described as such or audited, related to the spending plans now set out in the Autumn Statement and the new departmental reports. But these documents do contain a great deal of statistical information setting the plans in a wide-ranging historical context, they provide comparisons between expenditure plans and outturns for a number of years, and analyse features of special interest, such as capital spending, manpower costs and scientific research. It is an extensive system of financial reporting.

For day-to-day control the Treasury's financial information system supplies a running check throughout the year on the progress of spending, readily related to the planning figures, the Supply Estimates, and other relevant budgetary provisions.

This set of accounts and financial information has been criticized (a) because much of it is on a cash basis, which is felt to be self-evidently inadequate, and (b) because it shows inputs, in terms of money spent, and not outputs, in terms of what the schools, hospitals, scientific research, defence and other manifold activities of government have achieved. The second criticism is losing much of its force as the development and use of performance indicators and other measures of output have accelerated. The production of more informative and better presented departmental reports, in succession to the somewhat indigestible mass of Part II of the White Paper, is reinforcing the improvement. These reports should be a main focus of study for those wishing to assess progress in this area.

The criticism of cash – or receipts and payments – as the form of much government accounting often fails to apprehend the relevance of some important considerations and the irrelevance of others. To substitute an obligations basis, whereby expenditure is related to commitments, somehow defined, might achieve a more realistic presentation in some respects at the cost of lack of precision and argument about forward liabilities. Accounts showing how money has been spent in relation to funds voted cannot also show the full costs of services or projects including depreciation of assets and provisions for losses. Most government activities accounted for in cash terms are quite different from trading operations where it is essential for survival to calculate expenditure and fix prices with adequate regard to the full annual costs, capital and current, being incurred. Capital expenditure on a warship or the new British Library should not be incurred without applying appropriate criteria, and it makes the same kind of demand on the construction and engineering industries as capital spending by business. The resulting equipment should be run as efficiently as possible, but it does not result in a stream of saleable products to generate profit, and the criteria for judging it will not be commercial criteria. The total cash spent by public bodies, for whatever purposes, is of importance for the government's monetary policy as it affects the money supply. Spending by a private company has no comparable significance and has to be judged differently by its contribution to profitability over a period of years and by any shorter-term problems of cash flow to which it may give rise.

These arguments, sound in themselves, leave room for manoeuvre in applying commercial concepts to public operations, for example in capital accounting and accommodation and staff costs. For a long time, ready reckoners have been available in the Civil Service to enable officials to calculate quickly, not just the pay bill of extra people, but the full staff costs including superannuation. If the Army provides quarters for its servicemen it is necessary to know the current cost of construction and management in deciding what rents to charge, subsidized or not. It may be operationally acceptable to move part of the Ministry of Social Security out of London at a big saving in accommodation costs, whereas a few hundred people in the Treasury or the Foreign Office may be inhabiting office space in Westminster at extremely high, but unavoidable, opportunity cost. Now that 'provider markets' are developing in the NHS it may be necessary to value hospitals, but it serves no practical purpose to depreciate the latest battle tank or guided missile over an arbitrary period of years.

More sophisticated accounting systems need to be applied to all types of government operations where they can contribute to better decision-making or improved public information. This has been done for a long time where trading activity is involved, and has been emphasized by the establishment of the statutory trading funds. It is an important aspect of better management information in the context of the financial management initiative and the establishment of executive agencies (see below), and it is increasingly being met by internal management accounts for particular services within departmental responsibility. Examples among many are the annual report of the Home Office's prison service which gives the costs of running the system, and the Ordnance Survey's published commercial accounts, both of which are linked to their management accounting systems. Even where Parliament's main control over Supply-financed, i.e. non-trading, agencies continues to be through the annual cash Estimates and Accounts, the aim will be to supplement these with suitable commercial-type accounts. The questions always to be asked are: 'What purposes is the accounting treatment intended to serve?' and 'How will a particular presentation improve decision-taking?', not 'What are the professional accounting rules for this type of expenditure?', because they may or may not, in the public sector, be relevant.

DEVELOPMENT OF MANAGEMENT IN THE CIVIL SERVICE

There has been a sustained attempt during the 1980s to change the attitude of the Civil Service towards its responsibilities for the management of those services which the government provides, and the way it is organized to discharge them. The emphasis has been on the importance of the management role; the need to give those in charge of blocks of expenditure at various levels in government the maximum scope for the exercise of their own judgement, with a corresponding degree of personal accountability; and the provision of the necessary financial and other information to support the necessary decisions. It is believed that agreed policies can be carried out in alternative ways and with greater or lesser expenditure for essentially the same results, in contrast to the long accepted conviction by most civil servants that once 'policy' had been decided there was minimal scope for administrative savings in executing it. Policies themselves are not immune from challenge by officials, if by policies is meant particular methods or systems for securing the objectives set by ministers. The move to establish executive agencies to be responsible for the delivery of government services, discussed below, reflects the promotion of individual responsibility for securing agreed objectives within the degree of freedom of action which can be given to individual managers.

These changes are often viewed as the introduction of business or commercial values and methods. If by this is meant a greater awareness of costs, including the cost of capital and staff time, recognition of the need to streamline working methods, devising and using adequate information systems to assist decision-making and managerial control, and promoting personal responsibility, it is correct. But the provision of public services has to meet objectives which do not constrain private business, notably public accountability through ministers, and equitable treatment of individual citizens in their dealings with the state.

One manifestation of this new thinking was the efficiency studies instituted by Sir Derek (now Lord) Rayner which examine in depth specific activities with a view to cutting costs and staff and tightening methods of work without detriment to results. These studies are now carried out by small departmental teams under the guidance and supervision of the Efficiency Unit of the Cabinet Office, responsible to the Prime Minister.

THE FINANCIAL MANAGEMENT INITIATIVE

Another important and related development was the financial management initiative (FMI). The public expenditure survey, Ministers' decisions thereon, periodic policy reviews and the discipline of cash limits should suffice to determine and control the total of public spending and its allocation between competing services. The vote accounting system and the associated parliamentary and audit procedures should guard against spending without constitutional authority and misappropriation of public funds. But essential as they are for these purposes these arrangements are insufficient to secure maximum efficiency and cost-effectiveness in day-to-day management in departments. The government's financial management initiative was designed to meet this need. It was first described publicly in 1982 in the government's reply to a report from the Parliamentary Treasury and Civil Service Committee on efficiency and effectiveness in the Civil Service (Cm 8616). It is both in financial and a management initiative. Its object is to promote in each government department an organization and a system in which civil servants in a managerial capacity at all levels have a clear view of their objectives, well-defined responsibilities, and the necessary information to help discharge them. Clearly the nature of these responsibilities will vary greatly according to the particular job. Senior officials in the Treasury, responsible for advising on matters of monetary policy, may have virtually no expenditure under their direct control and few staff. A principal in the Department of Social Security may supervise the distribution of millions of pounds in benefits and have scores of people working on their detailed administration. A project manager in the Ministry of Defence may be in charge of the development and procurement of a complicated weapons system for whose success a variety of military, scientific, industrial, financial and administrative skills have to be satisfactorily combined. The management approach, and allocation of budgetary and other managerial tasks, must be adapted to the reality of each such situation.

Adequate, timely and relevant financial information is clearly one important requirement for successful day-to-day management. The annual appropriation accounts obviously cannot meet it. Nor for that matter can the commercial accounts produced by bodies which operate as trading funds. Even if their structure was fully consistent with the allocation of responsibilities within departments, these accounts could not display the necessary degree of detail, and in any case they are produced only annually after the end of the year to which they relate.

The Treasury's internal financial information system provides prompt expenditure figures throughout the year, but it was designed to meet broader objectives than those of middle managers responsible for specific parts of departmental programmes. Their need has to be met by the development and use of additional management information and accounting systems. They can vary in form from a full costing of a specific activity, say the acquisition, nurture and training of police dogs, to set against the outputs of these particular public servants, to the enumeration and costing of the multiple activities of a large department, such as the MINIS system (Management Information for Ministers) developed in the early 1980s in the Department of the Environment. The aims of this type of analysis are to know what is being done in the pursuit of policy objectives, what it costs, and whether an alternative procedure could produce efficacious results more cheaply: better value for money, not a poorer standard of service. But value cannot be judged without some measure of assessment of what is produced. Sustained effort is therefore necessary and is being applied to the development and improvement of measures of output and performance. The departmental reports contain numerous examples. More of these may now be confidently expected.

The FMI is not, however, simply a collection of financial and management techniques, however sophisticated. It also sets out to promote people's self-reliance and enthusiasm and to increase their job satisfaction, by giving them as much independence and personal responsibility for the achievement of their objectives and the management of their staff and budgets as is consistent with accepted policy and with their individual freedom of action. Granted that there are inevitable constraints on such freedom in large public service organizations, which have to operate within set policies and procedures and often with wide internal and external consultation, the FMI in practice is nevertheless demonstrating that there is more scope for it than had previously been thought. Progress on the FMI and its application in all the main government departments has been made public in successive White Papers.

EXECUTIVE AGENCIES

Early in 1988 a report by the Efficiency Unit to the Prime Minister was published: *Improving Management in Government: the Next Steps*. It summarized the progress made under the financial management initiative and related developments, criticized some continuing aspects of Civil Service organization, ethos and approach, and made recommendations for further change, including the setting up of agencies to deliver governmental services to the public.

In a statement to Parliament on 18 February 1988 the Prime Minister announced that the government had accepted four of these recommendations:

1. that to the greatest extent practicable the executive functions of government, as distinct from policy advice, should be carried out by units clearly designated within departments, referred to in the report as agencies, with responsibility for their day-to-day operations delegated to a chief executive within a framework of policy objectives and resources set by the responsible minister in consultation with the Treasury;
2. that the government should commit themselves to a progressive programme for attaining this objective;
3. that staff should be properly trained and prepared for the delivery of services 'inside or outside central government';

4. that a 'project manager' at a senior level should ensure that the programme of change takes place.

These decisions initiated a major change in the organization of central government, and the weight which has been put into their implementation speaks for itself. Departments are progressively being split into a central core, responsible for advice on policy, and where applicable one or more executive agencies responsible for the management and delivery of services to the public. Ministers remain responsible for their departments as a whole; all staff are still civil servants; the Treasury retains an essential role in the central control of resources and the design of measures to ensure parliamentary and public accountability. 'Hiving off' is therefore an inappropriate term to describe this reform; but that is not to diminish its significance. If sensibly and successfully developed it should improve both the efficiency and the esteem of the Civil Service, while preserving its standards of ability and integrity.

The main features of the agency system include:

1. setting clear objectives, and allocating adequate resources to enable them to be achieved, either through the Supply procedure – Votes – and cash limits, or through trading funds in the case of agencies of a trading type;
2. appointing a chief executive with the maximum freedom of action in using his resources consistent with the constitutional position outlined above and the preservation of essential common features in the civil service;
3. establishing agreed performance targets, both financial and non-financial, to judge the degree of success in meeting the aims of the agency;
4. working out a 'Framework Document' – the capitals underlining its significance – to define the above points with the necessary precision; to relate the agency's responsibilities to those of the department; and to lay down the arrangements for accounting, reporting and accountability, financial and otherwise.

This framework is to be utilized with regard to the widely differing nature of the operations to be managed by agencies, for example the administration of social security benefits by a staff of 79 000, as compared with the Vehicle Certification Agency with a staff of 50, or the Royal Mint's manufacturing business with 950. The problems of establishing a new internal relationship between departments and their agencies are not minimized, nor is the need to continue to provide attractive and if possible enhanced career opportunities for all staff concerned. Policy cannot be rigidly separated from administration; experience with the delivery of services may throw up defects in the policy framework itself. All these issues and others are discussed in the two succinct reports mentioned in 'Further reading' below.

SUMMARY

This chapter has explained the government's central role in planning and controlling the expenditure of the public sector. This objective has been related to the economy as a whole, to the government's financial relations with local government and the public corporations, and to their own spending policies. The objectives and greatly changing methods of departments in the day-to-day management of their programmes has been summarized. The framework of public accountability, the role of Parliament and of the select committees, and the supporting structure of government accounts and financial reports have been described. Important changes in the reporting system, superseding the long-standing Public Expenditure *White Paper*, have been explained. The significance of the 'Next Steps' agencies has been emphasized.

FURTHER READING

Study of the main government documents published each year – the *Autumn Statement*, the *Financial Statement* and *Budget Report*, the departmental annual reports (from 1991) – will give a full and up-to-date picture of the presentations summarized in this book. *Government Accounting* (HMSO) describes the basic accounting system, including the Supply Estimates and Appropriation Accounts. The annual *Supply Estimates Summary and Guide* (HM Treasury) gives full details each year, relates the Estimates (Votes) to the cash limits and planning total, and explains the parliamentary procedure. The House of Commons Treasury and Civil Service Select Committee reports on topical issues of expenditure policy and control; the Public Accounts Committee concentrates on financial management. *The Financing and Accountability of Next Steps Agencies* (Cm 914, 1989), and *Making the Most of Next Steps* (Report to the Prime Minister, HMSO, 1991), explain the development of agencies. The interplay of political, departmental and administrative aspects of public expenditure is discussed with considerable insight by Heclo and Wildavsky (1981) in *The Private Government of Public Money*. *Getting and Spending* (Pliatzky, 1982) gives a personal account of life in the Treasury by a former senior official who was concerned with the present author over several years in advising ministers on public expenditure matters. The work of Thain and Wright on public spending is appearing as this book goes to print and provides recent insights into the process of policy formulation.

GLOSSARY*

Accounting Officer An officer appointed, normally by the Treasury, in compliance with Section 22 of the Exchequer and Audit Departments Act 1866, to sign the Appropriation Accounts and any other accounts within his responsibility. By virtue of that duty, he has the further duty of being the principal witness on behalf of the department before the Committee of Public Accounts to deal with questions arising from those accounts and from the Comptroller and Auditor General's reports to Parliament under the National Audit Act 1983.

Ambit (of a vote) The description in Part I of a Supply Estimate, or a Supplementary Supply Estimate, which describes and limits the purposes for which provision is made. The Ambit appears in a schedule to the Appropriation Act and Parliament authorizes specific sums of money to each Ambit.

Appropriation Account An end-of-year account of money voted by Parliament which compares the Supply Estimate with actual payments made and receipts brought to account, and explains any substantial differences. An Appropriation Account is prepared for each Vote.

Appropriations in aid Receipts which, with the authority of Parliament, are used to finance some of the gross expenditure on the Vote, thus reducing the amount to be issued from the Consolidated Fund to the Vote.

Capital expenditure Expenditure on new construction, land, extensions of and alterations to existing buildings and the purchase of any other fixed assets (e.g. machinery and plant) – including vehicles – having an expected working life of more than one year. Also includes expenditure on stocks, and grants and lending for capital purposes.

Cash limit The limit on the net amount of cash that can be spent on certain specified services during one financial year. The limit will usually be equal to the Vote total but will be lower than this when agreement has been reached to reduce provision, for example, to offset an increase elsewhere.

Class A group of Estimates whose coverage corresponds to the voted expenditure element of one of the Departmental Reports.

Consolidated Fund The Exchequer account into which are paid gross tax revenue, less repayments, and all other Exchequer receipts not specifically directed elsewhere. Issues from the Fund are made to meet expenditure shown in Supply Estimates.

Consolidated Fund extra receipts Receipts related to expenditure

* Taken from *Summary and Guide to the Supply Estimates 1991*, Cm 1454.

in the Supply Estimates which Parliament has not authorized to be used as appropriations in aid.

Contingencies Fund A fund which can be used for urgent expenditure in anticipation of provision by Parliament becoming available. It is limited to 2% of the previous year's total authorized Supply provision. Drawings on this fund must be repaid when Parliament has voted the additional sums required.

Economic classification An analysis of public sector accounting transactions according to their economic character. It is based on the classification used by the Central Statistical Office for compiling the accounts of national income and expenditure.

Estimate Day A day set aside by Parliament for the debate of main or Supplementary Supply Estimates.

Executive Agencies In February 1988, the Prime Minister announced that the government had accepted the main recommendations of the report by the Efficiency Unit entitled *Improving Management in Government: the Next Steps*. To the greatest extent practicable, the executive functions of government, as distinct from policy advice, would be carried out by clearly designated units, referred to as Agencies. The main aim of the Next Steps initiative is to deliver services more efficiently and effectively, within available resources, for the benefit of tax payers, customers and staff.

Financial year The year from 1 April one year to 31 March of the next.

Grant Money voted (i.e. granted) by Parliament to meet the services shown in Supply Estimates. Also used in individual subheads of Supply Estimates to describe an unrequited payment to an individual or body in the private or public sector. See also **Grant in aid** and **Subsidy**.

Grant in aid A grant from voted monies to a particular organization or body where any unexpended balances of the sums issued during the financial year will not be liable for surrender to the Consolidated Fund.

National Audit Office This Office carries out the audit of every Appropriation Account other than its own, other public accounts, and some international (e.g. UN) accounts.

Net subhead A net subhead is created when receipts are offset against expenditure in a specific subhead, rather than appropriated in aid of the Vote as a whole. In most cases the receipts equal the expenditure and only a token £1000 is shown to be voted.

Outturn Actual expenditure.

Planning total The aggregate of the elements of public expenditure which the government plans and controls to achieve its wide objective for general government expenditure.

Reserve The public expenditure planning total includes a Reserve which provides a margin for uncertainties and is intended to cover any future additions to departmental spending, whether these result from policy changes, new initiatives, contingencies or revised estimates of demand-led programmes.

Running costs Running costs are the gross costs of the administration of central government, including the pay of civil servants and those members of the armed forces engaged in support activities, and all associated administrative expenditure, including the costs of accommodation, travel, training, etc. Accruing superannuation liability costs for Civil Service staff under the Principal Civil Service Pension Scheme are excluded, as are pensions in payment.

Section A group of subheads in the same Vote. Sections provide a means of summarizing an Estimate if, for example, it covers more than one area of public expenditure, and provide a link to the Departmental Report.

Subhead Expenditure within a Vote which is separately identified in the Supply Estimate and Appropriation Account.

Subsidy A grant (i.e. an unrequited payment) to a producer or trader which is deemed to benefit the consumer by reducing the selling price of the product or service. See also **Grant**.

Supply Estimate A statement presented to the House of Commons of the estimated expenditure of a department during a financial year asking for the necessary funds to be voted.

Token subhead See **Net subhead**.

Token Vote In some cases receipts of a kind that could be appropriated in aid of the Vote are expected on a scale equal to or greater than the expected gross expenditure. In these circumstances, sufficient of the expected receipts are shown as appropriations in aid to leave only a nominal balance, usually £1000, to be voted as Supply. Part III of the Estimate shows the balance of the receipts expected which are payable to the Consolidated Fund as extra receipts (see above). In addition a Supplementary Estimate for a token sum may be presented, for example to transfer some existing provision to a new service in the same Vote.

Vote An individual Supply Estimate.

Vote on account Money granted by Parliament to carry on public services from 1 April of the next financial year until the passing of the Appropriation Act, which authorizes the issue of the amount required for the full year.

5

Local government and its financing

Local government is a key part of the democratic system within the United Kingdom. Its scale and significance also means that it is an important part of national public expenditure planning and economic management with many formal and informal relationships with government.

Management in local government is also complex, not only because of the wide range of services and activities undertaken but also because of the interaction with central government, a changing society and environment, the local community and community interests and the influences of political party organization. Reflecting this, each local authority will have its own unique way of managing which generates a variety adding to the challenges facing both elected members and employed officials alike. This chapter gives an in-depth analysis of how local government is financed and the current challenges at a time of considerable change. It also gives a flavour of general management issues by:

1. providing a brief summary of the history of local government;
2. examining the legislative relationship between central and local government;
3. giving an analysis of the internal management arrangements of local authorities and the importance of political awareness and sensitivity.

BACKGROUND

There is little doubt that local government has experienced much change over the last decade. At the time of writing a fundamental review of local government structure, outside the metropolitan areas, is planned and there is all party commitment to further changes in local taxation related to the recognized weaknesses of the community charge.

In addition there are also trends emerging from a changing society and environment, with new views on management structures and the shape of services for the 1990s. The themes include:

1. moves away from direct service provision and towards a role concentrating on service specification and purchase;
2. encouraging voluntary community initiatives, sponsoring voluntary agencies and the development of the commercial sector's ability to supply services previously managed directly by local government;
3. further development of general management skills as opposed to professional and service based management;
4. improved and clearer accountability to the community with more community choice through competition in service provision;
5. encouragement of an internal commercial culture.

THE NEED FOR LOCAL GOVERNMENT

Virtually all developed countries have a system of municipal or local government although its scale and autonomy varies. This approach to regional democracy reflects the belief in the need to provide services in a way which reflects local circumstances and choice.

The balance of power with central government and the extent of local discretion tends to vary over time but the basic principles supporting the need for locally provided services remain. In the UK, local authorities are the only elected political bodies outside Parliament. As a result they perform several important functions:

1. democratic involvement; by providing the means by which people can take part in decisions concerning the services in their own area;
2. spreading political power; by providing a large number of points where decisions are taken, by people of different political persuasion and background, there is a counterweight to the uniformity inherent in central government decisions;
3. enhances accountability; because it brings those who are responsible for decisions closer to their electors;
4. improves effectiveness; because services can be adjusted to reflect local needs and preferences and more responsibility can be decentralized;
5. limits central government overload; by devolving functions to more local management;
6. provides a vehicle for developing new approaches and pioneering ideas. The scope for this is limited in a central organization concerned to apply policies uniformly.

(Precised references from Layfield Committee (1976), p. 53.)

Within this framework, the system is fairly typical in international comparison. However, a factor seen to be important, in local government's ability to spread political power and exercise discretion in carrying out its functions, is the ability to raise a significant proportion of its revenues locally through local taxes. This is seen as one of the difficulties with the community charge and the proposed council tax, as the yield is not seen as being a significant proportion representing less than 20% of total revenues.

HISTORY AND LEGISLATIVE FRAMEWORK

Local government in the UK is not homogeneous. There are different systems in England, Wales, Scotland and Northern Ireland. This paper focuses on England and Wales. Scotland has a similar structure but a different legislative framework.

The unwritten constitution has long recognized local government as a means of enabling villages, towns and counties to provide certain services for their area. The present structure has a lengthy evolution dating back to the pre-nineteenth century shire counties, boroughs and parish councils.

The general framework in place at the end of the nineteenth century endured largely unchanged until the 1960s. In the larger towns and cities a county borough council was responsible for the provision of all local government services, including education, police, fire, water and sewerage. Elsewhere the structure contained several types of authority within a two-tier structure, with the county council being responsible for major services such as planning, education and social services and police. Beneath the county council, in the smaller towns, were municipal borough and urban district councils which provided all other services. Parishes in urban areas had no councils and did not provide any services. Outside the towns, there were rural district councils. Within rural districts there were parishes, often with their own parish councillors, which performed a few very local functions.

In London, by the mid-nineteenth century, there were some three hundred different active bodies providing a variety of services and a metropolitan board of works providing infrastructure, especially sewerage. These bodies were successively combined so that by the end of the century there was a two-tier structure of 28 metropolitan boroughs and the London County Council.

British local government derives its legitimacy and power from Acts of Parliament. For all its actions it must look to an Act of Parliament for authority.

The dependence of local authorities on the legislative framework, in being able to identify specific legal powers for all its actions, finances and contractual relationships, is demonstrated in a 1991 case related to borrowing and lending powers. The House of Lords, following a series of court judgements and appeals declared that the use of interest rate 'swaps' was illegal and could not be enforced by the banks. Eighty banks faced losses of approximately £500 million on swap transactions as a result of this decision. The ruling declared the swap transactions to be *ultra vires*, that is councils had no power to enter into such agreements. Recognizing the financial emphasis of this publication, the case is explained at some length on pages 121–123.

Turning to powers of taxation, Edmund Burke remarked that, 'to tax and to please is a power not given to man'. Nowhere is this problem more evident than in local taxes and the regular government intervention to refine the tax system or the means of supplementing it through government grant. In the past twenty years there has been either a major committee of inquiry or a Green Paper on local taxation every five years and, since 1979, over forty-six separate pieces of legislation affecting local government (S. Platt, 'Skeleton Service', *New Statesman*, 17 June 1988).

There are four key dates in the present structure of local government:

1963 This year saw the creation of the Greater London Council. This defined the area of Greater London and organized it into 32 larger boroughs and the City of London.

1974 Following the Report of the Royal Commission on Local Government in England (the Redcliffe Maud Report) in 1969, the Local Government Act 1972 established a two-tier system consisting of metropolitan counties and districts in six areas (the West Midlands, Merseyside, Greater Manchester, West Yorkshire, South Yorkshire and Tyne and Wear) and a two-tier system of shire counties and districts in the rest of England and Wales. The new structure came into existence on 1 April 1974.

1985 The Local Government Act 1985 abolished the Greater London Council and the metropolitan county councils. The services previously provided by the metropolitan counties were transferred to a system of joint boards with representatives nominated by the boroughs and metropolitan districts.

1990 the Inner London Education Authority (ILEA) was abolished and its services transferred to the inner London boroughs.

The trend over the last decade has also been to remove a number of services from local government. The major area identified for growth has been personal social services, where the 1988 Griffiths Report on Community Care recommended transfer from the health service of major responsibilities. However, it is interesting to note that many major industries and services had their early development within local government, for example, electricity, gas, water and health. The process of evolution of local services is continuing with Community Care, aspects of economic development and environmental protection and improvement.

LOCAL AUTHORITY FUNCTIONS AND ASSOCIATIONS

An analysis of the main responsibilities of each type of authority is given in Fig. 5.1. This is not a definitive list but indicates the range of duties undertaken and the tremendous impact they have on local community life. These responsibilities are at any time subject to legislative change. A recent example was the announcement by the Secretary of State for Education on 21 March 1991 of the government's intention to remove sixth form and further education colleges from the control of local authorities from April 1993. In addition, and perhaps more important is the general policy emphasis of the Conservative central government aimed at reducing local government's role as direct providers of services to one of emphasis on enabling and purchasing. This conceptual change is dealt with later on p. 114.

Although the challenges and policy issues faced by local authorities vary from area to area, there are also many they have in common. One is the relationship with government and government departments and the ability to communicate and influence that relationship.

Because of these common interests and needs, associations have emerged which represent groups of local authorities and organize collaborative work in a way which enables the sharing of experiences and cooperation in tackling new challenges. In England there is a different association for each type of authority, namely:

The Association of County Councils (ACC)
The Association of District Councils (ADC)
The Association of Metropolitan Authorities (AMA)
　(representing metropolitan districts and London boroughs).

In London, political differences have also led to the grouping of councils into two additional associations:

The London Boroughs Association (LBA)
The Association of London Authorities (ALA).

Membership comprises nominations from the member authorities. This inevitably leads to a political structure where a majority party view will generally predominate on major policy issues. These associations are also at the apex of a whole host of formal and informal networks between local authorities. For example, there are also related national bodies representing each area of professional work, such as the Association of Directors of Social Services and the Society of County Treasurers; each has important informal affiliations with the relevant association.

Fig. 5.1 Main functions of local authorities as at 1 April 1991. The aim of this list is to give a brief summary of the distribution of the main functions. A detailed summary can be found in Byrne (1990). In London and the metropolitan counties joint boards, committees or authorities carry out a number of county-wide functions.

Function	Metropolitan		England and Wales non-metropolitan			London		Scotland	
	Joint	District	County	District	Joint	Joint	Borough	Region	District
Community charge collection		x		x			x	x	
Consumer protection		x	x				x	x	x
Education		x	x				x	x	x
Environmental health	x	x		x			x		x
Fire service	x		x			x		x	
Housing		x		x			x		x
Industrial development		x	x	x			x		x
Libraries		x	x				x		x
Passenger transport	x		x	x				x	
Planning									
Strategic plans		x	x				x	x	
Development control		x		x			x		x
Police	x		x			(Central government)		x	
Recreation		x	x	x			x		x
Refuse disposal	x		x			x			x
Social Services		x	x				x	x	
Transport and highways									
Policy and principal roads		x	x				x	x	
Non-principal roads		x	x	x			x	x	
Water								x	

Local Government Management Board (LGMB)

The associations, through their member authorities, also sponsor professional advice and consultancy effort on behalf of local government as a whole through the Local Government Management Board. This was created in April 1991 and combined the roles of three previously separate organizations – the Local Government Training Board (LGTB), the local authority employers' organization (LACSAB) and a management/computer consultancy (LAMSAC).

The new body brings together, on a national basis, advice and support for local government across the whole range of management and personnel issues. The Chief Executive of the Board, Michael Clarke, has pointed out that he sees the relationship between the Board and the Associations as critical with the Board setting a framework in which local authorities can operate more effectively.

Audit Commission

The Audit Commission was established under the Local Government Finance Act 1982 with responsibility for appointing the external auditors of all local authorities in England and Wales. The Act also gave the Audit Commission a remit to analyse the arrangements taken by an authority to ensure economy, efficiency and effectiveness (the 3Es). The Audit Commission's concern for the 3Es and Value for Money has been an integral part of its work and this has been extended also to cover the National Health Service where, since 1 October 1990, it has been given responsibility for appointing external auditors.

Each year the Commission selects a number of aspects of local government for in-depth review. In 1990–1, for example, heavy emphasis was put on the police service with the publication of six papers examining various aspects of service management including performance review and income generation.

INTERNAL MANAGEMENT

The ultimate decision-making body of each local authority is a meeting of the full council of elected councillors. Subject to the overriding authority of the full council, each council establishes its own formal organization, decision-making processes and internal management arrangements. These form a series of laid-down powers and procedures whereby authority is delegated to standing committees, subcommittees or paid officials. Standing Orders and Financial Regulations govern the rules of debate, how and where issues are brought before the council and even the procedures by which the council enters into contracts with third parties.

The formal structure therefore covers a series of committees and subcommittees which are allocated responsibility for overall policy and management of specific service areas.

The committee structure itself has its origins in over a hundred years of developing legislation which includes some prescription as to appointment and membership. By way of example, the Local Government and Housing Act 1989 requires the pro rata representation of political groups on committees. Section 113 of the Local Government Finance Act (1988) requires that the Treasurer or Director of Finance of each council be a member of one of the chartered accountancy bodies.

Figure 5.2 shows the council and committee structure for the Shire County of Cheshire. It also serves to illustrate the diversity of council services and the necessity for councillors to concentrate on particular aspects of council business. The committees tend to span areas of service or have a resourcing and corporate management responsibility through, for example, the Policy Committee or its subcommittees. In Cheshire's case the Policy Committee takes on the corporate policy-making role and decides the medium-term strategy and budget allocation for each service area.

It is argued that the committee system has focused individual councillor attention on too narrow a stream of council business and even day-to-day workings of departments, at the expense of the full range of councillor roles. Achieving a balance between the need to fulfil the representative role on behalf of the councillor's own local community and the ability to have space for learning, direction and review are all features under consideration in most authorities and nationally. These features are forcing the re-thinking of committee structures and the effective use of councillor time.

All councillors will on occasions be faced with conflicts and tensions in forming a view on what is in the best interests of the council as a whole and what is in the best interests of that councillor's own local electors. There will also be times when a councillor will find the internal party organization imposing pressure on the ability to speak and vote freely. Senior officials working closely with council policy-making and supporting the administration and decision-making process must understand and be able to recognize these tensions.

Management developments

The interrelationship between officers and members of the council provides another interesting and less than absolutely clear dimension

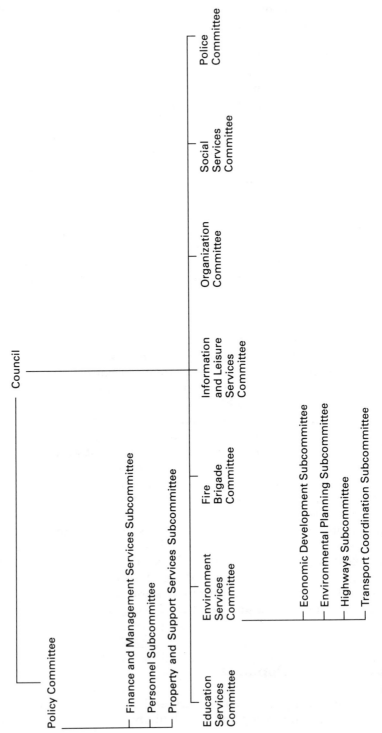

Fig. 5.2 Cheshire County Council – main committee structure.

to working relationships and transacting business. Again, ultimate authority is with the council and committees, but developed mutual respect and trust of leading members and the Chief Officer team can improve policy-making and the smooth management of policy development and service delivery.

The Widdicombe Report (1986) examined the roles of officers and members and, more recently, the present government has returned to this in their consultation paper issued in July 1991 on the internal management of local authorities. In the way the council has to have a means of determining authority-wide policy through the Policy Committee, Widdicombe emphasized the role of the Chief Executive and the management team of senior officers of the council. The relationship between the members of the senior officer team and the way the Chief Executive leads that team in dealing with current issues and organizing the advice and information for elected members is a key aspect in effectively supporting political management. The elected members generally must feel confident in the advice that they receive, and that their officers operate in an impartial, fair and open way.

The above comments serve to emphasize that elected members and full-time officials have to balance their identity with specific services and also with corporate priorities. This has been a continuous challenge and a recurring management theme over the past three decades. Other key contributions to this debate were from the Committee on the Management of Local Government (1967) (the Maud Report), and the Bains Report which both emphasized the greater need for a corporate approach.

The greater emphasis on corporate identity stressed by Maud and Bains has been recognized by organizational changes, with the development of more effective corporate management teams and the strengthening of the leadership role of the chief executive. However, the effectiveness of these organizational changes is inevitably dependent on the skills and commitment of individuals in each authority. The ability of chief officers and leading members to bring about a clear understanding of their roles, communicate effectively and operate at a strategic level is essential in determining priorities and allocating resources.

The importance of political sensitivity as a key management skill in local government cannot be over-emphasized. Widdicombe recommends the acquisition of 'political sensitivity' as esssential to officers and the Local Government Training Board has suggested that a management syllabus on this theme should include:

1. the structure and process of political decision-making;
2. how local government politics are changing;
3. developing sensitivity to the politics of your own authority;
4. improving communications in a political setting;
5. being able to handle the stress implicit in a political management system;

6. acknowledging the legitimacy and necessity of political control;
7. being prepared to face the dilemmas which can arise.

Structural changes facing local government

The Conservative government, during 1991, issued three consultation papers covering the structure, internal management and the financing of local government. The last of these covers the commitment to introduce a new Council Tax to replace the community charge and is explained on p. 135.

The papers on structure and internal management are part of a wider government initiative aimed at improving the efficiency and effectiveness of public services. In addition to the three consultation papers a White Paper entitled *The Citizen's Charter* (1991) has also been issued and encapsulates a number of management themes which emerged in the 1980s. It is reflected by corresponding publications by the other two main political parties covering very similar themes in relation to citizens' rights, namely the Labour Party's *Citizen's Charter* and Liberal Democrats' *Citizen's Britain . . . Policies for a People's Charter*.

These 'charters' put emphasis on devising ways and means of improving quality, choice, standards and value in the provision of public services. In general they are trying to develop pressures on public sector 'providers' which simulate the benefits of markets in the shape of competition and choice. As part of this process, local authorities will be encouraged to set and declare priorities, declare target standards of service and subsequently how effective they have been in meeting them. This is not a new challenge but the commitment from all three political parties demonstrates the general consensus but obviously with different emphasis reflecting political ideology. The 'charters' also include similar demands on other public services and recently nationalized public utilities.

In the consultation paper (DoE, 1991) The Structure of Local Government in England, the government clearly favours a move to unitary authorities which it argues will improve accountability, coordination and reduce bureaucracy. The whole issue is dependent on the timing of a general election but the first of the new unitary authorities could be established by 1 April 1994 with a rolling programme of area by area reviews resulting in further change in the mid- to late 1990s. Restructuring proposals to establish unitary authorities have been announced for Wales and, in the case of England, a Local Government Commission is to be formed which will review arrangements on an area by area basis.

The consultation paper (DoE, 1991) The Internal Management of Local Authority in England, incldues a brief history of management structure, the advantages and disadvantages of present arrangements and leads into an outline of potential options for change. As with the paper on structures, the report is simple in style and does not strongly favour any particular course. The options are also clearly placed in the context of councils as enablers rather than providers.

Options specifically identified are as follows.

1. Adapting the committee system. This could involve allowing delegation of decisions to committee chairs and reconsidering the need for minority representation. Safeguards to ensure public debate on issues and to protect minority parties might be needed.
2. A cabinet system. Executive and representational roles could be split. The leader of the controlling party could appoint members to particular portfolios and this executive body would take responsibility for most functions while some matters such as approving a budget would have to go to full council.
3. A council manager. An officer could be appointed to take over day-to-day running of a council with members retaining overall policy responsibility.
4. A directly elected executive. This would involve separate elections to the council and to the executive.
5. A directly elected mayor. An individual would be elected separately from the council to take over its executive role. This could involve the elected mayor making political appointments.

The paper says there may be a case where a small number of members are taking on significantly increased responsibilities for salaries to be paid.

LOCAL GOVERNMENT FINANCE

The past decade has seen little stability in local government finance with several changes in the method of distributing government grant, the abolition of domestic rates and the introduction of the community charge which, in turn, is to be replaced by a new property-based council tax in 1993. The remainder of this chapter explains the position in 1992 and reviews the planned changes.

Income and expenditure

Local government is big business and represents major investment in the nation's physical and social infrastructure. In 1991–2 total spending was £62 billion. Of this about 9% was capital investment and the remainder running costs and debt charges. This represents more than a quarter of total public expenditure and about 10% of the Gross Domestic Product (GDP). The proportion of GDP is somewhat

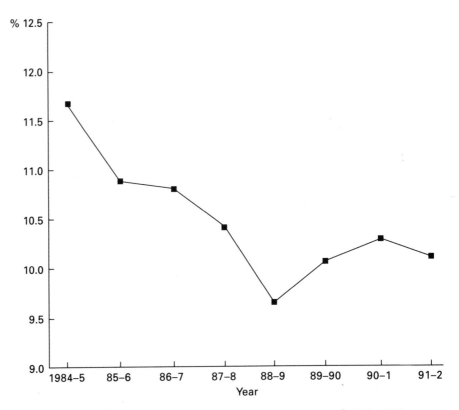

Fig. 5.3 Local government expenditure as a proportion of GDP: UK.
(Sources: *Public Expenditure Analyses to 1993–94* – Statistical Supplement to the 1990 Autumn Statement; *The Government's Expenditure Plans 1990–91 to 1992–93*.)

lower than existed earlier in the 1980s and follows the general thrust of government policy aimed at containing and reducing the relative size of the public sector. To achieve this, local government has been growing at a lower rate than the economy as a whole, as is illustrated in Fig. 5.3.

The major services and their relative costs

In the main, local authorities are involved in providing personal local services and therefore tend to be labour intensive. Almost 70% of annual revenue expenditure is devoted to salaries, wages and related employee costs. The major exception to this general rule is in housing where longer term capital investment in the form of house building and maintenance is more prominent. As shown in Fig. 5.4, Education dominates revenue expenditure and represents more than a third of total local government spending.

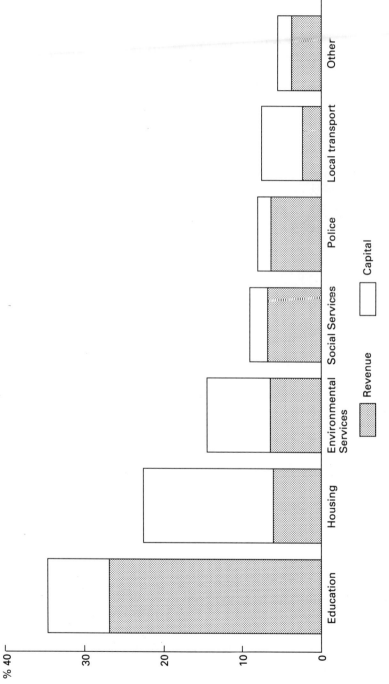

Figure 5.4 Revenue and capital expenditure by service, 1988–9: England. Data shown as a percentage of total combined expenditure.

(Source: DOE, *Local Government Financial Statistics*, England, No. 2, 1990.)

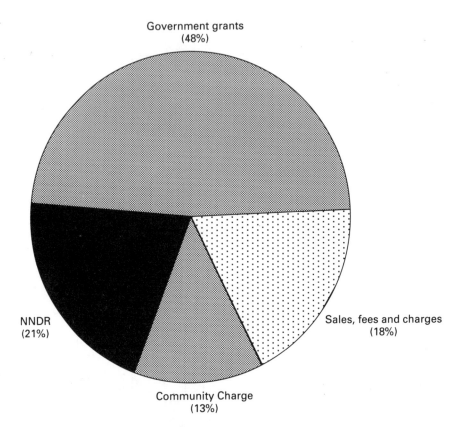

Fig. 5.5 Sources of revenue, 1991–2: UK.
(Sources: *Financial Statement and Budget Report 1991–92*; DOE, *Local Government Financial Statistics, England*, No. 2, 1990.)

Where the money comes from

There are four principal sources of revenue for local authority services:

1. government grants;
2. national non-domestic rates (NNDR);
3. community charge;
4. sales, fees, and charges paid by service users.

   Government grants and non-domestic rates represent two-thirds of total income in 1991–2 as shown in Fig. 5.5. In both cases the total amount available and how it is distributed is wholly under the control of central government and outside the control of local authorities. There are also many external constraints on the ways in which local authorities can raise money through direct fees and charges. This leaves the community charge as the only substantial means of raising local tax revenues. Even in the case of the community charge, the amount levied by each authority is greatly influenced by Government through 'capping' (see p. 125) and other factors.

Government grants

Government grants are of two main types:

1. specific grants;
2. block Grant or general revenue support grant (RSG).

Specific grants tend to be given where the Government wishes to have a direct influence on the standards and policy direction of specific services, as is the case with the probation and magistrates courts services, or where Government wishes to encourage the rapid development of particular services, as with recent grants for services to deal with drug and alcohol misuse. They are paid as a proportion of the total cost of a service. Eligible expenditure is strictly defined and grant claims are subject to close scrutiny through external audit. The largest specific grant-aided service is the Police, where a specific grant of 51% of approved expenditure is available.

In contrast, revenue support grant, which represents about a third of total income, is paid as a general contribution to the overall running costs of local government. The mechanisms for distributing the grant have been designed so as not to be directly related to the level of expenditure on particular services. The aim is to avoid giving direct incentives to increase expenditure and earn more grant. Likewise, non-domestic rates, which represent approximately 21% of total income are distributed in the form of a general grant. These two sources, together with community charge, some 13% of total income, are explained in more detail on pp. 128–37.

Fees and charges

Fees and charges represent some 18% of total income and are raised in a variety of ways including, for example, income from car parking charges, college tuition fees and charges for the residential care of elderly people. The single largest category is rent income from local authority housing, a service which by law is managed and financed separately from other services. A ring-fenced set of housing accounts is maintained by each housing authority keeping general council finances separate from those available for housing, with the aim of preventing cross-subsidization.

Capital investment and government controls

In common with the private sector, local government can arrange funding for longer term (capital) investment through borrowing. This spreads the cost over several years with the aim of matching the benefit flowing from the investment. Because of the need for central government to influence this borrowing, as part of the management of the public sector borrowing requirement, there are Government controls. These controls encourage local authorities to find ways other than borrowing in order to finance their longer term investment. The general shape is summarized at Table 5.2. Borrowing represented about 46% of total funding in the financial year 1986–7 (most recent year available) but the balance is not believed to have changed significantly since that year.

As with other Government controls, there have been a number of changes in approach over the last decade. The system that operated during the 1980s exerted control over 'prescribed expenditure' which was, very broadly, a cash limit on total local authority expenditure as opposed to new borrowing. The Government 'limit' could be supplemented by a set proportion of receipts from the sale of property or other investments. However, the system proved to be unsatisfactory as many arrangements fell outside the definition of 'prescribed expenditure' and were 'escaping' the controls through barter arrangements and leasing. By the time expenditure financed from capital receipts was added, total local authority expenditure bore little resemblance to the total anticipated by Government.

Recognizing these 'weaknesses', the Local Government and Housing Act 1989 introduced a new system of controls, this time over borrowing and other forms of credit arrangement. The control process begins when individual Government departments assess the expenditure requirements of local authority services within their area of responsibility. This is achieved by a variety of methods including responding to bids by individual authorities and allocation by formula. The departments then issue 'annual capital guidelines' corresponding to the main service blocks, i.e. education, housing, etc.

From the guideline figure is deducted a Government estimate of the authority's receipts from the sale of property. What remains is the basic credit or borrowing approval which sets the total value of credit arrangements which the authority may enter into in relation to that year's investment programme. As a rule the basic credit approval is not restricted to use on particular services.

There are also some specific grants for the financing of capital investment, mainly for roads, and the balancing item is the extent to which the authority is able to supplement its capital financing directly from its revenue budget. The scale of the revenue supplement is largely a matter for local council judgement having regard to the impact on the community charge.

Obviously the scale of borrowing and longer term financing will affect the charge on the revenue budget. The charge in relation to leasing will normally reflect the payments to the lessor over the leasing period. In the case of borrowing, the council will establish a pattern of principal repayments which takes into account the useful life of the asset. Interest charges are also incurred based on the amount still outstanding. There is a further overall government control in that the total of the principal repaid from the revenue account must not be less than 4% of the total outstanding debt at the beginning of the financial year. The developing scene in relation to accounting policy for capital assets is further developed in Chapter 6. The approximate pattern of financing is summarized in Fig. 5.6 below.

	%
Borrowing	46
Leasing	21
Capital receipts (sale of assets)	20
Contribution from revenue budget	7
Specific government grants	5
Other contributions (developers etc.)	1
Total	100

Fig. 5.6 Financing capital investment.

This general system of government influences and controls can be seen to overcome two of the major difficulties of the previous approach. First, there is control at the level of borrowing, not at the level of expenditure. Second, account is taken of the capital receipts available to authorities.

An outcry followed the implementation of the new controls, as many authorities found themselves unable to finance their planned capital programmes. It remains to be seen whether such tight control over capital expenditure can be maintained in the longer term.

BORROWING, LENDING AND CASH FLOW MANAGEMENT

The above brief outline of the means of financing longer term investment serves as a useful introduction to the general topic of borrowing and cash flow management. Although the impression could be gained that there are earmarked loans to assets, this is not the case. An authority can determine its own financing strategy and borrow for any amounts and periods, so long as it does not exceed the total limit for long-term borrowing. In addition, there is power to borrow for revenue purposes 'in anticipation of future revenues' such as community charge income due. The authority will aim to have a mix of long-term borrowing (over one year), at fixed and variable rates of interest, and short-term borrowing. The mix is aimed at minimizing the financing costs, in the shape of the average interest payments, having regard to the general volatility of interest rates. Day-to-day borrowing and lending of temporarily surplus funds by local authorities is also on a major national scale with annual turnover of the order of £100 billion.

This management of long-term debt and day-to-day borrowing and lending is a further illustration of the financial autonomy of local authorities. It also serves as a major contrast to other public sector bodies, such as the National Health Service, whose funding is managed within central government accounting.

Although local authorities have powers to borrow from a wide range of sources, in practice over 90% is borrowed from central government through the Public Works Loan Board (PWLB). This reflects the extremely competitive borrowing terms offered by the PWLB by virtue of a Government subsidy. This subsidy is gradually being withdrawn causing a reduction in PWLB competitiveness. This will cause authorities to look elsewhere in the money market over coming years. Total local authority borrowing at March 1991 exceeded £53 billion which represents approximately a quarter of the total National Debt.

Emphasis was made on page 106 of the need for a local authority to be able to point to a legislative enabling power in relation to all its actions. Because of the controversy through 1990 and 1991 in relation to borrowing and lending powers this section has been developed to demonstrate this particular aspect of local government financial management.

The general pressure on public expenditure had led to attempts by some authorities to be creative in the management of their debt 'portfolios' and cash surpluses which in turn led to questions about legality. The most notable instance is the use made by a number of local authorities, in particular the London Borough of Hammersmith and Fulham, of 'interest rate swaps'. A swap is a transaction with a bank, by which each party pays to the other an amount representing interest on the same notional principal sum – but based on different interest rate terms and periods; typically one amount is calculated on a fixed interest rate and the other is calculated on a short-term variable interest rate. Each party will have a different view on how short-term rates will move relative to the fixed rate. As the settlement is on a net payment basis and no principal sum changes hands, it is possible to enter into swaps involving a huge underlying principal sum.

The legal case with Hammersmith and Fulham Borough Council involved deals based on principal sums totalling several billion pounds;

the actions were ruled to be beyond the powers of the Borough and the Borough was therefore freed from its obligations to the banks. The banks experienced significant losses as a result.

The finding that it is illegal for local authorities to enter into interest rate swaps has caused banks to adopt a more cautious approach towards lending to local authorities. Only straightforward borrowing and lending transactions are now possible and some banks are reluctant to lend to local authorities at all. This is seen as merely a temporary reaction.

In 1991, it was also brought home to all lenders that loans to banking institutions were not risk free; three banks registered in the UK failed, notably the Bank of Credit and Commerce International. The importance of local authorities to the banking sector was apparent from the immediate impact on the money market of the so-called 'flight to quality', as authorities moved their surplus funds away from the secondary banking sector. Renewed emphasis has been placed on the responsibility of the Finance Director to have a clear, considered policy for lending money to other bodies.

RELATIONSHIPS WITH CENTRAL GOVERNMENT

The relationship between central and local government, particularly on financial issues, has been a source of concern throughout the modern history of local government. The key issue is the role of central government and the degree of control exerted over local government.

Central government's perception of its role was set out clearly in its response to the Layfield Committee (1976) Local Government Finance: Report of the Committee of Enquiry. The principal elements identified were:

1. to ensure that local services reflect national priorities and national policies and are provided at broadly comparable standards;
2. to ensure that, in aggregate, local government's spending plans are compatible with the government's economic objectives;
3. to ensure that activities of one authority do not have adverse effects on the area of another;
4. to promote cooperation between local authority and other complementary services;
5. to ensure that the financial arrangements promote efficiency;
6. to safeguard the interest of vulnerable minority groups whose interests may get a proper hearing only at national level;
7. to encourage and maintain local democracy.

With the passage of time it has become clear that some of these elements have been accorded higher priority than others. It is also clear from the actions of government that a new responsibility must be added to the list:

8. to ensure that local government does not set a rate of local tax which is higher than central government considers reasonable.

The ability to control local government expenditure and income is of paramount importance and it is this feature which we will now concentrate upon.

Control of local government expenditure

The case is often argued that central government has a duty to control aggregate local authority expenditure. It is asserted that only central government is in a position to assess the competing claims on national resources. In the case of local authority borrowing it is held that the scale is such to demand close control by central government. It is also clear that these arguments depend upon the stance adopted towards monetary and fiscal policy.

Perhaps more fundamentally, it would appear that government's role in ensuring compatibility between local spending plans and economic objectives directly conflicts with its role in encouraging local democracy. It is on these grounds that tight control of local authority expenditure is open to the most telling criticism. As Barlow (1981) concludes:

> If local democracy is to be valued highly, then this freedom (to make choices about the provision of services) is essential to local government, and if local government is to be preserved, local authorities should no longer accept unequivocally the argument that control over their levels of expenditure by central government is essential to economic management (p. 12).

Whatever the rights and wrongs of the situation, the 1980s and early 1990s witnessed a determined, and ultimately successful, attempt by central government to achieve control over local authority spending.

Expenditure control via the grant mechanism

The main tactic used by central government throughout the 1980s was to seek expenditure restraint through pressure from ratepayers. This was to be achieved through manipulating the levels of grant paid to authorities. By forcing a higher proportion of costs on to ratepayers, the government hoped that they would force authorities to hold down expenditure. Three mechanisms were involved:

1. under the block grant system, introduced in 1980, the proportion of grant paid to an authority was reduced if it spent significantly more than the government's assessment of what was needed;

2. the government progressively reduced the overall proportion of local authority expenditure met by grant from 60% in 1980–1 to 32% in 1990–1 (both figures net of fees, charges and specific grant);
3. the government introduced a system of expenditure targets (calculated independently of the assessment in 2.) which, if exceeded, resulted in a grant penalty. This mechanism was abolished in 1986–7.

Despite these pressures local authority expenditure continued to exceed government estimates, heralding the introduction of a much more direct form of control – capping.

Capping

The Rates Act (1984) gave the Secretary of State for the Environment the power to limit rate increases either in individual authorities or across the board. This required him to designate the authorities to be capped and to define the criteria used in selecting them. The criteria were stated in terms of:

1. excess of expenditure over government assessment; and
2. increase in expenditure over the previous year.

Councils had the right to appeal against capping but were reluctant to do so because under the legislation this gave the Secretary of State additional powers to impose direct conditions on local budgets and financial management.

Rate capping directly affected up to twenty authorities each year and undoubtedly it also influenced those authorities who were close to the capping threshold. However its impact in restraining local government expenditure in aggregate is debatable as those well below the declared threshold experienced pressure to raise their spending.

What is not a matter of doubt is the dramatic impact that capping has had under the community charge regime. The new powers under the Local Government Finance Act 1988 are similar to the old ones, although the procedures are simplified. In addition, the power to cap an authority can now be exercised *during* the financial year in question.

Most important of all, in October 1990, for the first time, the Secretary of State announced in advance the criteria to be adopted in designating authorities for the following financial year. Moreover the criteria announced were particularly strict, allowing most authorities little additional expenditure over and above an increase for inflation. The result was that among authorities subject to the capping rules, there was a clear convergence of budgets just below the capping threshold. Among shire counties, 22 of the 39 authorities budgeted within

0.1% of the capping limit. Accordingly, in 1991–2 local authority budgets in aggregate were set just 0.4% above the government's expenditure assessment.

Apparently not satisfied with even this outcome, the government in 1991 abolished the *de minimis* rule which had previously exempted smaller authorities from the capping legislation (if their budgets were less than £15 million). This single act appears to demonstrate that the government was no longer concerned with regulating council spending primarily in the interests of the wider economy.

Other legislation

Through legislation the four successive Conservative governments since 1979 have shifted the balance of power in the financial management of local authorities. This has been achieved largely in pursuit of central government's role in promoting efficiency. Two major principles have guided the quest for efficiency:

1. that efficiency is promoted through the introduction of market disciplines; and
2. that decisions should be made as close as possible to the point of service delivery.

Principle 1. is evident in the compulsory competitive tendering (CCT) legislation, which compels authorities to put council services out to tender. The council's own workforce has then to compete with the private sector for the business. By 1991 this legislation applied to a number of areas, mainly affecting the manual workforce:

1. highway maintenance;
2. building maintenance;
3. refuse collection;
4. cleaning of buildings;
5. ground maintenance;
6. vehicle maintenance;
7. catering services (including school meals);
8. sport and leisure management.

Recent proposals suggest that CCT will be extended to encompass white-collar support services, including legal and financial services.

The second principle is evident in the legislation for the local management of schools and colleges. This requires the delegation of budgets on a formula basis to individual establishments. Although certain expenditure decisions remain the prerogative of the education authority, most are now made in the school or college, including decisions as to how many teachers to appoint and their salary.

The result in both cases has been to reduce the scope for local authority discretion in financial management. It has been further reduced by the powers given to schools to opt out of local authority control and will reduce still further if the government enacts proposals to remove all further education and sixth form colleges from local authorities.

PUBLIC EXPENDITURE PLANS

Central government departments consult local authorities routinely on matters of concern to them, for example, when proposing legislation which would impose new duties. This type of consultation takes place as and when required and tends to be conducted from long-distance.

A very different model operates for consultation on public expenditure plans. It is both more formal, operating within definite time-tables, and much more intimate, involving face-to-face meetings. At its heart is the Consultative Committee on Local Government Finance (CCLGF). This comprises representatives of the local authority associations and of the government, including the Secretary of State for the Environment.

The CCLGF is supported by a network of officer working groups which prepare the ground for these meetings. Although the Committee normally meets only twice a year the working groups are busy all year round. The first CCLGF meeting in the cycle, normally in June/July, is primarily concerned with ascertaining views as to the required aggregate level of local government expenditure in the following year. It is followed soon after by the Secretary of State's announcement of aggregate assumed spending levels and the amount of government support to be provided.

The second meeting, in September/October, is more concerned with the distribution of government support. Again, it is followed by a formal announcement by the Secretary of State. At this stage provisional grant figures are supplied to individual authorities for consultation. Final grant figures are normally announced in January for the financial year commencing in April.

The outcomes of these processes are fed into the government's own financial planning system, the Public Expenditure Survey. The principal document is the *Autumn Statement*, published around November, which summarizes the government's plans for the following three years. Further details are supplied in the *Statistical Supplement* and the Department of Environment Annual Report, both published in the following January/February. These documents describe in the main only the government contributions to local authority expenditure, and exclude self-financed expenditure, for example that raised from the community charge/local tax.

The plans described in these documents are of very limited value to individual local authorities. They are designed, quite naturally, to suit the purposes of central government control and accountability. They are not designed primarily to aid local authorities. The major drawbacks include the following:

1. the plans are on a cash basis, blurring the distinction between inflation and volume changes;
2. only very limited information is provided, all at aggregate level;
3. in view of the current importance of local government in national politics, the plans are subject to sudden and dramatic change. For example, the decision was announced in the March 1991 budget to provide £5 billion additional finance to local authorities despite no such provision having been made in previous plans (see p. 131).

For these reasons the publication of government plans excites in individual local authorities little more than passing interest although at association or national level, where aggregates are more important, they have more relevance.

REVENUE SUPPORT GRANT (RSG)

There are a number of reasons why a contribution is made out of central taxation towards the costs of local authority services. Prominent among those reasons are the following.

1. To promote geographical equity. The underlying objective of the RSG system is to permit the same level of community charge (or other local tax) to be set throughout the country for the same standard of service.
2. To promote accountability. Government, through its actions, imposes many costs on local authorities, particularly where services are national in character. For example in education the government introduced the National Curriculum. Likewise the Environmental Protection Act (1990) imposed new duties upon local authorities. It is therefore only right that government should contribute to the cost rather than leave the local council to account for the initiative to the local electorate.
3. To promote progressiveness in the tax system. Local taxes, such as rates, the community charge or the proposed council tax, tend to be insufficiently progressive, imposing a great burden upon members of the community with lower incomes. By making a contribution from the much more progressive system of central taxation this aspect of inequity is reduced.
4. To promote acceptability of local taxes. Local taxes are highly visible. Unlike income tax or national insurance, most people re-

ceive an annual bill for their local taxes. They also tend to lack buoyancy, which implies that the tax rates have to be increased annually. They are therefore unpopular and paying a subsidy out of central taxation helps to make them more acceptable.

Features

RSG was introduced in 1990–1 as the successor to block grant. Entitlement is calculated annually and is fixed at the outset. In general no action of a local authority can have any impact on the level of its RSG. The aim of RSG is to compensate for differences between areas in terms of:

1. need to provide services; and
2. taxable capacity.

Thus, an area with high need for services will receive extra grant. An area with a high taxable capacity, for example a large number of community chargepayers, will receive less grant. Equalization of taxable capacity is achieved relatively simply through the final calculation of RSG entitlement, as described below. Compensating for different levels of need is a highly complex matter involving standard spending assessments.

Standard spending assessments

The standard spending assessment (SSA) represents the government's view of the appropriate level of revenue expenditure for an authority. (Strictly, it represents expenditure financed from RSG, non-domestic rates and community charge/local tax. Expenditure financed from fees and charges and from specific grant is excluded.) It comprises a series of separate assessments, covering seven major service blocks and, in Education and Social Services, a number of sub-blocks:

1. Education:
    (a) primary;
    (b) secondary;
    (c) post-16;
    (d) under 5;
    (e) other.
2. Personal Social Services:
    (a) children;
    (b) elderly;
    (c) other.
3. Police.

4. Fire and civil defence.
5. Highway maintenance.
6. All other services.
7. Capital financing.

The service assessments are derived from, in essence, relatively simple formulae which take account of the social, demographic and geographical characteristics of the area. In general the formulae represent the number of prospective clients or some other indicator of need for a service multiplied by the appropriate unit cost. The individual service assessments are then aggregated to arrive at the authority's SSA.

Because of the burden placed upon SSAs in the system of local government finance, great emphasis was placed on the need for stability and simplicity. As a result many of the measures of need are regarded as fairly crude, and despite protests from many quarters in local government there have been few changes of note in the assessment methodology. Nevertheless the annual calculation of SSAs is of prodigious complexity, on account of the need to incorporate new indicator data (many of which are revised annually) and the need to ensure that SSAs in aggregate conform to the government's view of the appropriate level of total local government spending. It is in the latter process that much of the subjectivity and political involvement in the system can be identified.

Once SSAs have been determined, compensation between areas for different levels of need is simply achieved through the calculation of RSG entitlement.

Calculation of RSG entitlement

The first feature to bear in mind is that the calculation of RSG is a top–down approach. It begins with a government assessment of the appropriate level of total local government spending, not with an objective assessment of the needs of individual authorities. The government assessment is reflected in its announcement of Total Standard Spending for the year. This is expenditure to be financed from:

1. specific grants;
2. RSG;
3. non-domestic rates;
4. community charge/local tax.

Before RSG entitlement at local level can be ascertained the government must determine the level of non-domestic rates for the year and the amount it regards as appropriate to be raised from the community charge/local tax. Having done so, the calculation of

RSG is very simple. In any authority area the assumed income from non-domestic rates and community charge/local tax is calculated. RSG is simply the difference between this figure and the SSA, i.e.

RSG equals SSA
          minus income from non-domestic rates
          minus assumed income from community charge/
           local tax.

It can be seen that, all else being equal, areas with a higher SSA will receive extra RSG, thus compensating for differences in need. Similarly, areas with a greater taxable capacity, and able to generate a higher level of local tax income, will receive less RSG.

Trends in RSG

In 1980–1 rate support grant, the forerunner of RSG, represented 60% of local government expenditure (net of fees, charges and specific grant). By 1990–1 the proportion had fallen to 32%. This trend was consistent with the government aim of reducing the scale of public expenditure and with the use of the grant system as a means to influence local authority expenditure.

In 1991–2, as a direct result of the immense unpopularity of the community charge, there was a dramatic reversal of the long-term trend, with the infusion of an additional £5 billion in grant. This was financed by an increase in VAT from 15% to $17\frac{1}{2}$%. At the same time, the government gave a commitment to maintain in future years the balance between central and local funding at the new level (Fig. 5.7). The injection of grant was tied to a reduction in community charge levels of £140. The price to be paid by local government was two-fold.

1. Following the introduction of central control of business rates it entailed a further increase in the 'gearing-ratio'. The result was that a 1% increase in local authority expenditure would require an increase in the community charge of 4.6%.
2. It reduced the tax base for the community charge/local tax to such a low level that, in the opinion of the Audit Commission, it was no longer viable in the long term as a tax source. This represented a potential threat to the independence of local authorities as tax-levying bodies.

THE LOCAL TAX BASE

The financial autonomy of local authorities dates back to the six-teenth century when parishes were first required to impose a compul-

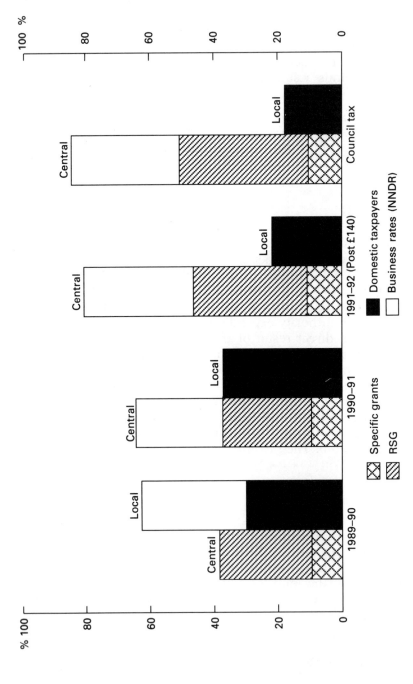

Fig. 5.7 Sources of finance: England.
(Sources: ACC, *Revenue Support Grant, England, 1991–92*; DOE, Press Release No. 251, April 1991; CIPFA, *Finance and General Statistics, 1989–90*).

sory levy for poverty relief. Over time a number of separate rates were added to finance different services. By the mid-nineteenth century local councils began to displace parishes as the main unit of organization. However, it was 1925 before the modern system of rating emerged with a unified rate set for each district. Many changes followed prior to its abolition in 1990 in England and Wales, and 1989 in Scotland.

Rates were basically a tax levied on property. Each property was assessed by an independent valuer and a rateable value assigned. This was simply a notional annual rent. The actual rates payable by the property occupier were set annually. Each tier of local authority ascertained the total sum to be raised from rates, having taken account of all other sources of income. Knowing the aggregate rateable value for all property in the area, the total rate income required for each tier could be expressed as a multiplier of the rateable value. This multiplier, the rate poundage, was then applied to each property in the area and the individual rates bills were established. Domestic properties, however, received a discount in the rate poundage of 18.5p in the pound, financed by government grant. The rates were collected on behalf of each tier by the rating authority, being the district or borough council in England and Wales and the regional council in Scotland.

Since the early nineteenth century government grants had been provided to meet part of the cost of local services and reduce the call on the rates. From 1979 onwards central government began to use rates as a means of restraining local government expenditure by reducing the amount of grant paid. This coincided with a period of high inflation and, since rates lacked buoyancy, the consequence was a series of high rate rises. These rises, coupled with constant government publicity about alleged local authority 'overspending', were expected to result in political pressure upon local authorities to reduce expenditure.

Instead the result was that the system of local government finance fell into disrepute. This reached its peak when in 1985 the five-yearly reassessment of rateable values took place in Scotland. A significant proportion of households suffered very large rates increases. The ratepayers' expression of outrage produced overwhelming political pressure upon central government. In anticipation of a general election they promised to abolish rates and introduce a fairer system.

The government's first step towards reform was the publication of the Green Paper (DoE, 1986) *Paying for Local Government*. Its conclusion was that domestic rates should be replaced by a flat rate community charge. In reaching that conclusion it explicitly rejected the findings of the Green Paper (DoE, 1981) *Alternatives to Domestic Rates* and the subsequent White Paper (DoE, 1983) *Rates*. Of rates the White Paper noted:

They are highly perceptible to ratepayers and they promote accountability. They are well understood, cheap to collect and very difficult to evade. They act as an incentive to the most efficient use of property.

The White Paper had rejected a community charge as unworkable.

... the tax would be hard to enforce. If the electoral register were used as the basis for liability it could be seen as a tax on the right to vote. A new register would therefore be needed but this would make the tax expensive to run and complicated.

The crucial issue which changed the government's mind in 1986 was that of accountability. It felt that accountability to ratepayers was insufficient. Of the 35 million local electorate who enjoyed the benefit of local authority services, only 18 million were liable to pay rates and only 12 million actually had to pay the full amount without rebate.

Only two other forms of local tax had been considered as serious possibilities. A local sales tax was rejected on several grounds.

1. It would not be readily perceptible, so would not enhance accountability.
2. It would require complex administration.
3. The yield would be uneven geographically (favouring regional shopping centres) and uneven over time.

A local income tax was also rejected.

1. It would require an increase in income tax, contrary to government policy.
2. It would not be readily perceptible.
3. There would be substantial collection costs.
4. As a redistributive tax it was considered inappropriate for local government.

Accordingly the community charge was introduced in 1989 in Scotland and a year later in England and Wales.

The central features were:

1. virtually every adult was liable and was billed individually;
2. the maximum rebate was 80%, requiring everyone, however low their income, to pay at least 20%;
3. the registers of liable adults were updated continuously.

In England, a peculiar feature which blurred accountability was that the separate tiers of local authorities did not each set their own community charge. District councils alone determined the level of community charge to be set, based upon the individual requirements of all the local authorities covering the area. They were also responsible for collecting the community charge and for managing the collection funds which were central to this system. Under these arrangements, RSG and non-domestic rates were not paid to the separate tiers, but were all paid into the district collection fund, along with all community charge income. The county, district and parish councils or other authorities then precepted upon the collection funds for the total amount required to meet their net expenditure on services for the year.

From the outset a large number of weaknesses were apparent and the practical difficulties encountered in implementation were immense. These were exacerbated by a fundamental contradiction in the government's policy aims. Rates were unpopular because they were too high, largely resulting from government reductions in grant. However the government continued cutting its grant contribution during the implementation of the community charge. The aim was still to try to control local authority expenditure through pressure from local residents. At the same time, the removal of non-domestic rates from local control meant that any shortfall in government funding would not now be shared by business ratepayers, but would fall wholly upon community chargepayers. The rates burden, which was rejected by ratepayers as too great, was deliberately converted into an even greater burden on community chargepayers.

The combination of the basic weaknesses and the pursuit of this policy resulted in almost universal condemnation of the community charge:

1. it was regressive and perceived as more unfair than rates;
2. charge levels far exceeded government estimates;
3. 'losers' outnumbered 'gainers' by two to one;
4. administration costs more than doubled;
5. non-payment levels reached crisis point, particularly in Scotland.

Crucially the government was held to blame and in 1991 in a dramatic U-turn, it announced the impending abolition of the community charge. In the meantime it injected an additional £5 billion in grant while promising to maintain that level of support in future years. As a result the average community charge in England and Wales fell from £360 in 1990–1 to £240 the following year.

The government published its proposals for a replacement to the community charge in April 1991. In the consultation paper (DoE, 1991) A *New Tax for Local Government* it suggested a return to a property-based tax to be called the council tax. It would nevertheless include a personal element to retain a vestigial link with its predecessor. The main features of the proposed tax were:

1. each household would receive a single bill;
2. the bill would reflect the capital value of the property and the number of resident adults;

3. each property would be assigned to one of a number of bands according to its market value;
4. the council tax would be the same for all properties in the same band in any area;
5. the tax bands would remain in constant proportion to each other, as defined by government;
6. tax bands would increase at a lower rate than the average property value in each band, i.e. progressiveness would be limited;
7. single adult households and students would receive a 25% discount off the bill;
8. each tier of authority would set its own council tax (and hence receive RSG and non-domestic rates in its own right).

Many features were welcomed by local authorities, particularly the return to a property-based tax and return to a tax set independently by each tier of authority. Equally there were many features of concern:

1. the retention of a personal element implied complex and costly administration;
2. the use of property bands could provoke numerous and costly appeals by owners of property near the band thresholds;
3. most tellingly, the system would require a 5.4% increase in council tax for a 1% increase in net expenditure.

This level of gearing turned the spotlight back on the issue of accountability. Local government would raise only about 12% of its gross expenditure through the council tax, and would be subject to the same strict capping controls as under the community charge. Central government would directly control over 70% of local authority income, and would have a substantial influence over the remainder through regulation of fees and charges. Under this regime the concept of local accountability could be little more than illusion. A tax on this relative scale certainly raises local awareness but responsibility between local and central government would be far from clear. It remains to be seen whether the Audit Commission was correct in its assessment that the proposed council tax system is unsustainable in the long term.

Non-domestic rates

Prior to 1990 rates were levied upon all non-domestic property in a similar manner to household rates. The rate set was the same as that for domestic property, except for the general reduction of 18.5p in the pound applied to domestic property.

In the Green Paper (DoE, 1986) *Paying for Local Government* several criticisms of locally-controlled non-domestic rates were advanced. The crucial criticisms, however, were that:

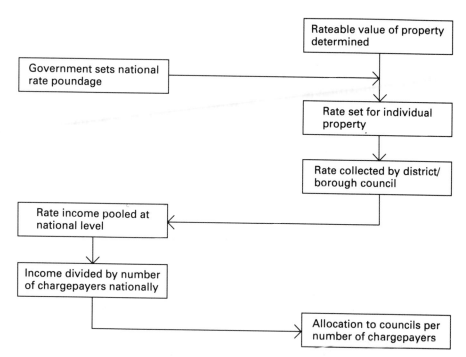

Fig. 5.8 The national non-domestic rating system, England (NNDR).

1. in some areas increased council spending was financed dispro-
   portionately by local businesses (on average 60% of expenditure
   financed from rates was paid by the non-domestic sector);
2. businesses in high rate localities were believed to be at a competitive disadvantage.

The fundamental point in the first criticism is that because businesses have no vote in elections there was little incentive for local
politicians to reduce the rate level. On the other hand, if the full cost
of council spending increases were passed on to the local residents,
pressure on the council to reduce spending would increase.

Accordingly the government abolished locally-controlled non-
domestic rates and replaced them in England and Wales with a single national rate set by government. Enshrined in the legislation was
a provision limiting the maximum annual increase in the rate poundage to the annual increase in the retail prices index. (Slightly different
arrangements were applied in Scotland.) (See Fig. 5.8.)

Non-domestic rates are nevertheless still collected by district/
borough councils. The proceeds are pooled and then redistributed to
councils in proportion to numbers of community chargepayers. In
fact, given the system of RSG entitlement, the redistribution mechanism is of little consequence, since any shortfall in rate income is

made good by RSG. A change will however be necessary on the re-placement of the community charge and the abolition of the charge register.

As can be seen from this description, there was an explicit govern-ment aim to load a higher proportion of any increased spending on to local domestic taxpayers. This mirrored the tactic of reducing the proportion of expenditure met by grant. The impact in both cases was to greatly increase the 'gearing ratio'. Under the proposed council tax the gearing ratio will increase still further. It is concern over this feature which is prompting calls by local authority associations for the return of non-domestic rates to local control.

CONCLUSION

During the 1980s there was a steady decline in the relationship between central and local government. Central government was de-termined to impose its will and assert its constitutional power over local authorities. Financial management was the very core of the debate and the primary aim, on both economic and political grounds, was to control local authority expenditure.

This objective was eventually achieved, but at great cost in terms of local democracy.

Adding to the strains was the introduction, contrary to the wishes of almost all in local government, of the community charge.

The debate continues and will inevitably also be clouded by the effects of further structural change both through the current move to unitary authorities and also transfers of functions to and from local government.

A decade of change seems to have resolved little in terms of clarifying local accountability. At national and local level there is much unease about the soundness of the current proposals for the council tax and whether the high gearing that will result can provide a solid basis for a local tax system.

SUMMARY

This chapter has reviewed the structure, functions and financing of local government. Emphasis has also been placed on the constitu-tional and financial relationships between central and local govern-ment. Major changes in financing from 1991 were considered, their rationale and potential problem areas. The chapter concluded with examination of the local tax base and the planned introduction of the council tax.

FURTHER READING

The financing of local government is the subject of continuous amendment. *Public Finance and Accountancy* (CIPFA), *Local Government Chronicle* and *Municipal Journal* are regular publications addressing current news and topics. In addition, the Chartered Institute of Public Finance and Accountancy (CIPFA) publishes a large quantity of relevant material both within the 'Financial Information Service' and on an *ad hoc* basis. Useful summaries are contained in the following annually produced publications: *Local Government Trends* (CIPFA), *Public Domain* (Public Finance Foundation). The Green Paper (DoE, 1986) *Paying for Local Government* provides a fascinating insight into the subject.

6

Local government accounting, reporting and budgeting

Chapter 5 considered the structure and financing of local government. In this chapter attention is focused on the financial accounting and reporting requirements to which local authorities are subject, looking in turn at statutory requirements, accounting standards and other forms of guidance on best practice. The chapter also considers the specific requirements that govern the accounting and reporting of local authority housing and direct service organizations; the basis of accounting for local authorities' fixed assets, and the current proposals for change in this area; and the requirements for local authorities' annual reports. The chapter concludes with a review of local authorities' budgeting and budgetary control arrangements.

The basic principles discussed in this chapter are common to all local authorities. However, it should be borne in mind that local authorities in different parts of the United Kingdom are subject to separate and, in certain instances, quite different legislation. This chapter has been written from the perspective of local authorities in England and Wales, and most references to specific legislation apply to English and Welsh authorities only. For those interested in practice in Scotland, a source reference is included in the section on 'Further reading' at the end of this chapter.

INTRODUCTION

For a variety of reasons, reflecting in part both the history of the development of local government and the specific legal framework and financing regime that governs their activities, the form of local authorities' published accounts and the accounting principles and practices followed in preparing them have developed separately from those in the private sector. These differences of form and practice used to be defended on the grounds that local authorities are different from commercial enterprises and that, therefore, the accounting principles and practices adopted in the private sector do not necessarily apply.

Increasingly, however, this argument has come to be questioned. In its place there is a growing recognition that accounting is a common discipline and that the same principles and practices should apply to all enterprises whether in the private or public sectors. This is not to deny that a different approach may be justified in particular circumstances, but there has been a marked shift in emphasis. The presumption now is that generally accepted accounting practices, or 'gaap', will apply to local authorities, rather than vice versa, and any departure from them needs to be justified rigorously by reference either to first principles or, more pragmatically, to statutory requirements. This has proved a healthy development for the general standards of financial accounting and reporting by local authorities. This growing convergence has been given practical expression in the work that has been undertaken on the application of accounting standards to local authorities, culminating in the development of a 'franked' SORP issued by CIPFA in April 1987 and subsequently revised. The development of accounting standards for local authorities is considered in further detail below.

However, one fundamental distinction that relates to the 'culture' of financial reporting does remain. In the private sector, the publication of a company's annual report is a major event for the company. The detailed information in it will be pored over by institutional investors, specialist analysts and the financial press, and their conclusions can have significant practical effects, for example on the share price and on financial institutions' perception of the financial health and well-being of the company. In this sense, a company 'lives and dies' by its published results and a commensurate amount of care and attention is devoted to their preparation throughout the organization, right up to and including the board of directors. What might be regarded as relatively straightforward technical changes, e.g. in accounting policies, can have a far-reaching impact on the company in a very real, practical sense, insofar as they affect reported profits.

In the case of local authorities these external pressures do not, on the whole, apply. The level of public interest in the published annual report, of which the financial statements normally form part, as reflected in enquiries or requests for information from local taxpayers, consumers of services or other interested parties, is generally low, despite the successful efforts of many local authorities to improve the quality and accessibility of their annual reports. Often this relative lack of interest is also reflected among the elected members of the local authority itself. Although it is quite clear in law that it is the authority that is responsible for preparing and publishing its accounts, they tend to be regarded in practice as 'the treasurer's or director of finance's accounts'. There is not an equivalent degree of ownership of the accounts by the authority as is the case with the directors of a limited company.

Clearly, the analogy between an elected local authority and a company's board of directors is not a precise one. The different approach reflects in part the perceived complexity of a local authority's accounts to the lay members of what is essentially a political body, but also the special status, enshrined in legislation, that is accorded to the local authority's chief financial officer, who has responsibility for the administration of the authority's financial affairs. This serves to reinforce the view that the accounts are a highly specialized matter, and best left to 'the experts'. Nevertheless, it is surely a paradox that most surveys of the users of local authorities' annual reports and accounts have cited the authority's own elected members as the perceived main user group, yet as part of the management of the local authority they are accountable for the activities of the body and the report should properly be regarded as their report to their constituents, the local community and the users of the local authority's services.

One other factor that should be borne in mind when comparing local authority and private sector practice is that for local authorities the annual report comprises only one link in a chain of accountability. In addition to publishing their results, local authorities also publish their financial plans in the form of the annual budget and they are required to include summary financial information in the bills sent to community chargepayers and non-domestic ratepayers. It is perhaps inevitable that decisions over the future allocation of resources and tax levels should excite more interest than a retrospective statement of the way in which monies raised were actually spent. In addition, local authorities' accounts are openly available for public inspection. Section 17 of the Local Government Finance Act 1982 provides that 'at each audit . . . any person interested may inspect the accounts to be audited and all books, deeds, contracts, bills, vouchers and receipts relating to them'. It also gives local government electors the right to question the auditor about the accounts and, in certain circumstances, to make objections on particular matters.

Nevertheless, the published financial statements remain the single most important vehicle by which local authorities can demonstrate accountability both for the stewardship of public money, i.e. how the various resources available to the authority have been applied and whether it has complied with its statutory obligations, and for performance in the provision of services, i.e. how the resources have actually been used.

Much has been written about the objectives of local authority financial reports, and the potential users and their information needs. However, the purpose of a local authority's published accounts is expressed most simply and succinctly in the revised *Code of Practice on Local Authority Accounting* issued by CIPFA in 1991, as:

> . . . to give electors, those subject to locally levied taxes and charges, members of the authority and other interested parties clear information about the authority's finances. It should answer such questions as:
>
>> What did the authority's services cost in the year of account?
>>
>> To what extent was income greater or less than the cost of services in that year?
>>
>> What were the authority's assets and liabilities at the year-end? (CIPFA, 1991a).

However, if the elected members of an authority find the prospect of coming to grips with the accounts daunting, what chance has the local taxpayer or consumer of services? In this respect, it is interesting to note that the Departmental Committee on Accounts remarked in 1907 that 'it is generally agreed that as wide publicity as practicable should be given to the accounts of local authorities and that they should be published in such a form as to be intelligible to ratepayers possessed of average ability but without special knowledge of accountancy'. Similarly, the Layfield Committee reported in 1976: 'we believe that there is an obligation on local authorities to devise a means of providing the electorate with financial information about services in reasonably simple and straightforward terms'. Since 1976 much progress has been made in the development of accounting standards for local authorities and of local authorities' annual reports, but the objective articulated in 1907 still remains to be accomplished.

Local authorities are required by statute to maintain a variety of separate funds and accounts for different functions or activities. In many cases all that is entailed is the need to maintain a separate record of income and expenditure for control purposes, e.g. to demonstrate that the net expenditure on a particular activity does not exceed specified limits, to identify certain categories of income and expenditure of a discretionary nature or in respect of certain trading activities or as the basis for claiming government grants. In the majority of cases, these accounts will not be included separately in the authority's published statement of accounts, although where material the net expenditure or a summarized statement of income and expenditure will be disclosed in a note to the accounts. The main accounts that different groups of local authorities are required to maintain and that form the core of the published financial statements are:

1. the General or County Fund, which comprises the income and expenditure relating to the generality of the local authority's services that fall to be funded in part by the local taxpayer in the form of community charges and non-domestic rates;

2. the Housing Revenue Account, which comprises the income and expenditure relating to the provision of council housing and related housing services, which fall to be funded in part by council tenants in the form of rents;
3. the accounts of the authority's various direct service organizations (DSOs) established under the compulsory competitive tendering provisions of the Local Government Planning and Land Act 1980 and the Local Government Act 1988; these are internal trading organizations that are required to be run on commercial lines and that generate income in the form of fees and charges for contracted services provided to other parts of the local authority's organization;
4. the Superannuation Fund, the local authority's pension fund, which comprises income in the form of employers' and employees' pension contributions and investment income from invested funds, and expenditure in the form of benefit payments to pensioners and related expenses.

The specific accounting requirements in respect of the Housing Revenue Account and DSOs are dealt with in greater length below. In general, however, the form and content of the financial statements to be published in respect of each of the various funds and accounts maintained by a local authority are subsumed within the general provisions regarding the financial accounting and reporting of local authorities.

THE FRAMEWORK OF FINANCIAL ACCOUNTING AND REPORTING

The financial accounting and reporting of local authorities is governed by a framework comprising: statute and regulations; professional accounting standards (SSAPs) and statements of recommended practice (SORPs); and other professional guidance and advice on 'best practice'. Together these elements comprise an interlocking hierarchy as set out in Fig. 6.1.

Clearly, within this hierarchy statutory requirements have the greatest formal authority, but in general these have been defined only in broad terms and relatively loosely, and most of the specific accounting requirements with which local authorities must comply are set out in the SORPs developed for local authorities. The relationship between these two 'tiers' of accounting requirements is now specifically recognized in legislation and is discussed in further detail below. However, both of these top tiers rest on a broad foundation of lower order guidance on detailed aspects of local authority accounting, for example the standard objective and subjective classification of income and expenditure developed by CIPFA, and 'best practice' guidance on specific issues, such as accounting for overheads.

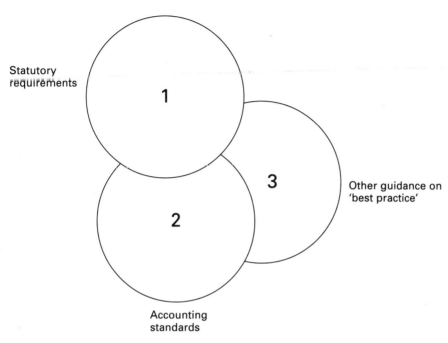

Statutory
requirements

Other guidance on
'best practice'

Accounting
standards

Fig. 6.1 The framework of local authorities' financial accounting and reporting.

Each of the three elements in the accounting framework is considered in turn below.

THE STATUTORY BASIS OF FINANCIAL ACCOUNTING AND REPORTING

The most important statutory requirements in this context are those that relate to the preparation, audit and publication of statements of accounts. The starting point here is the Local Government Finance Act 1982 which empowers the Secretary of State by regulations to make provision with respect to *inter alia* 'the form, preparation and certification of accounts and of statements of accounts'. These provisions are set out in the *Accounts and Audit Regulations 1983*, as amended (DOE, 1983). These Regulations are something of a mixed bag, covering four main areas: the keeping of accounts; internal and external audit matters; the public's right to inspect the accounts and question the auditor; and the publication of accounts, in addition to the preparation of the statement of accounts themselves.

In this last category, the Regulations require the accounts to be prepared as soon as practicable after the end of the financial year and not later than six months after that date, i.e. by 30 September, and to be published not more than nine months after the end of the period, i.e. by 31 December.

The Regulations go on to specify that the statement of accounts shall include:

1. summarized income and expenditure accounts for each of the authority's separate funds and undertakings for which it is required by statute to maintain separate accounts;
2. a summarized statement of capital expenditure analysed by services, and showing the sources of finance;
3. a consolidated balance sheet;
4. balance sheets for any fund which is not included in the consolidated balance sheet;
5. a statement of source and application of funds,

together with prior period figures in all cases. The statement of accounts is also required to include 'particulars of the main principles adopted in its compilation', including any changes of accounting practice that in the opinion of the authority have had a significant effect on the published results for the period. These 'main principles' are subsequently specified to include:

1. the basis on which debtors and creditors outstanding at the year end are included in the accounts;
2. the nature of substantial reserves, provisions, contingent liabilities and deferred charges;
3. the basis on which provision is made for the redemption of debt;
4. the basis on which capital expenditure is recorded;
5. the basis of valuation of land and buildings, and investments;
6. the basis of provisions for depreciation; and
7. the extent to which central administration expenses are allocated over services.

A local authority's statement of accounts is required to 'present fairly' the financial position of the authority at the accounting date and its income and expenditure for the year. In practice, the 'presents fairly' basis of accounting is not significantly different from, and no less onerous than, the 'true and fair view' basis of accounting adopted in the private sector. In one sense, the distinction is simply one of semantics, intended to avoid the Companies Act connotations of the phrase 'true and fair view'. However, it does have one practical effect, namely that SSAPs, which were developed for application to financial statements prepared to give a true and fair view, do not apply directly to local authorities, but have to be applied indirectly through the medium of SORPs.

It is interesting to note that the 'presents fairly' basis of accounting is not enshrined in primary legislation. Rather, it derives from the

Code of Audit Practice for local authorities prepared by the Audit Commission and approved by Parliament under Section 14 of the Local Government Finance Act 1982 (Audit Commission, 1990). This Code is an important document in the framework of local authority financial accounting and reporting, and its provisions have provided an effective stimulus to the widespread application of, and compliance with, professional accounting standards by local authorities.

The current version of the Code of Audit Practice, which came into effect in November 1990, requires the auditor, in reviewing the financial statements for the purposes of expressing his audit opinion, to be satisfied that:

1. the provisions of the *Code of Practice on Local Authority Accounting* issued by CIPFA have been complied with 'except in situations in which for justifiable reasons it is impracticable or, exceptionally, would be inappropriate or give a misleading view';
2. any accounting policies that have a material effect, but which are not covered by the CIPFA Code of Practice are appropriate to the circumstances of the authority and 'comply with good practice';
3. the figures are not over- or understated by a material amount;
4. the description of the figures is neither misleading nor ambiguous;
5. there is compliance with statutory and other requirements applicable to the accounts of the authority;
6. there is adequate disclosure of all appropriate material items;
7. the information contained in the statement of accounts is suitably classified and presented.

If the auditor is not satisfied on any of these counts, 'the opinion should be qualified'.

The Local Government Finance Act 1982 also introduced the concept of 'proper [accounting] practices'. Section 15 requires the auditor to be satisfied that the accounts are prepared in accordance with the Accounts and Audit Regulations and comply with the requirements of all other applicable statutory provisions, and 'that proper accounting practices have been observed in the compilation of the accounts'.

The statutory element of the accounting framework was reinforced by the Local Government and Housing Act 1989. Sections 41 and 42 of this Act now require all expenditure of a local authority to be accounted for in accordance with 'proper practices'. Section 66 of the Act defines 'proper practices' as:

> those accounting practices which the authority are required to follow by virtue of any enactment; or which, whether by reference to any generally recognised published code or otherwise, are regarded as proper accounting practices to be followed in the keeping of the accounts of local authorities . . .

It goes on to state that in the event of a conflict in accounting practice arising between statute and code then only those practices falling within statute are to be regarded as proper practices.

Rather more light is shed on the distinction between statutory and non-statutory proper practices in Annex D to Circular 11/90 on *Local Authority Capital Finance* issued by the Department of Environment in August 1990 (DOE, 1990). It specifies those parts of the 1989 Act that are deemed to be statutory proper practices in relation to capital. However, it also identifies those published documents that 'may be regarded as non-statutory proper practices in relation to capital', which include:

1. the relevant parts of the then extant SORP on *The Application of Accounting Standards (SSAPs) to Local Authorities in England and Wales* issued by CIPFA in April 1987; and
2. the relevant sections of the *Code of Practice on Local Authority Accounting* issued by CIPFA in July 1987.

It also makes the significant point that 'from time to time these documents may be revised and the contents of any revision would become proper practices'. The 1989 Act and the clarification afforded in the Annex to Circular 11/90 are highly significant so far as the future development of professional accounting standards for application to local authorities is concerned.

The Act means that, while the Government can legislate to have accounts kept in a particular way if it chooses to do so, in the absence of specific legislation the accounting profession is free to develop what it regards as proper practice. More significantly, where the accounting profession has issued recommendations on the appropriate standards of financial reporting by local authorities, they now effectively have statutory backing as a non-statutory proper practice with which local authorities must comply. This represents a public recognition of the efforts of the profession to raise by means of self-regulation the standards of financial reporting by local authorities and has given a tremendous boost to the continuing efforts to bring about further improvements, for example in relation to local authorities' capital accounting.

ACCOUNTING STANDARDS FOR LOCAL AUTHORITIES

Code of Practice on Local Authority Accounting

In November 1985, the Secretary of State for the Environment issued proposals that would have altered fundamentally the relative 'weight' of statutory requirements and professional accounting standards within the overall accounting framework. These were issued in the form of draft revised Accounts and Audit Regulations that would have prescribed not only the form and content of the financial statements, but also the terminology used, thereby reducing local authorities' published accounts to mere pro forma statements. The proposals were greeted with widespread criticism from the local authority associations, and CIPFA and the accounting profession generally. In the face of such opposition, the Secretary of State invited the local authority associations, together with the Audit Commission and the professional accountancy bodies, to bring forward their own proposals to secure improvements in the standards of external financial reporting by local authorities.

In response, CIPFA and the Audit Commission developed the *Code of Practice on Local Authority Accounting* (the *Code of Practice*), which was published in July 1987. The *Code of Practice* was endorsed fully by the local authority associations, and the Audit Commission advised its auditors that 'the provisions of the Code represent best practice for the purpose of expressing the audit opinion'. As we have seen, compliance with the *Code of Practice* has subsequently been formally incorporated into the Audit Commission's own Code of Audit Practice. In November 1987, the *Code of Practice* was 'franked' as a SORP by the ASC. The publication of the *Code of Practice* and the public expressions of support for it from all those with an interest in local authority accounting standards, marked the high point of professional self-regulation, and the high levels of compliance achieved in practice since its implementation are a measure of the success of this approach.

A revised version of the *Code of Practice* was published in April 1991 (CIPFA, 1991a), to reflect several pieces of legislation affecting the financial affairs of local authorities enacted since 1987. The revised *Code of Practice* applies to accounts prepared for the financial year 1990/91 onwards. Its provisions have also been extended to cover Scottish local authorities for the first time, with effect from 1991/92.

The overriding requirement of the *Code of Practice* is that the statement of accounts should 'present fairly' the financial position and transactions of the authority. It states that:

> 'fair presentation' will normally be achieved by compliance in all material respects with local authority accounting practices and in particular with this Code of Practice as regards form and content and the broad accounting concepts outlined [in the Code]. Where the requirements of the Code are not met, then full disclosure and, where relevant, quantification of the departure in the Statement of Accounts is required.

It goes on to state that:

the Statement of Accounts will reflect the ongoing activities of authorities and the exercise of their fiduciary duties. This includes compliance with the Code of Practice. The Code requires accounting practices to be applied consistently, but in appropriate circumstances these policies may properly be changed. The overriding requirement remains that the Statements of Accounts 'present fairly'.

The *Code of Practice* specifies which accounts shall be published as part of the statement of accounts, and defines the minimum requirements for disclosure and presentation (subject to materiality) of the information to be included in each account. However, the layout and terminology used are at the discretion of local authorities themselves 'within the general framework and requirements of the Code', and 'an authority may add such additional information or statements as are necessary to ensure fair presentation of its financial position and transactions'.

The *Code of Practice* also specifies the accounting concepts and principles, in accordance with which the accounting statements should be prepared, in order to 'present fairly'. It identifies five basic accounting concepts, as follows:

1. matching;
2. consistency;
3. prudence;
4. substance over form;
5. materiality.

Of these, matching, consistency and prudence are derived from **SSAP 2**, *Disclosure of Accounting Policies*, and the materiality concept is common to all accounting standards. The concept of 'substance over form', which requires the accounting statements to be prepared 'so as to reflect the reality or substance of the transactions and activities underlying them, rather than only their formal character', reflects concern at the time that the original *Code of Practice* was being developed at the prevalence and proliferation of various off-balance sheet transactions, such as advance and deferred purchase schemes, which enabled local authorities to exploit loopholes in, and thereby evade, government capital expenditure controls. The concept of substance over form is intended to bring such transactions back on to the balance sheet, to ensure that the financial statements 'present fairly' all of the transactions and obligations entered into by the authority.

The *Code of Practice* also sets out a number of 'accounting principles', consistent with these basic concepts, in respect of specified areas of income, expenditure and balances. Perhaps the key principle is the distinction it draws between reserves and provisions, which is fundamental to ascertaining the true cost of services in the year. Provisions are defined as amounts set aside 'for any liabilities or losses which are likely to be incurred, or certain to be incurred, but uncertain as to the amounts or the dates on which they will arise. Provisions may also be made for irregular, but recurring types of expenditure'. Reserves are defined as amounts set aside for purposes falling outside this definition of provisions, and transfers to and from reserves are required to be distinguished from expenditure on services disclosed in the statement of accounts. The key distinction, therefore, is that provisions are included in the cost of services for the year, whereas reserve movements appear as separate appropriations.

The *Code of Practice* specifies that the statement of accounts shall comprise:

1. an explanatory foreword;
2. a statement of accounting policies;
3. the accounting statements relevant to the authority's functions:
    (a) General or County Fund summary revenue account,
    (b) Housing Revenue Account,
    (b) Collection Fund,
    (c) General Fund balance sheet or consolidated balance sheet (excluding the Superannuation Fund and the Collection Fund),
    (d) statement of revenue and capital movements,
    (e) summary DSO revenue and appropriation account,
    (f) Superannuation Fund: statement of revenue income and expenditure and net assets statement;
4. notes to the accounts.

The requirement to include an 'explanatory foreword' in the statement of accounts reflects the importance attached to interpretation and explanation of the accounts. The purpose of the foreword is:

to offer interested parties an easily understandable guide to the most significant matters reported in the accounts. It should provide an explanation in overall terms of the authority's financial position, and assist in the interpretation of the accounting statements.

It is intended that the foreword should be 'concise and restricted to significant matters'.

The statement of accounting policies is intended 'to explain the basis of the figures in the accounts'. The *Code of Practice* outlines some of the key policies that it will be necessary to disclose in conformity with this requirement. This requirement is consistent with the requirements of SSAP 2, *Disclosure of Accounting Policies*, and with the statutory requirement under the *Accounts and Audit Regulations 1983* as amended, to disclose 'particulars of the main principles adopted' in compiling the statement of accounts.

Tabel 6.1 Information to be disclosed in the General or County Fund summary revenue account

---

Gross expenditure (including provisions), income and net expenditure on services

Interest and investment income

Surplus or deficit from trading undertakings, DSOs or other operations, including subsidiary and associated companies

Contributions to or from reserves

Subsidy receivable from the HRA, where appropriate

Exceptional/extraordinary items

Net receipts from Collection Fund or precepts receivable

Government grants (not attributable to specific services)

Surplus or deficit for the year

Change in General or County Fund balance

Source: CIPFA, 1991a.

The *Code of Practice* specifies the minimum disclosure requirements for each of the accounting statements required. However, where an authority feels that 'a more informative presentation of activities' would be given by disclosing the information by way of a note to the accounts, it may do so. This exemplifies how the *Code of Practice* is intended not to be regarded as an accounting 'strait-jacket', but rather to secure improved standards of financial reporting by encouraging individual local authorities to consider how the needs of the users of their accounts can best be met and to experiment with different forms of presentation within the overall framework laid down. The minimum disclosure requirements for the General or County Fund summary revenue account, the General Fund balance sheet or consolidated balance sheet and the statement of revenue and capital movements are set out in Tables 6.1, 6.2 and 6.3 respectively.

Of these statements, perhaps that requiring particular comment here is the 'statement of revenue and capital movements'. This statement summarizes the expenditure and income of the authority for both capital and revenue purposes, analysed on a subjective basis, eliminating internal transfers between accounts. The statement fulfils the legal requirement on authorities to prepare a statement of source and application of funds and it is consistent with SSAP 10, *Statements of Source and Application of Funds*. It is intended to show consolidated information which is not shown in any other accounting statement, summarizing where the money came from and how it was spent, bringing capital and revenue expenditure together in one place to give an indication of the volume of the authority's financial activity.

Table 6.2 Information to be disclosed in the General Fund balance sheet or consolidated balance sheet

---

Fixed assets
- Council dwellings
- Other land and buildings
- Infrastructure
- Vehicles, plant, furniture and equipment

(to be included at historical cost less capital discharged, on a net or gross basis)

Deferred charges
- Improvement grants
- Other

Investments (long-term)

Long-term debtors

Current assets
- Stocks and work in progress
- Debtors
- Investments (short-term)
- Cash and bank

Current liabilities
- Temporary borrowing
- Creditors
- Bank overdraft

Provisions

Borrowing (other than temporary)

Deferred liabilities (including deferred capital receipts)

Deferred credits

Provision for credit liabilities

Fund balances and reserves

Source: CIPFA, 1991a.

SORP on *The Application of Accounting Standards (SSAPs) to Local Authorities in Great Britain*

The *Code of Practice* is supported by a number of detailed accounting recommendations that have evolved as best accounting practice over many years. In particular, it is complemented by the SORP on *The Application of Accounting Standards (SSAPs) to Local Authorities in Great Britain*, prepared jointly by CIPFA and the Local Authority (Scotland) Accounts Advisory Committee (LA(S)AAC), which was 'franked' by the ASC in July 1990 (CIPFA, 1990a).

Table 6.3 Information to be disclosed in the statement of revenue and capital movements

---

Expenditure
  Revenue
        – Employment costs
        – Other operating costs
        – Interest and lease payments
        – Housing benefits

  Capital
        – Acquisition of fixed assets
        – Long-term investments
        – Deferred charges
Total revenue and capital expenditure

Income
  Revenue
        – Government grants
        – Charges for goods and services
        – Net rents (after rent rebates)
        – Net receipts from Collection Fund
        – Other income

  Capital
        – Sales of assets
        – Capital grants
        – Other income
Total revenue and capital income

Shortfall/excess

Financed by/utilized in
        – Net change in long-term borrowing
        – Net change in short-term indebtedness
and changes in other current assets/liabilities
being increase or decrease in
        – Stocks and work in progress
        – Debtors
        – Creditors and provisions
        – Cash in hand and at bank

Source: CIPFA, 1991a.

Although SSAPs were developed for application to 'all financial statements whose purpose is to give a true and fair view' and thus do not apply directly to local authorities, CIPFA takes the view that accounting standards and the principles that underlie them are generally applicable to the public sector, and to local authorities in particular, except where they are clearly inappropriate, for example as in the case of SSAP 3, *Earnings per Share*. This view is reflected in the SORP. Of the twenty SSAPs extant at the time the SORP was prepared, only five are deemed to be not applicable to local authorities;

the remainder are applicable either in whole or in part. The SORP follows a common format for each SSAP:

1. an explanatory note on the general principles of the SSAP;
2. discussion of the relevance of the SSAP to local authorities;
3. a formal statement on the application of the SSAP;
4. a note of any relevant statutory requirements and other matters relating to its application in practice.

The SORP is intended to complement the statutory requirements on preparers of accounts, and serves further to define proper accounting practices within the context of the *Code of Practice*. The explanatory foreword to the SORP states that 'in applying the SORP it is important to have regard to the spirit of the SORP and the reasoning behind it. It is not intended to be a comprehensive code of rigid rules'.

As in the case of the *Code of Practice*, CIPFA is committed to maintaining the SORP up to date to reflect legislative changes, new or revised accounting standards to be issued in the future by the new Accounting Standards Board and developments in its own recommendations on best accounting practice for local authorities.

The SORP supersedes an earlier version developed by CIPFA in 1987 for application in England and Wales. The extension of the coverage of the revised version to Scotland reflects the success of the efforts of the Public Sector Liaison Group of the ASC to encourage a harmonized approach to the development of accounting standards for local authorities throughout Great Britain.

OTHER PROFESSIONAL GUIDANCE

CIPFA's standard classification

A central feature of local authorities' financial accounting is that they account for revenue income and expenditure 'segmentally', i.e. net expenditure is analysed objectively over individual services. Given that one of the central aims of the *Code of Practice* is 'to narrow the areas of difference and variety in accounting treatment and thereby to enhance the usefulness of published statements of accounts', it is important that local authorities should adopt a common objective analysis and that the reported costs of individual services are determined in a comparable manner. In practice, this is achieved by compliance with CIPFA's 'standard classification', the latest version of which was published in 1988 (CIPFA, 1988). This forms the basis of all local and national financial accounting for local authority services and for associated statistical collections. Indeed, it also provides

Table 6.4 CIPFA's standard classification: objective analysis of main services

Highways
Transportation
Schools
Continuing education
Other education
Libraries, museums and art galleries
Social services
Housing General Fund services
Cemeteries and crematoria
Coast protection
Environmental health
Land drainage
Leisure
Planning and development
Community charge collection
Registration of births, deaths and marriages
Registration of electors
Smallholdings
Trading services
Waste collection and disposal
Civic ceremonials
Corporate management
Police
Fire service
Magistrates' courts
Probation service
Coroner's services (including mortuaries)
Prosecuting solicitors
Civil defence
Trading standards

Source: CIPFA, 1988, as amended.

the framework for local authorities' budgeting and budgetary control arrangements.

The standard classification comprises both an objective and a subjective analysis. The objective classification breaks local government activity down into services, divisions of service, and sub-divisions of service. The main services, which will be reported in the General or County Fund summary revenue account, are set out in Table 6.4.

In practice, these main services will tend to be combined in the summary revenue account into a single line for each of the authority's committees, which are responsible for managing an individual service or group of services.

The subjective analysis breaks down local authority income and expenditure into the nine main types of resources used in providing local authority services, as follows:

1. employees expenses;
2. premises related expenses;
3. transport related expenses;
4. supplies and services;
5. agency and contracted services;
6. transfer payments;
7. central, departmental and technical support services;
8. capital financing costs;
9. income.

Each of these main subjective headings, or 'standard groupings', is then broken down further into sub-groups and 'detail heads'.

The origins of the standard classification can be traced back to 1889. However, CIPFA's commitment to updating it regularly to reflect new service developments and legislation has ensured its continuing relevance and it remains an essential element in the framework of local authority accounting, and forms the basis for all inter-authority comparisons.

Accounting for overheads

In determining the costs of individual services as defined in the standard classification, the accounting treatment of one particular category of expenditure is critical, namely the costs of central, departmental and technical support services, or 'overheads'. In any local authority the level of expenditure incurred on these activities and services is likely to be significant, and how this expenditure is accounted for can have a considerable impact on the reported costs of services. The lack of a standardized approach in this area can undermine inter-authority comparisons and impair the usefulness of associated statistics.

Over recent years, CIPFA has devoted a considerable amount of time and effort to developing guidance on the proper accounting treatment of these costs, and its thinking has evolved markedly in that period. Its current requirements are set out in an Institute Statement issued in March 1991 (CIPFA, 1991b). The Statement identifies three different types of 'overhead'.

1. Support services. These comprise services which support the provision of services to the public; they may be either provided internally or bought in from external providers, to help the users of support services to carry out their own main functions. Examples of support services include accountants, architects, computer staff, engineers, lawyers, personnel officers, valuers.

2. Management. This is defined as 'direction, supervision and guidance by members of the organization superior to those whose overheads are under consideration'; local authorities and their committees comprise the two top levels of management in local government.

Management in turn comprises:

(a) corporate management, which is defined as including all activities that local authorities engage in specifically because they are elected multi-purpose authorities, e.g. meetings of the council and corporate policy committees, and the costs associated with them; and
(b) service management, the management of specific services to the public, DSOs and support services.

The final category of 'overhead' is:

3. Regulation. This comprises *inter alia* all the duties which local authorities are required by statute to carry out in order to maintain the standard of services provided to the public, either by its own staff or by third parties.

The statement requires the costs of support services to be apportioned to all those services which use them, on the principle that all users should pay for the support services that they use. These users might include other support services. A consistent basis of apportionment should be used, and the basis adopted should be disclosed in the statement of accounting policies. The costs of service management and of regulation should be included in the reported costs of the services to which they relate, while corporate management should be reported separately as an objective expenditure head in its own right. The statement will apply to accounts for the financial year 1991/92 onwards, so it is still too early to judge whether this particular accounting problem has finally been resolved.

SPECIFIC ACCOUNTING REQUIREMENTS

Housing Revenue Account

The specific financial accounting and reporting requirements for the Housing Revenue Account (HRA) reflect its special legal status and the fact that housing is subject to a separate financing regime. The Local Government and Housing Act 1989 in particular provides for the 'ring fencing' of the HRA, preventing any subsidy of housing rents being made from the local authority's General Fund, and imposes on housing authorities a duty to budget so as to avoid a debit balance on the account. The Act requires the HRA to be kept in accordance with

Table 6.5 Information to be disclosed in the Housing Revenue Account

Income
    Dwelling rents (gross)
    Charges for services and facilities
    Housing Revenue Account subsidy receivable
    Contributions towards expenditure
    Housing benefit transfers
    Credits from housing repairs account
    Investment income
      – Mortgage
      – Other
    Transfer from General Fund

Expenditure
    Repairs and maintenance or contribution to housing repairs account
    Supervision and management
    Capital expenditure charged to revenue
    Rents, rates, taxes and other charges
    Rent rebates
    Housing Revenue Account subsidy payable
    Provision for bad or doubtful debts
    Capital financing costs

Change in reserve balance

Source: CIPFA, 1991a.

proper practices, as defined in statute or that are generally accepted as proper accounting practices, and the Secretary of State is empowered to give directions as to which practices are to be followed. These are set out in Schedule 4 of the Act which prescribes the main headings and defines the items to be included under each heading on the face of the account.

The *Code of Practice on Local Authority Accounting* reflects these statutory requirements, but leaves the format of the account to the discretion of the authority, allowing it to arrange the information required in the most informative way. The minimum information to be disclosed is set out in Table 6.5.

DSO accounts

The other main set of accounts of local authorities that are subject to specific accounting requirements are those of their direct service organizations (DSOs) set up under the compulsory competitive tendering provisions of the Local Government Planning and Land Act 1980 and of the Local Government Act 1988. These are statutory trading units of the local authority that are required by law to compete for work in specified service areas in competition with private

Table 6.6 Local authority services subject to compulsory competitive tendering

1980 Act
General highways and sewers work
Building construction work costing more than £50 000
Building construction work costing less than £50 000
Building maintenance work

1988 Act
Refuse collection
Cleaning of buildings
Street cleansing
Schools and welfare catering
Other catering
Ground maintenance
Vehicle repairs and maintenance
Management of sports and leisure facilities

sector contractors. The main services subject to compulsory competitive tendering, for each of which local authorities are required to maintain separate accounts, are set out in Table 6.6.

Local authorities are required to keep separate DSO revenue accounts for each description of work. The 1980 Act requires each DSO revenue account to show 'a true and fair view' of the financial results for the year. The 1988 Act requires such accounts to 'present fairly' the financial results. CIPFA's *Code of Practice for Compulsory Competition* 1991 (CIPFA, 1991c) states that 'authorities will in general satisfy both requirements' if they follow:

1. good accounting practices;
2. the *Code of Practice* itself;
3. the *Code of Practice on Local Authority Accounting*;
4. the recommendations of CIPFA on accounting generally.

The *Code of Practice on Local Authority Accounting* requires the accounts of DSOs to be included in the financial statements either in aggregate, to show the combined income and expenditure from operations of all DSOs, or, alternatively, by disclosure of turnover, total expenditure and the surplus or deficit for each DSO separately. The information to be disclosed in the summary DSO revenue and appropriation account under the first option is set out in Table 6.7.

Local authorities are free to decide how any surpluses on DSO revenue accounts should be treated. They may:

1. distribute them in whole or in part in accordance with profit-sharing schemes;
2. transfer them to the General or County Fund;

Table 6.7 Information to be disclosed in the summary DSO revenue and appropriation account

Expenditure
  Labour
  Materials
  Sub contractors
  Transport and plant
  Overheads
  Movements on work in progress
  Movements on provisions for future losses

Income
  Charges to other accounts of the local authority
  Charges under agency agreements
  Charges under works contract

Appropriations
  Surplus or deficit for the year
  Contribution to or from the General or County Fund
  Movements on DSO reserve

Source: CIPFA, 1991a.

3. transfer them to DSO reserves, which in England and Wales form part of the balances on General or County Funds;
4. return them to clients.

Deficits cannot be carried forward, but must be charged to DSO reserves if these have sufficient balances, or to General or County Funds.

The DSO revenue account is kept on similar lines to other local authority accounts. However, each of the DSOs, with the exception of those in respect of building cleaning and the management of sports and leisure facilities, is required by directions and specifications made under the 1980 and 1988 Acts to earn a rate of return on any capital employed, calculated on a current cost accounting basis, of at least 5%. In the case of building cleaning and the management of sports and leisure facilities the requirement is simply that the revenue account should break even.

The rate of return is determined by expressing the current cost operating surplus for the year as a percentage of the current value of capital employed by the DSO. The current cost operating surplus or deficit is calculated by adjusting the surplus or deficit on the DSO revenue account. All capital, renewal or financing charges are added back, and interest credits are deducted. Depreciation charges based on the replacement value of the assets used for direct service work are deducted, together with a stock adjustment (if material) along the

Table 6.8 Example of a calculation of the DSO rate of return

	£
Surplus on DSO revenue account	80 300
Add back	
Interest charged during the year (via transport and plant charges, and stores on-costs)	15 100
Capital financing charges (via ditto)	10 500
Contributions to replacement reserves (via transport and plant charges)	40 800
	146 700
Deduct	
Depreciation (calculated on a CCA basis)	(32 200)
Current cost operating surplus	114 500
Capital employed on	
Depot land – average of market value on 1 April (£165 000) and on 31 March (£175 000)	170 000
Store's land – average of direct service portion (67%) of market value on 1 April and 31 March (direct service portions £120 000 and £134 000, respectively)	127 000
Buildings, vehicles and plant	189 700
Stock (average of balances on 1 April and 31 March)	124 200
	610 900

Return is therefore at the rate of $\frac{114\,500}{610\,900} \times 100$, i.e. 19%

Source: CIPFA, 1991c.

lines of the now withdrawn SSAP 16. The capital employed in the year is defined as the average aggregate depreciated replacement cost of land, buildings, plant and vehicles used by the DSO, and the replacement value of stock held. An example of a rate of return statement is set out in Table 6.8. If DSOs fail to make the required rate of return, the Secretary of State has the power to close them down, and this has happened in some cases.

Local authorities are required to prepare separate reports for each DSO. The report must be prepared by 30 September and copies must be sent to the Secretary of State and the authority's auditor by 31 October. Reports must also include copies of DSO revenue accounts and rate of return statements. Local authorities are free in all other respects to decide what information to include in their DSOs' reports. Provided they include the statutory minimum information, they may exclude information which private contractors would not normally include in their annual accounts and reports prepared under companies' legislation.

CAPITAL ACCOUNTING

Perhaps the one area where local authority accounting departs most from generally accepted accounting practice and relevant SSAPs is in respect of accounting for fixed assets. The principal difference derives from the fact that local authorities do not depreciate their fixed assets. This has implications both for the revenue account and balance sheet aspects of accounting for fixed assets. For historical reasons, in part related to the nature of the controls on local authority capital finance, the system has developed of accounting for capital financing transactions in the revenue account, rather than accounting for the use or consumption in the provision of services of the assets themselves. Thus, service revenue accounts are charged with debt (or loan) charges in respect of loans raised to finance the acquisition of capital assets, comprising both interest on the balance of the loan and an element of principal in order to repay the loan over a predetermined period. In practice, local authorities' borrowings are pooled through a 'consolidated loans pool', which then 'lends on' to individual services and, therefore, it is not possible to link directly any external loan with a particular asset. The loans to which the loan charges relate (both interest and principal) are thus essentially notional accounting entries.

The legal basis for this practice was restated in the Local Government Act 1972, which required:

> where expenditure incurred by a local authority for any purpose is defrayed by borrowing, the local authority shall . . . in each year, debit the account from which that expenditure would otherwise fall to be defrayed with a sum equivalent to an instalment of principal and interest combined such that if paid annually it would secure payment of interest at the due rate on the oustanding principal, together with the repayment of the principal not later than the end of the fixed period.

This requirement was designed to ensure that authorities made proper prudent provision for the repayment of debt and, because the charges were reflected in the level of expenditure upon which local taxing decisions were based, to generate the cash flows necessary to pay off the debt. The Local Government and Housing Act 1989 subsequently replaced this requirement with the current requirement simply to make a 'minimum revenue provision' (MRP) for the repayment of debt, calculated in accordance with a laid down formula, thereby breaking the statutory link between capital financing and individual service revenue accounts.

Fixed assets may also be financed directly from revenue, in which case the cost of the asset is written off in the period in which it is incurred, or from capital reserves or capital provisions. Historically, the majority of local authorities' fixed assets were financed from loan, but this is now increasingly less the case. Increasing pressure on local authorities to realize surplus assets and, for housing authorities, the obligation to sell houses to sitting tenants under the 'right to buy' legislation, has meant that many local authorities have significant capital reserves, and the proportion of capital expenditure financed from loan has declined markedly. Other forms of capital financing have also been used increasingly, in particular leasing and various forms of creative financing techniques, such as advance or deferred purchase and barter transactions.

Each of these different sources of financing will impact on the revenue account in different ways. At one extreme, the revenue account may bear the total cost of assets acquired in the year, because the assets have been financed from revenue; at the other, it may bear no charge at all, because the assets have been financed from accumulated capital receipts.

In short, the cost of capital assets used in the provision of services is reflected in local authorities' revenue accounts in an inconsistent and almost arbitrary way. Charges to revenue bear little relation to the useful economic life of the asset, over which the local authority may expect to derive benefit from it in the provision of services. Thus, although the revenue account reflects correctly the cost of financing transactions, it is misleading in respect of the quantity of capital consumed in providing services. While the current system may satisfy certain basic stewardship criteria, it does not promote accountability for the use of capital resources. Moreover, comparability is significantly undermined. Although one authority may appear to be spending more on a particular service than another, this may simply reflect the fact that the first authority has a policy of financing assets from loan or from revenue, whereas the second authority has financed its assets from capital reserves.

The accounting treatment of capital assets in the balance sheet is similarly related to their financing. Thus, rather than being included in the balance sheet at cost or valuation, they are reported at cost net of 'capital discharged'. 'Capital discharged' reflects the extent to which the local authority's assets have been 'paid for' either by repaying the 'loans' raised to finance them or from revenue or capital reserves. The amount at which assets are included in the balance sheet is thus simply the amount of capital that remains to be repaid in future periods, i.e. the net notional loans outstanding. Because assets financed from revenue or from capital reserves are fully 'paid for' at the date they are acquired, they will not appear in the balance sheet at all. By failing to record on any generally accepted measurement basis such a significant part of the authority's asset base, the local authority balance sheet fails to meet one of the most basic objectives of a balance sheet, namely to record the assets and liabilities of the reporting entity at the end of the financial year.

The deficiencies of the current system of accounting for local authorities' fixed assets are well documented and widely acknowledged. CIPFA has sponsored a number of major reports on how the current system might be improved, including Jack Woodham's seminal paper *Local Authority Accounting I – Accounting Principles*, published in 1975 (CIPFA, 1975), which advocated the adoption of depreciation accounting, and *Capital Accounting in Local Authorities* (the 'Pearce Report'), published in 1983 (CIPFA, 1983), which advocated the adoption of a system of asset rental accounting. Both papers, which essentially approached the problem of capital accounting from quite different perspectives, sparked off a major debate within the profession on the most appropriate way forward.

However, this debate did not lead to action and by the time the *Code of Practice on Local Authority Accounting* was being developed in 1986/87 no practical progress had been made. Given the timescale within which the *Code of Practice* was developed, it was not possible to address and resolve this intractable problem in any meaningful way. Thus, the *Code of Practice* was developed on the basis of existing practices of accounting for capital. This means that the accruals concept is applied only to operating income and expenditure and interest charged to the revenue account; capital income and expenditure are accounted for on a cash basis. The *Code of Practice* requires revenue accounts to be charged with amounts that cover the minimum revenue provision required by statute; charges to services may be made on the basis of outstanding debt or 'on any other appropriate economic basis'. The *Code of Practice* also includes recommendations on how the financial information included in the balance sheet may be supplemented to provide the user with more information on an authority's fixed assets, by including a 'statement of fixed assets', a list of the principal assets held by the authority, appropriately classified, 'to provide a straightforward but informative picture of the fixed assets of the authority'.

However, so far as capital accounting was concerned, the *Code of Practice* was intended to represent only an interim 'holding statement', pending the development of proposals for a new system. To take this work forward, CIPFA, together with the local authority associations and the Audit Commission, established the joint Capital Accounting Steering Group (CASG), chaired by John Parkes of Humberside CC. The CASG published its initial proposals in the form of a 'Consultative Implementation Manual' in February 1989 (CIPFA,

1989). Aspects of the proposals were then tested at a series of 'pilot' sites. In the light of the findings of these pilot studies and comments received from commentators on the draft proposals, the CASG revised its proposals in a number of areas, although the proposed accounting framework remained the same. Its revised proposals were published in September 1990 in the form of the 'Final Report', on which CIPFA invited further comments (CIPFA, 1990b).

In summary, the CASG's proposals would have replaced the current system of accounting for capital financing transactions in the revenue account with one based on accounting for the economic cost of capital assets used in the provision of services. The economic cost would be reflected in a charge to revenue comprising depreciation (for all assets other than land) and a charge for the cost of capital employed, calculated by applying a real rate of interest (the Treasury's discount rate of 6%) to the amount at which the asset is included in the balance sheet. To avoid impacting on the total net expenditure of the local authority, and thereby the level of local taxation, it was proposed that the depreciation element should be netted off against the statutory minimum revenue provision. The cost of capital element would be credited to a central property holding account and thus be cancelled out within the revenue account.

Assets would be included in the balance sheet at depreciated replacement cost or market value, although short-lived assets, such as vehicles, plant and equipment, would be permitted to be carried at depreciated historical cost on grounds of materiality. Assets would need to be revalued periodically, at five-yearly intervals. Infrastructure assets, such as highways, would be treated differently. They would be capitalized at historical cost and amortized to revenue over a predetermined period. Housing was excluded altogether from the system, because of the perceived legal difficulties arising from the introduction of the new system of housing finance and the 'ring fencing' of the HRA under the Local Government and Housing Act 1989. It was proposed that the new system should be implemented with effect from 1993/94.

The main objections from local authorities to the proposals were practical, rather than technical. In order to implement the system, local authorities would need to undertake a comprehensive valuation exercise of all their assets and make arrangements to have these valuations updated on a regular basis. Although in practice this exercise could be simplified, practitioners expressed concern about the likely costs involved in implementing what elected members would regard as purely technical accounting changes at a time when local authority spending is already subject to extreme pressure and local authorities are having to make painful decisions about cutting expenditure on 'front line' services. The timing of the implementation of any change was also questioned given the pace of recent and prospective changes affecting local government finance and services, with which local authorities were already having to cope. The apparent complexity of the accounting entries required also generated a great deal of comment, particularly the difficulty of explaining them to elected members and service officers, especially when the net effect on the revenue account was 'nil'! In this context the exclusion of housing, which accounts for some 60% of metropolitan authorities' assets and 80% of district councils' assets, from the scope of the proposed system also made little sense.

CIPFA considered carefully all of these comments and in May 1991 it issued a Statement setting out formally its response to the proposals set out in the Final Report and the comments received on it (CIPFA, 1991d). The Statement endorsed the basic principles that underlay the proposals as being technically sound and providing the basis for a new system of capital accounting by local authorities. It summarized these principles as follows:

1. accounting for capital financing transactions should be separated from accounting for the cost of assets used in the provision of services;
2. the balance sheet should include meaningful information about the assets held by the local authority;
3. service revenue accounts should bear a proper charge for the cost of capital assets used in the provision of the service;
4. the charge to revenue should be determined by reference to the amount at which the asset is included in the balance sheet.

The Statement stated the Institute's belief that a new system of capital accounting is 'essential', and expressed CIPFA's wish to see a new system of capital accounting based on these principles implemented in 1994/95. However, CIPFA decided to defer its final decision on the details of any new system until spring 1992. It was argued that this deferment would give time for a new working group to follow up the concerns and positive suggestions made by commentators on the Final Report; to undertake the necessary further work to resolve the outstanding detailed technical issues; and, above all, to find ways in which the new system can be implemented relatively simply and at minimum cost to local authorities. In this respect, the working group will re-examine the basis for determining charges to services for capital for external financial reporting purposes, with a view to simplifying the detailed accounting requirements of any new system and, together with the Royal Institution of Chartered Surveyors (RICS), consider the bases of valuation to be adopted and the need for and frequency of revaluations, and develop guidance on practical methods of valuation. CIPFA also proposes to set up a full scale implementation study to test thoroughly its proposals 'on the ground', to identify the likely costs of, and practical problems associated with, implementing the new system. One other advantage of the delay is that it will enable CIPFA to reflect the proposals of the Accounting Standards Board's statement of principles on asset values in the balance sheet which is expected to be published in draft early in 1992 and to assess the likely extent and practical implications of any reform of the structure of local government to emerge from the major review announced by the government early in 1991.

At the time of writing, work is in hand in taking the proposals forward. Whether a solution can yet be found to all of the various technical, practical and legal issues that surround this aspect of local authority accounting remains to be seen. One thing is clear: there is no easy solution; if there was, it would have been found many years ago. Perhaps above all, this issue highlights the difficulties of reconciling accounting principles with practical and political constraints in the public sector, where technical decisions on accounting standards can affect directly the levels of either local taxation or service provision at 'the sharp end'. In this context, there is no 'right' answer and, therefore, the more pragmatic approach now envisaged in the CIPFA Statement may hold out the best hope of making progress on this particular issue.

LOCAL AUTHORITY ANNUAL REPORTS

The publication of the statement of accounts is, as we have seen, a statutory requirement. However, the annual accounts form part of financial reporting in its wider sense and are normally published as an integral part of the local authority's annual report.

Paradoxically, there is no statutory requirement to produce an annual report as such, although Section 2 of the Local Government Planning and Land Act 1980 does empower the Secretary of State to issue a code or codes of recommended practice as to the publication of information by local authorities about the discharge of their functions, and Section 3 gives the additional power to regulate the manner, form and regularity of the publication.

Subsequently, a code of practice (the 'Code') on the publication of annual reports and financial statements by local authorities, *Local Authority Annual Reports*, was developed by CIPFA and the Society of Local Authority Chief Executives (SOLACE) and issued by the Secretary of State in 1981 (DOE, 1981). Although it is intended that every local authority in England and Wales should publish an annual report, the *Code* is not legally enforceable.

The *Code* recommends a basis for information to be published in an annual report, to ensure a broad consistency of practice and to ensure a minimum standard of content, in order to:

1. give local taxpayers clear information about the authority's activities;

2. make it easier for electors, local taxpayers and other interested
   parties to make comparisons of and judgements on the performance of their authorities;
3. help elected members form judgements about the performance of
   their authorities

The *Code* defines the objective of the annual report as being to integrate the local management and financial reporting of the authority
through the use of narrative and financial and statistical data. It should
account for the resource costs implicit in the policies of the authority
and, as far as practicable, the performance and efficiency of the authority. As such, it should be designed as a statement of stewardship
for the benefit of both elected members and the public.

In particular, the *Code* recommends that certain key statistics and
indicators should be compiled and published on a standard basis to
enable meaningful comparisons to be made both between authorities
and over time. Where a comprehensive report is produced, authorities are asked to pay particular attention to the question of public
understanding and access. They are also encouraged to consider draw-
ing together extracts of the information for wider circulation.

The *Code* recommends that the report should be produced as soon
as possible after the accounts are closed, and preferably within six
months of the end of the financial year, i.e. by the end of September.
The accounts may not have been audited by that time, but where
financial information is included the auditor may comment on the
report. The report should indicate whether the accounts on which it
is based have been audited at the time of publication.

In the decade since the *Code* was issued the overall quality of local
authority annual reports has improved considerably, and the best of
them compare favourably with the best of the private sector. A case
in point is Birmingham City Council which has consistently achieved
a high standard in producing reports which are stylishly and imagina-
tively presented, and highly informative. A number of local authorities
have also produced simplified newspaper-style reports in order to get
their message across to as wide an audience as possible. This trend
is generally to be encouraged as a means of disseminating information
about an authority's activities and performance to as large an audience as possible, and thereby investing the process of accountability
with real meaning.

LOCAL AUTHORITY BUDGETING

If the annual report is at one end of the cycle of accountability, the
financial planning process and the development of the annual budget
is at the other.

Financial planning process

Local authorities are multi-million pound organizations and it is essential that they should have a sound financial planning system. The objectives of the financial planning system include:

1. to help the elected members determine policy priorities and the timing of policy changes;
2. to demonstrate the cost of alternative policies;
3. to forecast the likely level of demand for services;
4. to provide a framework for the development of activity plans or business plans by individual services or trading units;
5. to match demand with available resources.

Financial planning is part of the corporate planning process and it will involve all of the senior service managers that comprise the local authority's management team and not just the chief financial officer. The financial planning cycle extends beyond the current and next financial year, as longer term forecasting is essential if the local authority's plans are properly to reflect the cost of policy changes and external factors, such as demographic changes. The planning horizon of the annual budget is too short for these purposes, although it is an important management tool and fulfils an essential control function.

During the 1960s and 1970s, under the influence of contemporary American theories, a great deal was written about the need for local authorities to have more sophisticated planning and budgeting systems. It was argued that there was a confusion between planning and budgeting and that as a result the essentially short-term process of budgeting was being used wrongly in place of longer term policy planning: local authorities were not sufficiently clear about their policy objectives and the needs for services; there was insufficient strategic thinking and long-term planning. However, experiments with 'planning, programming and budgeting systems' (PPBS) and variants on the theme, such as 'zero-base budgeting' (ZBB) and 'programme analysis review' (PAR) were short lived, and these techniques were never adopted widely. Nevertheless, local authority budgets do now tend to be prepared on a programme basis; an attempt is made to relate spending plans to service objectives and outputs; and plans are normally projected forward up to 3–5 years ahead. The current trend is towards the preparation of 'activity plans' for individual services and 'business plans' for trading or quasi-trading units. This in part reflects the more 'commercial' approach to the management and delivery of local authority services engendered by developments such as the introduction of compulsory competitive tendering. Such plans will normally incorporate both financial and non-financial objectives over different planning periods (short, medium and longer term) and provide the basis from which the detailed annual budget can be developed.

The budget development cycle

The annual budget is an expression in financial terms of a local authority's policies and plans. Its preparation and publication in the form of the annual 'budget book' is one of the most tangible outputs of the local authority's financial management system.

The most widely adopted form of budgeting among local authorities is 'incremental budgeting', whereby the current year's budget is taken as the 'base', which is then adjusted to reflect any ongoing additional commitments, such as the full year effects of previous policy decisions not reflected in the current year's budget or the full revenue effect of capital expenditure. The base will also need to be adjusted to reflect the effect of changing prices. The majority of local authorities prepare their annual budgets on a 'November price base', i.e. the level of prices on 1 November preceding the budget year, which starts on 1 April. This means that at the beginning of the new financial year the budget is effectively five months out of date. A central provision is needed, therefore, to cover inflation for the seventeen months to the end of the budget year. This will need to be allocated out over the detailed budget heads during the year, to provide a meaningful basis against which to monitor and control income and expenditure, for budgetary control purposes. The budgets for trading accounts and the HRA tend to be prepared at 'outturn prices', so that charges and rents are set at levels that reflect the likely level of inflation.

No two local authorities will prepare their budgets in the same way, but they do tend to follow a similar cycle. The local authority's financial year runs from 1 April to 31 March, and the annual budget development cycle, comprising planning, spending and accounting, is spread over a 3-year period, spanning some 30 months, as illustrated in Fig. 6.2.

In this example, year 0 is taken up with policy planning and finalizing the detailed budget. In year 1, actual expenditure will be monitored regularly against the budget, and the original budget will be revised to outturn prices and to reflect new commitments and other agreed variations. In year 2, the final accounts for year 1 are prepared, audited and published. The process of financial planning and budgeting is a continuous one, and no sooner is the detailed budget for one year prepared than the task of planning the following year's begins in earnest once again.

Alongside the revenue budgeting process, the authority will be developing its capital programme, identifying the need for new capital investment, determining priorities between competing schemes, and monitoring the progress of individual projects, all within the constraints of the government's capital expenditure control system. Clearly, new investment in capital projects will also have revenue effects, e.g. in the running costs of new buildings and in the form of capital financing charges on loans raised to finance them, so the link between

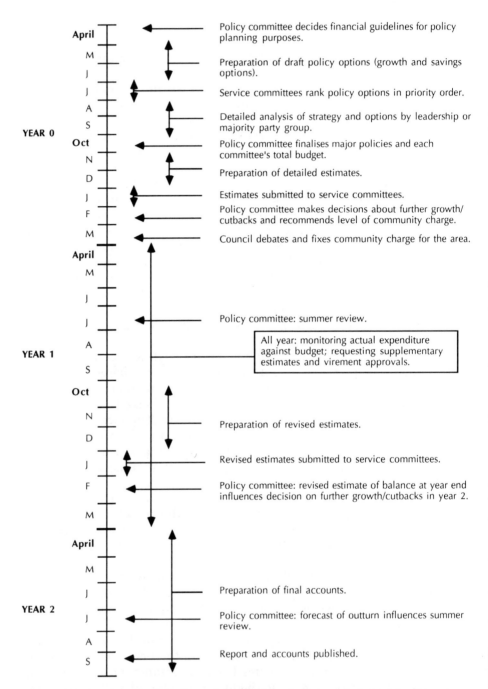

Fig. 6.2 A local authority's financial planning and control timetable. (Source: *Councillors' Guide to Local Government Finance*, CIPFA, 1991; CIPFA, 1991e.)

the capital programme and the revenue budget needs to be made explicit.

There are four key stages in the process of preparing the budget. In the first stage (covering the period April to October), the chief financial officer will issue detailed guidelines to the various spending departments on how they should compile the first draft of the detailed budget. Such guidelines will be consistent with the financial guidelines for policy planning purposes agreed by the authority's policy or finance committee. The chief financial officer will then compile a draft budget for the authority as a whole, after scrutinizing individual departments' budget submissions to ensure that they comply with the guidelines.

During the second stage (in October and November), the budgets for individual services will be scrutinized by the committees responsible for their management. The chief financial officer will also prepare a report highlighting the key trends in expenditure, and outlining the possible effects on individual services and the implications for the level of local taxation of possible variations in planned spending, such as may be necessary to comply with government revenue expenditure controls.

During the third stage (in December and January), the various service committees will carry out their final scrutiny of their budgets. The authority will also receive notification of the likely level of government grant, in the light of which the budget may need to be adjusted.

The allocation of government grant is a factor that is largely outside the control of the local authority, yet it is a key factor in the preparation of the budget. Decisions on the level of government grant are usually taken in the period November to January preceding the start of the new financial year. Once announced, the level of grant is unlikely to change significantly within the year, but there can be dramatic swings in the level of grant from one year to another.

The final stage in the process (in February and March) is the setting of the level of community charge (in the case of district and metropolitan authorities) or the precept (in the case of county councils). At this stage, the chief financial officer will consolidate the various service committees' budgets; determine the level of contingencies that needs to be provided for; and make any final adjustments to the budget in respect of the deficits or surpluses on the authority's trading accounts, the amount of interest receivable on the authority's revenue balances, transfers to or from reserves, and the use of, or contribution to, revenue balances. The use of balances will be determined in part by legal and prudent financial considerations, and in part by political considerations. It is illegal for an authority to budget for a deficit, and the local authority's auditor will comment if he considers that the level of reserves is either too high or too low.

The balance of expenditure, after deducting government grant receivable, including the authority's 'share' of national non-domestic

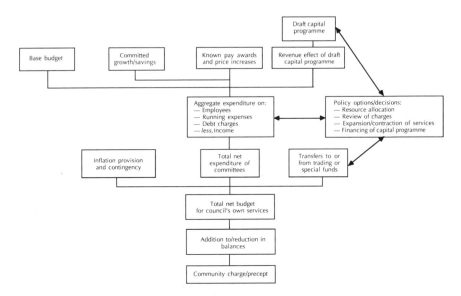

Fig. 6.3 Local authority budget development process. (Source: CIPFA, 1991e.)

rates (NNDR), must be financed by means of the community charge or precept. It is important to emphasize that the level of expenditure or financing decisions taken by the local authority do not necessarily determine the level of the community charge or precept. Under the current system of expenditure control it is quite possible for an authority to follow the government's expenditure guidelines and still have to increase the level of taxation above the rate of inflation. This might happen for a number of reasons:

1. the basis on which the government distributes grant or NNDR to local authorities may have changed from the previous year;
2. balances may have been run down in previous years and thus are no longer available to 'cushion' the level of local taxation;
3. the local authority may have provided for a higher rate of inflation than the government allowed for in fixing the amount of grant for local authorities.

The process of developing the budget and determining the level of precept or community charge is expressed simply in diagrammatic form in Fig. 6.3.

When the budget has been finalized and the community charge or precept has been fixed, the budget will be published in the form of the annual budget book. This may take the form of a summarized policy document, but more normally it is a fairly weighty document giving a detailed objective and subjective breakdown of the budget (usually on the basis of the main headings in CIPFA's standard classification) for cost centres or summary cost centres, for both the current year's revised budget and the 'original' budget for the following financial year. Normally, it will also show the previous year's actual figures for comparison. It may also show how both the revised and the original budgets have been built up from the current year's base budget, showing the major variations, analysed between price changes (inflation and pay awards), commitments and other approved growth items or savings, and other variations, with a brief narrative description of each. It may also include certain statistical data or performance indicators that underpin the budget, and the assumptions on the basis of which it has been developed, e.g. staff numbers or the expected level of demand for a particular service.

BUDGETARY CONTROL

Once the budget has been fixed, individual service chief officers are responsible for monitoring and controlling income and expenditure against the budget. Within each department of the authority there will be a structure of accountable cost centre managers, who will normally receive a regular (monthly) budget monitoring report that enables them to compare net expenditure to date with the approved budget. Most local authorities will have fairly sophisticated computerized financial information systems, which will profile the budget over the year to highlight variances and project the outturn for the year on the basis of the trends in expenditure to date. Some will also include details of commitments entered into and non-financial data relating to outputs and other performance measures. The cost centre manager will be expected to investigate any material variances and take corrective action as appropriate. The role of the chief financial officer in this process is to run the financial management system, and to monitor expenditure and forecast outturn at the corporate level.

Elected members will only normally become involved in this process if a major problem is identified, for example expenditure on a particular service is forecast to overrun the budget significantly, in which case a policy decision may be required to effect the necessary remedial action.

Local authorities differ in the extent to which cost centre managers are permitted to 'vire' budgets, i.e. to transfer resources from one detailed budget head to another. In some authorities, no virement at all is permitted, unless sanctioned by the elected members; others allow almost unlimited virement. As a general rule, virement should not be used to create new commitments, but it can reinforce financial accountability and serve to provide a powerful stimulus for managers to secure improved value for money.

In recent years, the trend has been towards more devolved systems of financial management. Devolving financial management responsibility means aligning responsibility for service delivery with accountability for the financial management of the resources used to deliver those services. This implies that the manager is responsible not only for keeping expenditure within agreed budgets but also for taking a proactive role in managing limited resources. This reflects not only current trends in management theory and the management culture generally, which emphasize that those nearest the point of service delivery are best placed to determine spending priorities and that the most effective decisions on the use of resources can be made at the 'local level', but also the recent changes that local authorities have undergone, such as the introduction of compulsory competitive tendering, the local management of schools, and the government's proposals on community care, all of which have caused local authorities to think about different methods of service provision and the organization, planning and financial management of services.

Ultimately, however, it is not sufficient just to measure whether income and expenditure on a service is contained within the approved budget. What is more important is: what outputs were achieved for a given level of inputs, and what outcomes flowed from them? Local authorities are thus increasingly concerned to measure their performance in meeting their policy objectives. Performance measurement focuses on two key elements of performance: efficiency and effectiveness. Efficiency can be defined as the relationship between inputs (the resources consumed) and outputs, i.e. maximizing outputs for a given level of inputs, or achieving a given level of output while minimizing the use of resources. Effectiveness relates to the extent to which local authorities are actually meeting their policy objectives. Effectiveness is the more nebulous concept and is not easily measurable. For that reason, more attention tends to be directed towards efficiency measures, in the form of statistical indicators, such as levels of usage and unit costs of services, which can be used as the basis for comparison between authorities.

As we have seen, the code of practice on annual reports requires local authorities to publish certain key statistics and performance indicators. Such statistics need to be interpreted with care and they provide only a relatively crude starting point for asking questions. Authorities are asked to provide comparisons with the national average for their class of authority and with other (usually neighbouring) authorities selected by the authority as having similar characteristics to its own. However, the quality or standard of service provided, and the extent to which clients or consumers of services are satisfied with the service provided, cannot be compared on this basis. Most statistics relate to the cost and scale, or volume, of service provided. At most, this provides only a very limited picture of performance and, as we have seen, the costs that form the basis of such measures are not always comparable, reflecting local authorities' different accounting policies, e.g. on the treatment of overheads, and the extent to which capital investment is financed from revenue or the assets used in the provision of its services are 'debt free'. The development of meaningful performance measures that can form a sound basis for comparison between local authorities is one of the key challenges for the future development of financial reporting by local authorities.

SUMMARY

This chapter has considered each of the elements comprising the framework that governs local authorities' financial accounting and reporting, namely statute and regulations, professional accounting standards and statements of recommended practice, and other professional guidance on best practice. It has outlined the specific accounting requirements affecting housing and direct service organizations, and the requirements for local authority annual reports, and has reviewed the debate surrounding the way in which local authorities account for their fixed assets. The final section outlined local authorities' budgeting arrangements, covering the financial planning process, the budget development cycle, and budgetary control.

FURTHER READING

There is no substitute for reading at first hand the primary sources referred to in the chapter. For a more general discussion of the financial accounting and reporting issues addressed in this chapter, CIPFA's *Local Authority Accounting Manual* (CIPFA, 1987) and *Local Authority Accounting Manual for Scotland* (CIPFA, 1990c) are recommended. The section on budgeting has drawn on CIPFA's *Councillors' Guide to Local Government Finance* (CIPFA, 1991e). A fuller outline is contained in Volume 4, *Budgeting* in CIPFA's *Financial Information Service* (CIPFA: Financial Information Service).

7

Nationalized industries

This chapter deals with a group of industries which, although significantly diminished in number by the privatizations in the 1980s, remains an important part of the public sector. The policy framework for their control and financing is examined first, together with the dilemmas which have arisen from the attempts over the years to establish the framework. The internal mechanisms of control and performance measurement are explored next, and finally the chapter examines the mechanisms and problems in external reporting by the industries.

INTRODUCTION

Despite major privatizations (denationalizations) in the 1980s, the nationalized industries covered in this part of the book remain, socially and economically, an important part of the British economy. Industries such as British Rail and the Post Office are household names because they deal directly with the public, while others such as the Civil Aviation Authority (which supervises the country's air traffic) or the British Waterways Board (which manages many inland waterways) are less familiar. The industries are often regarded as a group, and are usually treated as such in planning the country's financial and economic policy. But it is important to remember that they vary in many ways.

1. The degree to which there is restriction on competition. The framework for each industry is set by government and varies to reflect the policy on such factors as viability, safety, possible privatization, etc.
2. The industries vary greatly in size. British Waterways employs less than 3000 people, the Post Office more than 180 000;
3. Some have a record of profitable operation, while others have been consistent lossmakers.

Table 7.1 lists those industries which have their own identifiable and separate financing from central government. It is from these in-

Table 7.1 The main industries

British Coal	London Regional Transport
British Railways Board	Nuclear Electric
British Waterways Board	Post Office
Caledonian MacBrayne	Scottish Nuclear
Civil Aviation Authority	

dustries that the examples in this section of the book will be taken. There are a large variety of other publicly owned organizations which are funded by government departments. These include organizations as diverse as the Pilotage Commission and the Royal Mint. A full list is given in Appendix 7.1 at the end of the chapter. There are also organizations which are not formally nationalized, but where the state has a majority shareholding, as with the Rover Group before the company was sold to British Aerospace. These are not included because for most financial purposes they can be treated like private sector organizations which happen to have a controlling state interest.

There have been many changes in these lists of organizations. British Steel has been in and out of the public sector. British Aerospace was nationalized in 1977 only to have the shares sold back to the private sector in 1981 and 1985. In the 1980s a whole range of industries were privatized and to get some idea of the magnitude of the privatization programme it is only necessary to compare the list in Table 7.1 with the comparable table in the first edition of this book which came out in 1983. This included the British Airports Authority, British Airways, British Gas, British National Oil Corporation, British Shipbuilders, British Steel, British Telecom, British Transport Docks, Electricity Council and Boards, National Bus, North of Scotland Hydroelectric, Scottish Transport and South of Scotland Electricity as nationalized industries. Most of the industries have been sold in entirety to the private sector. Three of the existing nationalized industries are 'rumps' of entities, the bulk of which were privatized. These are Caledonian MacBrayne (originally part of Scottish Transport) and the two Nuclear Electricity generating companies (originally part of generating companies which used all types of fuel). So this is a group whose members are liable to change as a result of changes in government policy. Indeed, plans to privatize British Coal and parts of British Rail were proposed as this edition of the book was going to press. The industries covered in this section of the book may therefore be joined at any time by others or may be reduced in number by privatization.

The privatization programme has been driven by a number of motives. There has been the political impetus to reduce the size of the public sector and to spread private shareholding more widely. There have also been a number of economic motives. These have included the desire to move the commercial risk to the private sector, a drive to improve efficiency and an interest in increasing competition where possible. Finally, there has been the financial motive of raising extra revenue for the government from the sale.

The privatization programme has been important for those industries remaining in the public sector, even though privatization is outside the scope of this chapter. On one side they have felt the effect of the general drive for greater efficiency and reduced reliance on government financial support. Their relations with government departments too are better, mainly because of the emphasis on the economic rather than social role for the industries. On the other side there has been little incentive to make progress on developing a control framework from that set out in the 1978 *White Paper* which is still the basis of procedure. More prosaically there has been a tendency to make sure that the accounts of industries which are scheduled for privatization should show a suitably favourable picture.

Quite separately from privatization developments, the system of parliamentary and government monitoring and control described in the following sections also changes over time, so developments need to be watched carefully to make sure that what is described and analysed still applies.

Finally, a note on abbreviations. Those who work in or with an industry often refer to it by its initials, but apart from abbreviating some titles (British Railways Board to British Rail, etc.) initials have not been used in the text in order to maintain clarity and avoid jumbles of letters.

POLICY-MAKING

Government and Parliament

Public ownership means that the basis of all policy is the legislation which covers each industry, and the main details of what is in the legislation are examined in the section on external reporting. It is the minister who is formally responsible to Parliament for implementing the legislation and this responsibility means, for example, that the auditors report not to the management of the industry or to Parliament, but to the minister. In practice, this responsibility is not exercised entirely personally. Although the minister answers certain questions relating to an industry in the House of Commons, the day-to-day work is done under his authority by officials of the government department that 'sponsors' a particular industry. The sponsoring role means that the department is primarily responsible for government policy in relation to the industry and looks after its interests in discussions with the Treasury and other government departments. These

Table 7.2 Sponsoring departments

Department of the Environment	British Waterways
Department of Industry	British Coal, Nuclear Electric, Post Office
Department of Transport	British Rail, Civil Aviation Authority, London Regional Transport
Scottish Office	Caledonian MacBrayne, Scottish Electric

discussions will generally be between senior officials from the sponsoring department and senior management of the industry, but for matters concerning financing, capital expenditure monitoring and the accounts, Treasury officials are also likely to be involved. Table 7.2 gives a list of sponsoring government departments.

Parliamentary control is rarely exercised through the House of Commons as a whole, although on occasions there may be problems with an industry of such magnitude that there will be a debate on its position on the 'floor' of the House of Commons. Normally, however, parliamentary control over an industry is exercised through the departmental select committee monitoring its sponsoring department.

Select committees are in general more likely to be interested in general policy (including finance) than accountancy issues, though the Transport and Energy Select Committees have each undertaken investigations of the reports and accounts of certain industries. The Treasury Select Committee has also taken an interest in financial policy for the nationalized industries as a whole. Otherwise, finance and accounting matters come up at various times when chairmen and other board members of an industry are giving oral or written evidence before select committees. Because they are spontaneous, some of the answers given in oral evidence are revealing and make fascinating reading. But these investigations are not conducted primarily to provide entertainment. The select committee draws to the attention of the House of Commons as a whole those matters the committee feels require action. Often, however, a report itself will be enough to produce any changes which the industry's management or the government may agree to be necessary.

Policy through White Papers

The formal control mechanism through the minister and Parliament has, since 1961, been supplemented by White Papers outlining government policy towards the industries. The White Paper, *The Nationalised Industries* (Cm. 7131) issued in 1978 laid down a financial and economic framework within which the industries were to work. This is still the foundation of the policy, in part because privatization rather than improving the framework has for some time been the priority, in part because of the difficulty of finding a suitable alternative.

In practice, while some of the policies set out in the 1978 and earlier White Papers have become firmly established, others have been varied by successive governments because of changing ideologies or economic circumstances. So although the White Papers provide important guide-lines on government policy, day-to-day decisions will be based more on the needs of the moment. The effect of rapid changes in policy and the resulting conflicts are dealt with in greater detail later in this section.

Key areas covered by the 1978 White Paper were as follows.

1. **Financial targets**. After confirming that each industry would work to a specific financial target, the White Paper stipulated that:

   the level of each financial target will be decided industry by industry. It will take account of a wide range of factors. These will include the expected return from effective, cost conscious management of existing and new assets; market prospects; the scope for improved productivity and efficiency; the opportunity cost of capital; the implications for the public sector borrowing requirement; counter-inflation policy; and social or sectoral objectives, for e.g. the Energy and Transport Industries.

   For those industries not likely to make a profit, the White Paper said that the target would be set in terms of the amount of grant or deficit. The financial target was also said to be the 'primary expression' of financial performance.

2. **Investment criterion**. The legislation covering an industry generally requires that the minister approves programmes of major capital expenditure. The White Paper supplemented this by stating that the industries should earn a required rate of return (RRR) on new investment as a whole of 5% in real terms before tax. This figure was based on:

   the pre-tax real returns which have been achieved by private companies and the likely trend in the return on private investment. The cost of finance to the private sector has also been taken into account along with considerations of social time preference.

   The 5% figure was to be reviewed every three to five years (it was raised to 8% in 1989) and an appendix in the White Paper gave details of how the link between the financial target and the RRR was to be made.

3. **Non-financial performance indicators**. To supplement the

financial targets, the White Paper also stipulated that each industry should publish non-financial indicators of performance and service standards, to ensure that an industry should not be able to improve its financial performance simply by increasing prices or lowering standards of service. It was explained that the government had:

> asked each industry, in consultation with its sponsoring department, to select a number of key performance indicators, including valid international comparisons, and to publish them prominently in their annual reports. They would be supported by an explanation of why they had been chosen and of significant trends ... There will probably be some indicators common to most including, for example, labour productivity and standards of service where these are readily measurable.

Financial targets, the RRR and non-financial performance indicators were designed to be the three major elements of the control mechanism for nationalized industries. The White Paper also covered many other aspects of the relationship between industries and government of which other important financial and accounting elements included the following.

1. **Corporate plans**. Financial targets and investment strategies were to be part of the framework of the corporate plan whose importance was underlined by the statement that:

    > the government considers that the corporate plan, and the examination of strategic options, should have a central place in the relationship between the nationalized industries and their sponsoring departments.

2. **Audit committees**. The development of audit committees within the industries' own boards was welcomed, and their role in looking at efficiency and performance was emphasized.
3. **Pricing policy**. Prices were to be the result of the level at which the financial targets were set rather than of following the principle in an earlier (1967) White Paper that the nationalized industries should price to cover their long-term marginal costs.
4. **Inflation accounting**. The importance of inflation accounting was emphasized and the White Paper stated that financial targets 'should be put on some suitable inflation-adjusted basis'.
5. **Cash limits**. Flexibility was to be allowed on cash limits in view of the fact that, 'like private sector companies, their revenues and expenditures depend on trading conditions'. But while acknowledging that there might be conditions in which the cash limits should be increased, the White Paper also emphasized there was no guarantee that this would be automatic.

6. **Disclosure**. The White Paper provided that a large amount of information should be published in the annual report and accounts including:

   (a) the main points in the corporate plan and any government response to them;

   (b) the financial target and the accompanying parliamentary statement explaining it, including any sectoral and social objectives set for the industry as well as how financial performance compared against target;

   (c) the cash limit (later known as the external financing limit) set and how well the industry had performed against it;

   (d) the performance indicators and how well the industry had done against them.

It can be seen from this list that the White Paper was an attempt to provide a comprehensive financial and economic framework, and to ensure that the public was informed about what was going on through disclosure in the annual report and accounts.

Changes since the 1978 White Paper

A number of changes have taken place since the 1978 White Paper which have significantly altered the emphasis of the control mechanism. These have included the following.

1. The relative importance of the various control measures has changed, with what is effectively a cash limit on each industry's ability to obtain funds from the government assuming considerable importance in relation to the other elements in the White Paper's control mechanism. This external financing limit (EFL), is set each year for each industry.

2. As a means of providing external assessment, there are regular reviews of each industry by the Monopolies and Mergers Commission under the 1980 Competition Act at the government's request.

3. To add to the measures of control and act as a stimulus to greater efficiency, cost reduction targets have been set for a number of industries.

Financing the industries

Almost all the funds provided for the industries by the government are in the form of loans from the National Loans Fund administered by the Treasury. Interest is payable on these loans at the rate prevailing when the loan is taken out. The industries are also able to borrow on the home or overseas capital markets if they consider the terms more favourable and if government policy allows them to do so. These loans are usually guaranteed by the government and therefore count as part of government financing, even though the money may not come directly from public funds. In the case of overseas borrowing, the Treasury has a scheme whereby the industries are insured against losses that might arise for them if the pound depreciates against the currency in which the loan has been taken out. The industry pays the Treasury a premium for this service, exactly as it would do on any insurance policy.

The total of grants, net borrowing and leasing make up the industry's EFL which is determined each year, taking into account the capital requirements of the industry and the internal resources which it can generate.

EFLs are first published before the beginning of the financial year, usually in November, and the full table can be found in the *Autumn Statement* and its *Statistical Supplement*. Details of cash provided during the year are published in the following year's documents and also in the reports and accounts of each industry.

EFLs are by no means as severe a constraint as an overdraft limit for a private sector organization at a commercial bank. This is because the government does not have statutory powers to force the industry to keep within its EFL for the year, so the limit can only be maintained by agreement. In practice the government has a great deal more muscle, since ministers can withhold agreement for major investment decisions or borrowing. Nevertheless, in recognition of the fact that it is often difficult for an industry to keep within a fixed target set up months before the beginning of the financial year, there is some flexibility if, on the basis of discussions, there is a danger of a major departure from the industries' medium-term commercial interests or damage to explicit government objectives. An additional 'fine-tuning' formula was also agreed so that additional borrowing of 1% of the total of the turnover and capital expenditure for the year over and above the EFL would be allowed. The sting in the tail is that this amount is deducted from the limit for the next year.

The level at which the EFL is set will be determined by a large number of factors but will usually be a compromise between the claims of the industry for the cash to finance its current programme and the needs of governments to balance individual spending programmes, as well as keeping public expenditure as a whole under control. Starting from those two bargaining positions, there will be a great deal of discussion about the 'appropriate' level to be set for the coming year.

Policy issues

Conflicts between objectives

In theory there ought to be no difficulty in reconciling the objectives set out in the 1978 White Paper. The corporate plan should be the mechanism by which financial targets, non-financial performance indicators and the RRR are reconciled. In theory, too, the corporate plan ought to include sufficient provision of cash to ensure that the plan can be carried out. However, there are both theoretical as well as practical difficulties in reconciling the objectives.

Taking the relationship between the RRR and the financial target first, the White Paper suggests that an industry's revenue requirement should be the link between the two, the financial target on all assets being set to reflect the need to earn the 8% RRR on new investment. But one difficulty in linking them is the difference in the time scales involved. The financial target is supposed to last three to five years. The RRR, on the other hand, is assessed over the life of a project as a whole and indeed may be altered by the time a project with a long lead time comes on stream. With a regular ordering pattern, timing may not be such a problem, but if there is 'lumpy' investment, it is likely to be difficult in practice to match the two year by year. The calculation will be made even more difficult because estimates have to be made for the rates of return on 'old assets' and because the RRR is an average of 8%, so that in any one year the return is unlikely to correspond to the average even if it is exactly as planned.

A further problem is the reconciliation of financial and non-financial performance measures, and there may well be difficulty in succeeding both financially and against non-financial performance measures, particularly those on standards of service. For example, projects to improve British Rail's financial return may cause a deterioration in standards of service, so that running down the maintenance staff may save money, but may also result in more trains being cancelled. A similar conflict may arise between better performance against non-financial performance indicators and achieving an 8% RRR. It may be necessary to improve standards of service, but only by accepting projects that cause the industry to fail to meet the 8% target.

In theory, too, the primary position of the financial target should mean that, in case of any conflict, the non-financial performance criteria will have to take second place. In practice, the problem has not turned out to be reconciling the three targets, but reconciling all three with a target not given any prominence within the White Paper – keeping within the EFL. This was originally seen as a constraint rather than a target, but is as important as financial and non-financial targets.

The use of the 8% RRR

The idea of taking a standard required rate of return on new investment as a whole for all industries is conceptually difficult to justify. It is also difficult to apply in practice. Financial targets are supposed to be set in a way which mirrors the differences in the circumstances of each industry. But, curiously, the White Paper fails to follow the logic through and gives a standard RRR, no matter how risky each of the projects might be. It would seem more appropriate, at a time when capital is rationed, to take different rates of return depending on the risk. The idea behind taking a standard rate may well have been that capital should be rationed across all the industries using the same rate of return, to enable comparisons to be made between competing projects from every source. But without more information on the reasons it seems very difficult to justify the use of a standard rate on these grounds, and more probably the standard rate was included to avoid the difficult and embarrassing job of quantifying risk.

Methods of financing

The industries have often argued that using loan capital financing through the National Loans Fund as virtually the only way of providing funds is far too inflexible, and that the industries should be allowed to borrow directly from the market. On the face of it, this argument would seem to be reasonable, bearing in mind the very different circumstances of each industry, but there are some powerful arguments against a greater variety of financing methods. First, loan capital may be the only way by which a return can be assured on the money provided by the government. Attempts to use a kind of equity financing have on the whole fallen into disrepute because industries financed in this way have often not been able to pay dividends. And even those able to pay have been generally unwilling to do so because, with controls on external borrowing, they needed the cash for the internal financing of investment. Second, the justification for borrowing through the National Loans Fund (which means that the source is the money raised by the government for all its purposes) rather than letting the industries go straight to the market to borrow is that the industries with no independent credit standing would then be competing with central government. It is argued that it is therefore more economic to go through a central mechanism to ensure that rates are not bid up as public sector institutions compete with each other to raise funds. Third, the argument has been that since an industry's borrowings are guaranteed by the government, it would be wrong for them to go separately to the market and commit the government in such a way that it might break its overall financial limits.

Successive governments have rejected these arguments, mainly on the grounds that to give in to them would mean less financial discipline and a loss of control over their ability to get any return on the money which has been provided. Over the years the government has made some concessions, such as allowing the industries to borrow for varying periods of time, but the central arguments against greater flexibility have been upheld.

Flexibility in the control mechanism

Industries have also regularly complained that the system by which they are financially controlled is far too inflexible. This has applied both to the setting of financial targets and to EFLs.

In the case of financial targets, it has never been clear what the appropriate circumstances are for changing them. For example, will the target be adjusted if any industry consistently beats it or consistently fails to beat it? And what circumstances (domestic recession, world trade recession, bad weather) mean that the industry has to adjust to the target or that the target has to be adjusted? This is obviously an important issue in the way in which an industry responds to changing circumstances. After all, if the financial target has got to be maintained at all costs, this may mean that big savings have to be made and services may be cut with severe consequences for the consumer and maybe the economy. On the other hand, if it is entirely flexible, if could be argued that, once again, discipline is lost. In practice, the financial targets have rarely been adjusted in order to take account of changed circumstances, and there seems to be an 'unofficial' adjusted target for any year, which operates on the basis of an agreement between the industry and its sponsoring department but which is not published.

The second major area where the issue of flexibility has arisen is in the operation of EFLs. The nationalized industries have regularly complained about the difficulty of aiming at a precise target figure for financing which is a very small difference between large amounts of income and expenditure (both on current purchases and on capital expenditure). The chairman of one industry likened it to trying to land a jumbo jet on a postage stamp. The agreement reached in 1980 on increased flexibility for the industries meant that they had at least some margin of safety for financing. But even this formula has not satisfied many industries on the grounds that EFLs are not really a suitable method for controlling the industries anyway. Indeed, it has been argued that it is beyond the capability of any industry to forecast its capital requirements with such precision, bearing in mind not only the normal commercial uncertainties of the market-place, such as an unexpectedly steep recession, but also many factors outside their control, such as political turmoil in a key market or major currency fluctuations. The industries' difficulties are increased because even if they want to increase prices to meet the EFL, they often have to go through a lengthy enquiry procedure before they can do so.

In practice, EFLs have really not turned out to be such a harsh discipline because successive governments have either allowed the industries to overspend their EFL or have raised it when it has become clear that commercial circumstances have dramatically changed. So the system has been operated on the basis of an implicit ambiguity. The story of the 1989–90 British Coal EFL is an example, though an extreme one because of the magnitude and number of changes involved:

> The Corporation's external financing limit (EFL) for 1989–90 was adjusted on a number of occasions in response to the performance difficulties experienced. The EFL was initially set in October 1988 at £560 million. This was raised to £720 million in February 1989 to accommodate the effects of a price freeze conceded by the Corporation to the CEGB and other major customers in 1988–89, plus higher than expected cost inflation and interest charges and the impact of the Corporation's restructuring programme. By November 1989 it was apparent that the slippage of certain expenditure from 1988–89 to 1989–90, further increases in restructuring costs and interest rates, and weaker than expected performance at continuing mines had again increased the Corporation's cash requirements. The EFL was therefore raised by £423 million to £1143 million. In the event, there were further deteriorations in the Corporation's cash requirements resulting from continuing shortfalls in colliery output and sales, the latter largely due to the third mild winter in succession, and from lower than anticipated disposals of land reflecting difficult market conditions, and the Corporation breached its EFL by £149 million (Department of Energy Departmental Plan, 1991, Cm. 1505, p. 26).

The government has not officially been willing to be perceived to give much away to the industries, because they have not wanted it to be seen that the control mechanism has become slack. On the other hand, they have acknowledged by their action in raising limits that industries cannot in reality be controlled down to a very small amount.

The status of government minority shareholdings and 'golden' shares

As a result of its privatization programme, the government retained minority or 'golden' shareholdings in a number of former public corporations. The purpose of having minority shareholdings has never been completely clear though the explanations put forward have included:

1. a desire not to overload the market with too many shares when the organization was originally privatized;
2. an attempt to reassure the public/the unions/the employees that the government would still exercise influence over those that enjoyed monopoly status;
3. a means of protecting the organization from unwanted takeover, particularly by a foreign predator.

The 'golden' shares, on the other hand, were designed to allow the industries time to adapt to private sector conditions and act as a very tangible protection against takeover where the national interest was seen to be involved. Such shares gave the government power to outvote all other shareholders on specific issues. Jaguar, British Telecom and the water companies were among those which received golden shares.

However, the government has in practice made it clear that it has little interest in intervening in the affairs of privatized industries. With experience it is also clear that they have the means to intervene in other ways, for example through threat of referral to the Monopolies and Mergers Commission or through the time-honoured means of discreet ministerial arm-twisting. Although the timing of the sale of huge numbers of shares has to be judged with great care – witness the débâcle of the BP offering in October 1987 when the market price dropped below the offer price in the Stock Market crash – minority shareholdings have been progressively sold as a means of raising revenue. As for the golden shares, while some are open-ended, others have a built-in provision to be relinquished by the government after a period – usually 5 years.

INTERNAL CONTROL AND PERFORMANCE MEASUREMENT

This section concentrates on performance measurement rather than internal control because the details of how to operate the control mechanism, including budgeting, financial management, capital investment and internal reporting, are left very much to the individual industries.

There is no common system covering internal control, and practice varies between industries as much as it does between private sector organizations. This means that there is a fundamental distinction between the well-established rules and constraints for external reporting, which are common to all industries, and internal mechanisms which are a matter of individual management style.

Table 7.3 Some financial objectives in the legislation

British Coal
The revenues of the board shall be not less than sufficient for meeting all their outgoings properly chargeable to revenue account . . . on average of good and bad years.

British Railways Board
The combined revenues of the Board and its subsidiaries must be sufficient to meet the combined charges to revenue taking one year with another.

British Waterways Board
As for British Railways Board.

Civil Aviation Authority
Revenue is not less than sufficient for making provision for the meeting of charges properly chargeable to revenue taking one year with another.

London Regional Transport
So far as practicable the combined revenues of London Regional Transport and any subsidiaries of theirs are not less than sufficient to meet their combined charges properly chargeable to revenue account, taking one accounting year with another.

Post Office
To secure that its revenues are not less than sufficient to meet all charges properly chargeable to revenue account taking one year with another.

The measurement of performance links what the organization decides to do internally with how other people measure it. So while each industry has its own way of deciding how well or badly it is doing, in general it will tend to watch more closely those performance measures which the outside world is using. This section therefore deals with measures of performance that are commonly used to assess the industries.

Determining performance measures

The legislation

The legislation which set up each of the industries contains some statement about a financial objective. Often that objective is to break even (without the basis being specified) taking one year with another, although some are set profit targets. Table 7.3 summarizes the financial objectives of some industries as set out in the legislation.

In most cases, the legislation also gives the industries a variety of non-financial tasks, as for example:

It shall be the duty of the Railways Board . . . to provide railway services in Great Britain . . . and to provide such other services

Table 7.4 Some examples of strategic objectives

Nuclear Electric	The company's objective is to demonstrate that nuclear power is economic, safe and environmentally clean and to build public confidence. It aims to increase output, turnover and profit; to complete Sizewell B to time and cost; and to reduce the costs of waste management and decommissioning liabilities.
Post Office	Its objectives are to continue to work towards the separation of its businesses; and to seek to secure maximum efficiency through sustained and detailed cost control. The Post Office should make a profit each year in each of its constituent businesses and should ensure that its price structure is sensibly related to costs and avoids cross subsidy, particularly from monopoly to competitive activities.
Scottish Nuclear	The objectives of Scottish Nuclear are the continued safe operation of its nuclear power stations at Hunterston B and Torness, including improvement of the operating performance of the former; the achievement of improved financial performance within its operations; and the investigation of improved generating methods for the future.

Source: Cm. 1520, 1991, pp. 76–7.

and facilities as appear to the Board to be expedient and to have due regard . . . to efficiency and economy and safety of operation (British Rail: Transport Act 1962).

Such statements are of course only very vague and do not provide clear indications about what constitutes a good performance for an industry. Nevertheless they are important in establishing the background against which an industry's decisions are taken. It is also easy to see how these general objectives may clash with financial objectives, if an industry is required to break even while providing loss-making services.

The corporate plan

An industry's corporate plan, which will be seen and approved by the minister and the sponsoring department, usually contains a statement of broad objectives as well as a variety of specific objectives, some financial and some non-financial. Some corporate plans are published, others are not, but the context in which they are set is provided by the published strategic objectives which are published in the *Autumn Statement Statistical Supplement*. Some examples are given in Table 7.4.

Table 7.5 Performance indicators for the Civil Aviation Authority

A	– Airmisses
B, C	– Fatal and reportable accidents
D	– Pilot licence issues
E, F	– Air travel organizer's licences
G, H	– Punctuality
I	– Capital expenditure
K	– Overheads
L	– Profit and loss
M	– Computer availability
N	– Staff recruitment

Source: *Annual Report and Accounts 1990–1*, pp. 10–24.

Performance targets and aims

Almost all industries have a financial performance target, set by the minister in one of the three main forms:

1. return on assets;
2. profit as a percentage of turnover;
3. target profitability or loss.

Some examples are:

1. **Civil Aviation Authority**: 8% average current cost accounting return on average net assets 1989–90 to 1991–2, excluding activities determined by international agreement and the Highlands and Islands Airports.
2. **London Transport**: £70 million operating surplus by 1991–2 before depreciation and renewals.

Most of the targets have been set as a percentage return on net assets, as set out in the 1978 White Paper.

In addition to the financial targets, non-financial performance aims may also be set by the minister. The Post Office, for example, was set a five-year target to achieve (by 1994) a target of 90% next working day delivery for first class mail within a district and to neighbouring districts and 96% delivery within three working days for second class mail.

Such aims are in addition to the performance measures/indicators described in the section on policy-making. Both will be published in the report and accounts and Table 7.5 lists indicators for the Civil Aviation Authority.

Internally set targets

Most of the industries also set themselves targets as a means of measuring their performance. These are sometimes made public in the annual report and accounts and include a wide variety of different measures. As an example, the Chairman of the newly-created Nuclear Electric commented in the 1990/1 annual report:

> When the company was established, I set six clear objectives for us to achieve. These were: an increase in generation; an increase in turnover; an increase in profit; reduction in the fossil fuel levy; the continuation of work on Sizewell B power station to time and budget; and a reduction in the uncertainty and magnitude of back-end fuel cycle costs.

One target which is certainly regarded as important inside each industry is the self-financing ratio defined as either:

1. that proportion of capital expenditure over a period which is financed from internal resources, or;
2. that proportion of the total funds required for a period financed internally.

The 1978 White Paper specifically rejected this means of measuring performance, perhaps because there are so many different ways of defining it and of interpreting what the ratio means (see 'self-financing ratio', p. 195).

Types of financial performance measure

Return on net assets

The 1978 White Paper confirmed that this would be the 'main form' of target for profitable industries. The target level is set to reflect the different circumstances of each industry and is normally calculated on a current cost basis. In general the return is calculated before interest and tax since the operating management is not responsible for the way in which the industry is financed and therefore for the proportion of finance provided by interest-bearing loans. Table 7.6 shows the calculation for British Coal.

Profit margin

The 'profit' figure may be the same as that used in calculating the 'return for return on net assets', or may be a variation of it. Such variation might exclude income from investments, or include interest. Profit margin is much more rarely used as a financial target by the government than return on net assets, but it is almost always used within an industry as a measure of performance.

Table 7.6 Return on average capital employed and profit margin – British Coal

	£ million
1. Turnover	3950
2. Operating costs	3712
3. Operating profit	238
4. Interest	143
5. Profit after interest	95

Profit margin $\dfrac{238}{3950} \times 100 = 6.0\%$

6. Fixed assets (less depreciation)	1594
7. Net current assets	3137
8. Total assets less total liabilities	1225
9. Average of (8) and corresponding figure for previous year	1598

Return on average capital employed: $\dfrac{238}{1598} \times 100 = 14.9$

Source: *1990/1 Report and Accounts*, p. 64.

Self-financing ratio

Although not acknowledged by the government as a proper measure of performance, there is no doubt about its importance to the industries, and examining a series of ratios over a few years helps to build up a useful picture of an industry's ability to finance itself. Industries themselves vary in the way in which they use the ratio, referring sometimes to the proportion of its capital expenditure which it is financing internally and sometimes to the proportion of funds as a whole.

In assessing the ratio, it is necessary to take into account many factors, including the capital expenditure required to fulfil the industry's plans and the government's financing constraints, as well as their policy on prices and the level of the financial target set for the industry. These factors may mean that a high self-financing ratio is not necessarily 'good' and a low ratio not necessarily 'bad'.

Achieving a target of profit or loss

The requirement to achieve a certain level of profit or to contain loss to a certain figure is often, though not always, given to industries which are loss-making.

In assessing what an industry with this kind of target has achieved, once again changes in government policy and trading conditions since the target was set need to be taken into account. Either may change very rapidly and make it easier or more difficult for an industry to achieve the planned performance level.

Operating within the EFL

The importance of the EFLs and the problems surrounding their operation have already been discussed in the context of policy-making.

Measuring performance – an assessment

It can be seen that it is likely to be difficult to avoid conflict between different types of performance measures. The problem of reconciling non-financial with financial objectives in the legislation has already been mentioned. Combining these with the targets set by the minister, an industry may well have a set of objectives which are not reconcilable with each other. In this respect, the industries are very different from private sector organizations even though most private companies rarely have a single, 'profit maximizing', target and have other targets as well as acknowledging their obligations as members of the community and employers. Nevertheless, in terms of the sheer diversity of the measures, public sector enterprises generally have a more complex job to achieve satisfactory performance than those in the private sector. And it is because different groups in the community perceive success for the industries in very different ways that many of the industries' managers complain that they are being asked to do a task in which they cannot possibly succeed in everything required of them. This has an adverse effect on their morale and may make it more difficult to attract capable managers into the industry. It has certainly been a factor encouraging those in the industry to support the principle of privatization.

Another problem in measuring performance is that many of the industries are unique inside the UK; so there are no organizations with which they can be closely compared. In this respect also, therefore, nationalized industries differ from private sector organizations where comparisons between similar organizations are often regarded as the key indicators of success and failure. So the emphasis almost certainly has to be on the analysis of trends over time, or international comparisons and performance against target. But analysis of each of these has to be handled with great care.

1. Trends need to be interpreted in the light of changing commercial circumstances and government policies.
2. International comparisons are fraught with difficulty because of circumstances particular to each country and the fact that the

organizations are rarely comparable in what they do, so adjustments have to be made to the figures.
3. Targets may not be a good guideline because the level is to some extent the result of bargaining between the industry and the sponsoring department.

Of the three, the comparison between target and actual performance is probably the least complicated to interpret, and international comparisons the most complicated.

EXTERNAL REPORTING

Accounting and external reporting in nationalized industries are much closer to private sector practice than for most of the other parts of the public sector.

The rules governing external reporting

The starting point for nationalized industry accounting is that it should follow 'best commercial accounting practice', and indeed this phrase is sometimes included in the legislation 'Best commercial practice' and means taking into consideration (though not necessarily being bound by) four broad categories of regulation:

1. **The relevant current Companies Act(s).**
2. **Stock Exchange requirements**. Even though the industries are not quoted on the Stock Exchange, they will normally be expected to follow the relevant disclosure requirements of quoted companies.
3. **Professional regulation**. The industries are covered by the work of the Accounting Standards Board (ASB) and will be expected to follow Standard Statements of Accounting Practice (SSAP) and Financial Reporting Standards (FRS).
4. **General accounting practice**. The industries are covered by normal accounting conventions and will generally follow the latest practice of the accountancy profession.

Legislation

There is no standard wording in the legislation covering each industry (Appendix 7.2), but a number of items are always included, such as the appointment of auditors, the need to present information to the minister and the power of the minister to give directions on the form of the accounts, with the approval of the Treasury. An example (for British Rail and British Waterways) is that each Board:

1. shall cause proper accounts and other records in relation thereto to be kept; and
2. shall prepare an annual statement of accounts in such form and containing such particulars compiled in such manner as the minister may from time to time direct with the approval of the Treasury (Transport Act 1962).

Some passages in the legislation are open to differing interpretations, and this has led to trouble on occasions between the board of an industry and its sponsoring department. On the other hand the ministerial directions which most industries have received in the past few years, cover highly detailed items (particularly on the accounts) very precisely.

Self-regulation

A mechanism peculiar to the nationalized industries has grown up over the past few years using the Nationalized Industries' Chairmens' Group (NICG). The NICG has acted as a forum for discussion on a number of important policy issues, including European Community matters, which concern the industries collectively, and financial affairs are dealt with by their Finance Panel. The Panel has been particularly active in the field of inflation accounting and it was responsible for compiling a code of practice and a response to the Byatt Report (see below).

Looking at this system of regulation, it might be thought that the industries would be very constrained in what they could do. But one of the major problems in developing a framework of regulation for the industries as a whole is the sheer diversity of their activities. This means that the industries themselves are not likely to be agreed about what constitutes best practice, and it is clear from the way they report that there is much more flexibility than might at first appear possible. Furthermore, while ministers might seem to have almost total power over the industries in this area through their ability to issue directions, in practice there is a good deal of discussion and negotiation between an industry and its sponsoring department before a direction is issued.

DIFFERENCES BETWEEN THE ACCOUNTS OF NATIONALIZED INDUSTRIES AND OF PRIVATE SECTOR ORGANIZATIONS

There are two kinds of difference: the first in the underlying purpose of producing a report and accounts document, the second in the more detailed differences in the financial information shown.

The most obvious difference in the purpose of producing accounts is that while private sector organizations do so to conform with the Companies Acts, each nationalized industry has to conform with the legislation specific to that industry. This is not merely a technical difference, since it means that responsibility in the private sector is to the shareholders, while for the industries it is through the minister to Parliament. But behind these formal differences are the differences in the practical needs of users. *The Corporate Report* (already referred to in Chapter 2), took the view that reports, including those for nationalized industries, should be based on satisfying the information needs of users identified as:

1. the equity investor group;
2. the loan–creditor group;
3. the employee group;
4. the analyst–advisor group;
5. the business contact group;
6. the government;
7. the public.

Using this classification, it is clear that there are important differences between the user needs of the private sector, where the seven groups represent seven different interests, and the nationalized industries. Parliament can be said to be ultimately both the equity investor group and the loan–creditor group through its power to control funds, as well as having an important role to play as a watchdog over the interest of the public, but the government's role also spans these three functions. Moreover, through the sponsoring department the government is also to a large extent acting in the role of the analyst–advisor.

Apart from Parliament and the government, the public's interests are served by bodies set up specifically to look after consumers of a particular industry such as the Transport Users' Consultative Committee on behalf of the transport industries' customers and the Post Office Users' National Council for those of the Post Office. But it is the media which probably act as the most influential watchdogs, though their influence is generally more idiosyncratic than systematic.

It can be seen that the relative importance of groups using the accounts is very different compared to those concerned with the accounts of large private sector organizations. There are also great differences in how much information is available to the users. Unlike the private sector, where the report and accounts document is virtually the only source of information to all except the loan–creditor group (who need to have detailed financial projections directly from the organization to which they lend in order to safeguard their own funds), the sponsoring government department already has very detailed information. This includes not only information on past performance but also short- and longer-term projections, both financial and non-financial. The report and accounts document, therefore, may provide some additional useful information to the government but in practice it is Parliament, the media, consumer and employee organizations and the public at large for whom the document is crucial. Apart from answers to parliamentary questions, select committee investigations, annual departmental reports and other *ad hoc* reports, it will be their only public source of financial information. For this reason alone, the industries tend to regard a major purpose of the document to be to express their views about current problems and achievements, partly for public relations purposes, partly as a means of exercising indirect pressure on the government.

The difficulty of combining a campaigning and opinion-forming document with one which also provides a clear and dispassionate view of the industry to enable users to make up their own minds is obvious enough. Some of these more dispassionate purposes include helping the reader to:

1. evaluate an industry's performance over time;
2. establish its liquidity and possible future requirements for funds;
3. assess prospects and the vulnerability of the industry to outside forces;
4. have a basis for comparing it with other organizations;
5. act as a starting point to assess the effectiveness of the management;
6. find facts and figures about the industry.

The user group having rather different requirements is that represented by the employees who may well want the document for any of the purposes outlined above, but are likely to be primarily interested in the information as a means of establishing a wage-bargaining position.

Turning to the specific accounting differences between private sector organizations and nationalized industries, anyone comparing the main financial statements will find most of the items and the way they are presented to be very similar. But there are differences, and these are outlined below.

Profit and loss accounts

The major difference from the private sector is the prominence of current cost profit and loss accounts either as the main or as supplementary statements. Table 2.4 gave an example from British Rail. The rules for the format of the current cost profit and loss account were set out in 1981 in the *Code of Practice on Inflation Accounts* issued by the Finance Panel of the NICG. the contentious issues concerning this important area are set out later in the chapter.

The other main difference from private sector practice is in the amount of detail available in the profit and loss account and the treatment of grants. Because of the importance of accountability, the amount of detail given by the nationalized industries to support the profit and loss account is much greater than that available in private sector accounts. Many industries provide details of profitability by types of activity or even by location. The Post Office provides complete sets of financial statements separating counter services from letters and parcels. Even when industries do not go so far, the amount of supporting information is often extensive, covering the breakdown between different types of expenditure and other information not normally provided in the private sector. Figure 7.1 shows a breakdown of this kind for British Waterways. Note the separation of grant-aided and other activities and the importance of property transactions.

This information may not necessarily be attached to the profit and loss account, and may be in separate statements elsewhere in the report and accounts document. British Coal, for example, has for many years provided a particularly useful table analysing results by area. This shows how some areas cross-subsidize others.

Balance sheets

There are no major differences between private companies and nationalized industries here, though the balance sheets will reflect the prominence or otherwise of current cost accounts and differences in the form of capital structure, with loans as the main permanent means of finance.

Auditors' report

The form of statement reflects the fact that while auditors in the private sector report to the shareholders, nationalized industry auditors report to the minister. Assuming that the auditors have not qualified the accounts, their report will confirm to the minister that the accounts comply with the relevant legislation and any directions given. The complexity of the rules as a whole means that qualifications are more common for nationalized industries than for private sector organizations (see below).

Other statements and notes

As is made clear above, in general far more information is available in the statements supplementary to the accounts than is shown in the

	Waterways operation and maintenance (Statements B1 and B2)		Others activities (Statement B3)		Total	
	1990/91 £000	1989/90 £000	1990/91 £000	1989/90 £000	1990/91 £000	1989/90 £000
Turnover	15 070	12 687	12 059	11 455	27 129	24 142
Grants receivable	49 747	45 561	–	–	49 747	45 561
Total revenue	64 817	58 248	12 059	11 455	76 876	69 703
Major repairs and renovations	13 555	10 739	–	–	13 555	10 739
Other operational costs	48 664	43 862	3296	3129	51 960	46 991
Gross contribution	2598	3647	8763	8326	11 361	11 973
Administrative expenses	7777	7205	1234	947	9011	8152
Other operating income	(5179)	(3558)	7529	7379	2350	3821
	100	223	–	–	100	223
Operating profit/(loss)	(5079)	(3335)	7529	7379	2450	4044
Exceptional costs					(2758)	(3655)
Income from participating interests					5	–
Interest payable net of receivable					(487)	(1125)
					(790)	(736)
Investment property transactions					3065	4877
Exceptional sale of rights over operational property					–	6910
Profit for the financial year					2275	11 051
Property profits transferred to realized capital reserve					2086	10 878
Profit retained					189	173

Fig. 7.1 Identification of different types of activity: British Waterways profit and loss account, year to 31 March 1991.
(Source: *Report and Accounts*, 1991, p. 33.)

accounts of private sector companies. The greater detail may not only be the result of initiatives by the industries or ministerial direction but also the product of encouragement by a parliamentary select committee or of discussions with the sponsoring department. This requirement for greater public disclosure has not gone unchallenged. Some industries operating in competitive markets have objected to the amount of information they have to disclose.

Other items

In almost all other respects, the structure of the report and accounts document is similar to the private sector and items other than statistical material in the report and accounts will include the following:

1. the letter signed by the chairman formally submitting the report and accounts to the minister;
2. the chairman's statement, the length, style and content of which varies as much as similar statements for private sector organizations;
3. a summary of key figures or highlights at the beginning of the report – in some cases this may be purely financial, in other cases it may cover all aspects of the year's operations;
4. a review of the past year, usually covering finance, organization technical aspects, marketing and sales;
5. performance, the economic and social environment and recent research developments;
6. prospects for the year ahead, either as part of the chairman's statement or as a summary of the corporate plan;
7. members of the board and some details of the organization of senior management.

Most of this information is provided in a form which is at the discretion of the industry, though, as already described, the 1978 *White Paper* required publication of certain information, including the financial target for the year and the outturn, the cash limit and outturn, performance indicators and the main points of the corporate plan.

INTERPRETING THE FINANCIAL STATEMENTS

The immediate impression gained from reading the commentary accompanying the financial statements of most industries is that all is not only well but **very** well. 'Considerable further progress ... prospects for the current year are good', 'another successful year', 'continue to build on our recent successes' are typical phrases from recent reports. Even if things do not go so well, the tone is determined ('a difficult year') or euphemistic ('tensions in the past year' – a strike), or there is the implication that those things which went wrong were outside the control of management ('despite industry problems', 'despite turbulent conditions', etc.). It is unrealistic to assume that managements will not seek to blow their own trumpets, but the analyst of nationalized industries, as of private sector organizations, needs to interpret the figures with great care. Public relations statements can only be regarded as an opening bid on behalf of the management.

In interpreting the figures, a number of factors need to be carefully considered. Some of these factors are peculiar to nationalized industries, others apply to all commercial organizations but are more acute than for private sector organizations because of their size, complexity, history or position in the economy. For example, the statutes of most of the industries stipulate that they should 'break even taking one year with another'. Yet for a number of reasons (other than those which would apply anyway, such as the impact of inflation) it is unwise to rely on the profit and loss account to show whether the industries fulfilled that obligation or not.

In the first place, the magnitude of certain items and provisions for some nationalized industries may make it difficult to know how 'break even' should be interpreted. For example, British Coal made a £78 million profit in 1990/91, but only after 'exceptional reconstruction costs' of £4163 million had been provided in the previous year and a substantial proportion of the loan capital had been written off, giving it a £430 million reduction in the interest charge.

Second, for some industries the grant which forms a major part of income is not always clearly distinguished from trading operations. Thus Caledonian MacBrayne had a 1990 surplus of £22 000 after a 'revenue grant' of £5.7 million and British Rail's Regional services had a £25 million profit in 1991 after grants of £529 million had been included in a turnover of £832 million.

Third, other, special attributes of the industries make it difficult to evaluate the profit figures. In the case of the nuclear electricity industry, for example, there is the need to provide adequately – in practice on a highly uncertain basis – for the costs of decommissioning nuclear power stations and for the reprocessing of irradiated fuel. The amounts have varied significantly over the years, reflecting changing ideas on solutions to the problems. Less than £100 million a year was provided in earlier years but in 1990/91 Nuclear Electric (itself not the whole of the nuclear industry) provided £830 million.

Finally, the levels of depreciation charged on a conventional historic cost basis are, in many cases, a matter of historical accident. For some industries – London Regional Transport's tunnels for example – there is a justifiable assumption that all assets will not be replaced.

In others, such as the Post Office, open market values and replacement cost or modern equivalent asset values are used.

ISSUES IN EXTERNAL REPORTING

Uniformity of presentation and accounting treatment

There have been calls at various times to standardize the terminology used by the industries, the format of their accounts or the way in which items are treated within the accounts. The three cannot be treated entirely separately since in each case there is a question of whether the industries **ought** to be similar to each other as a matter of principle, rather than following the private sector practice of leaving it to the individual organization to decide, together with the auditors, on 'best accounting practice'.

Taking terminology first, the industries use a large number of different terms, particularly to describe profit or loss. The words surplus, revenue, income and profit are used to cover various concepts, no doubt in part reflecting different views about the objectives for a nationalized industry, bearing in mind that they are not generally trying to maximize their profits. Indeed, the objective may only be to break even over a number of years.

The question of these differences in the use of terminology is probably only important because profit is most often used to describe how well an industry is doing, and a large variety of terms may well confuse the reader. On the other hand it could be argued that it is for the industries themselves to decide what terms they should use and terminology is not a proper matter for anyone else.

But terminology is not nearly as significant as questions of whether there should be uniformity in format and accounting treatment. Following evidence to the Treasury and Civil Service Select Committee in the 1980/81 session, the Treasury submitted a memorandum on nationalized industry accounts. The Treasury stated that 'it has been the policy of successive governments . . . to reduce, so far as practicable, unnecessary diversity in the accounts of different industries'. It is clear that this is not going nearly as far as suggesting uniformity, and such a softly-softly approach seems appropriate, since accounting rules covering not only the nationalized industries but also private sector organizations are essentially a compromise between the desire to show uniformity where possible and the need to show diversity where essential. It is then up to the analyst to make adjustments when comparing organizations for particular purposes. The danger in a common format is that it would result in a distorted picture being presented because the diversity of the industries' activities could not be reflected in the financial information. The industries have also asserted that since it is normal to allow differences for private sector organizations, there is no reason why they should be treated any differently.

There have also been calls for more uniform accounting treatment, for example for the industries to depreciate similar items at the same rate. The fear that lies behind some of these calls is that accounting differences will distort policy decisions or that the industries will try to use accounting manipulation to meet a financial target. These fears should not be taken too seriously. The differences in accounting treatment are clear from the report and accounts, even though expertise may be needed to find and interpret all the relevant figures, and in general the figures are subject to far more public scrutiny than those of a private sector organization. The sponsoring department obviously also plays an important role in ensuring that accounting differences do not lead to distortions of policy, but as a more practical point it is doubtful in any case whether the government or Parliament has the right under existing regulations to impose strict uniformity for the accounts.

Auditing and value-for-money audit

Public sector audit as a subject is covered elsewhere in this book, but two issues are worth noting here. First, there is the difficulty faced by some auditors in being able to give an assurance that the accounts present a 'true and fair view'. Second is the need for a value-for-money audit.

A far higher proportion of nationalized accounts are qualified than is common in the private sector. This does not mean that the industries do not adhere to the rules but it illustrates the complexity of their commercial circumstances and the difficulties of fitting them into some parts of the framework of accounting rules. An example indicative of the kinds of difficulties faced by auditors in giving an unqualified audit report is provided by the British Waterways Board. The Auditors' Report states that 'Without qualifying our opinion above we draw attention to Note 19 to the accounts . . .'.

Note 19 states:

MAINTENANCE OBLIGATIONS
In June 1974, independent consultants were appointed by the Department of the Environment to study the costs of operating and maintaining the Board's waterways. This study, which took account of the Board's statutory and other obligations, identified a backlog of maintenance on the Commercial and Cruising

Waterways of £37.6 million at 1974 prices, equivalent to £178 million at 1990/91 prices. In addition, a maintenance backlog was identified on the Remainder Waterways. Excluded from the study were the Board's responsibilities in respect of certain major structures such as tunnels, public road bridges and reservoirs.

In recent years considerable progress has been achieved in overcoming the extent of the urgent items of maintenance backlog, including many subsequently identified failures. The Board continually reassesses the known urgent arrears of repairs and renovations and has ranked and phased them in order of priority. This provides the basis for the future engineering expenditure contained in the Board's 1991 Corporate Plan, in which funds in the order of £63 million have been earmarked over the next four years to cover both these identified works and others which will inevitably arise.

Thereafter, there will be a continuing need to allocate funds, at a reduced level, to major repairs and renovations to cover works which will continue to arise (*Report and Accounts*, 1990/91, p. 49).

Turning to value for money, nationalized industries are specifically excluded from investigation by the National Audit Office under Section 7 of the National Audit Act 1983, which covers examination into the economy, efficiency and effectiveness with which bodies mainly supported by public funds use their resources. However, there are two other mechanisms for conducting audits of efficiency. One is the Monopolies and Mergers Commission. The Commission has a programme of investigations initiated by government, which should include each nationalized industry every four years. These investigations can cover highly detailed matters as well as policy. A report on the Civil Aviation Authority in 1990, for example, recommended detailed cost breakdowns for users and a performance indicator giving trends in unit costs. The other mechanism for conducting efficiency audits is for the government to hire commercial consultants to conduct the work such as that for British Gas a few years before privatization.

Following an efficiency review, the minister in the relevant sponsoring department has the power to require the industry to take remedial action. In practice this power is not used and differences of view about the Commission's report will be settled behind the scenes by discussion after the industry responds to the findings. After about a year the industry reports on progress in implementation and a final report is made after three years. But the scope of any investigation is limited and in 1987 the role and efficacy of the Commission's work was questioned by the House of Commons Public Accounts Committee. While agreeing with some of the criticisms, there were those who said that the comments had to be seen in the context of the Public Accounts Committee's claim for the nationalized industries to be made more directly accountable to Parliament. This has been resisted as a matter of principle by the government and on practical grounds by the industries who have said that they already have quite enough monitoring mechanisms and it is unreasonable to add detailed parliamentary scrutiny to what is already in place.

Chapter 9 discusses the issues in this area in more detail with specific reference to the role of the National Audit Office.

Inflation accounting

As in the private sector, no subject has aroused more controversy in the field of accounting in the nationalized industries than the introduction of accounting for inflation. There have been a large variety of methods used over the years, including:

1. current costs on a CCA basis as the only accounts;
2. current cost accounts as the main accounts, with supplementary historic cost accounts;
3. historic cost accounts as the main accounts with supplementary current cost accounts;
4. historic cost accounts incorporating additional depreciation as a form of inflation adjustment.

These variations have included some industries providing only partial cost accounts (a profit and loss account or statement) and some including – and others not – a gearing adjustment (see Glossary at the end of the chapter) in the current cost accounts. The list is so varied because until 1981 there was no agreement on what form of inflation adjustment should be made by the industries. But in the NICG code of practice they were given three presentation options:

1. historic cost accounts as the main accounts with prominent supplementary current cost accounts;
2. current cost accounts as the main accounts with supplementary historic cost accounts;
3. current cost accounts as the only accounts accompanied by adequate historic cost information;

although there was a general provision allowing the industries additional flexibility.

The result was confusion. By the mid-1980s all industries were producing current cost information, though with varying degrees of prominence and a lack of uniformity. Most produced historic cost accounts with supplementary current cost accounts; some produced current cost accounts with supplementary historic cost accounts, while others produced only current cost accounts, though with some additional historic cost information. But despite the confusion, readers of these accounts at least had the opportunity to have inflation-adjusted figures if they wanted to use them and as far as inflation accounting was concerned, the nationalized industries could reasonably claim to be well ahead of the private sector. However, the basic problem, common to industrial and commercial companies generally, but particularly acute for the nationalized industries with their long-lived assets and dominant positions, remained: how to reconcile backward-looking accounts with forward-looking investment criteria? In 1986 a government advisory group, led by a senior Treasury official, Ian Byatt (who went on to become regulator for the privatized water industry) put forward a possible solution in a report which amounted to a comprehensive framework for adjusting accounts for inflation and reconciling the economic concepts used by the government with the accounting measures used by the industries.

The report confirmed that adjustments for inflation should be made using the current cost accounting system that had already been developed within the accounting profession, provided that additional financial information was made available. This information should not only use changes in an industry's operating capacity as the measure of financial performance. The report argued that the nation as an investor should also be able to assess changes in the real value of the industry's financial capital. The analysis covered pricing, the required rate for return on investment, the valuation of assets in the balance sheet, and the need for an interpretative section explaining the significance of the valuations.

If adopted, the report would have led to far greater consistency in the presentation of accounts, and would make evaluation of the industries' performances much easier. But in the event, despite the government's announcement in 1987 that discussions with the industries on the report had been satisfactory, there was no impetus to implement it. The report had received a lukewarm response from an accountancy profession embarrassed by failure to agree on overall adjustments for inflation. To this was added hostility from some nationalized industries which wanted to be treated as far as possible like the private sector and to be free of constraints. The importance of the report may be in the model it offers once the unresolved issue of accounting for inflation is again actively on the agenda, not only for the nationalized industries but also for the accountancy profession as a whole.

A major issue on inflation accounting has been the treatment of the gearing adjustment. The arguments have probably been more strongly rooted in differences about policy than principle – industries tended to advocate whichever course of action would put their results in the best possible light. The main argument for having a gearing adjustment was that the industries benefited from the falling real value of their loan capital in exactly the same way as private sector organizations and that this should be reflected in an allowance for that proportion of their net operating assets financed by borrowing. The main argument against was that although the industries are financed by a combination of loans and equity, the relationship between the two was much less clear than for private sector organizations because all the funds were derived from a single central source. Since these loans were the normal form of finance, treatment should not be the same as for the private sector where finance was through a combination of equity and loans, so a gearing adjustment was not appropriate. The compromise struck in a statement issued by the government in 1979 was that the gearing adjustment should go in a note, so that the information was available to make a calculation of profit including the adjustment while the profit would be declared without it. This decision meant in practice that industries were indeed treated differently from the private sector, though in practice some industries have found reasons not to provide the information agreed.

Another major issue arising from the discussion of current cost accounting is the implication it has for the industries' ability to fulfil their statutory obligations. The financial requirements in the legislation were generally drawn up at a time when historic cost accounting was the accepted form of financial reporting. It is unclear whether these obligations should be restated in current cost terms, quite apart from any financial target stipulated by the government. This may not be as simple as substituting one figure for another – there are complex technical problems involved in the calculation. Nuclear power stations, railway lines and air control computers are just some examples for which difficult decisions have to be made. Two key decisions are on the length of life of the assets and whether they will be replaced by assets of a similar kind. The importance of the technical decisions is magnified because many of the industries which have these 'difficult' assets are highly capital intensive, and the results of the decisions will have a major effect on profitability through the valuation of the asset base and the determination of current cost depreciation.

Deciding the framework of accounting rules

The framework of rules, incorporating legislation and ministerial direction, accounting practice and self-regulation, ought to mean that the industries have a clear basis for compiling their accounts. But over the years there has been a great deal of controversy about whether the framework is too loose and whether they should not be more closely controlled, as well as what the answers should be to some of the more contentious accounting issues already described. The industries themselves have been adamant that they should not be treated as 'special cases', but should be covered by 'normal' (i.e. commercial) mechanisms. What is clear from looking at the way in which the industries have presented their accounts over the years is that they have as much discretion as private sector organizations in applying the rules, and compliance with the requirements of *White Papers* and the self-regulation mechanism has been frankly patchy. It has also become apparent that there are few effective sanctions for non-compliance.

Suggestions on how to achieve closer control have involved using Parliament, the sponsoring departments or the Accounting Standards Board and its predecessor, the Accounting Standards Committee. But simply setting rules is not enough, as the history of the debate on inflation accounting shows, and agreement may not ensure compliance unless the industries enter into the spirit of any new arrangements. Here, progress will probably be determined by developments in the whole relationship between nationalized industries and the government. Seen in the perspective of this wider picture, problems over accounting rules are just one manifestation of a difficult and often ambiguous relationship. It may well be that clarity in the framework of accounting rules will only come with less ambiguity in the relationship as a whole, something which is not necessarily seen as wholly desirable by the industries or the politicians.

SUMMARY

This chapter, after introducing the context within which nationalized industries operate, dealt with the policy framework for controlling and financing them, then with internal mechanisms of control and performance measurement, and finally with external reporting. Analysing the issues and dilemmas of operating as a type of organization more akin to private sector organizations than most of the rest of the public sector, this chapter makes clear that there are a number of dimensions of the accounting and control framework which are not present in the private sector. It also pointed to the areas where dilemmas remain largely unresolved. The continuing programme of privatizations has made these dilemmas of less national significance, but recent developments in how nationalized industries account for inflation may turn out to be important for future developments in the private sector in the future.

FURTHER READING

There are four major sources for further reading on nationalized industries: the reports and accounts, the relevant sections of the annual departmental reports, official reports and other sources. Because of its importance, the third group is given fuller treatment than normal in this section. As with the other chapters, the final group is included in the bibliography at the end of the book.

Annual reports and accounts

These are invaluable as source documents for facts about the industries as well as indicators about government policy and the industries' responses. The majority of the industries make a small charge for the document and most must be ordered from HMSO or through bookshops, though some are available from the industry's head office.

The industries have a March year-end and publish their reports and accounts in July or August.

Official reports

In looking at any individual industry the latest relevant reports of House of Commons select committees, the Monopolies and Mergers Commission and other official bodies such as statutory Users' Councils should be examined. Some of the more general matters are covered in the following, all published by HMSO.

HM Treasury (1984) *Nationalized Industry Legislation: Consultative Proposals*. Reproduced in Energy Select Committee, Session 1983/ 4, HC 302.

HM Treasury (1986) *Accounting for Changing Costs and Economic Prices* (Byatt Report).

HM Treasury (1991) *Economic Appraisal in Central Government: Technical Guide for Government Departments*.

House of Commons Public Accounts Committee, Session 1983/4. *The Monitoring and Control Activities of Sponsoring Departments – Departments of Industry, Transport and Energy*. HC 139.

House of Commons Public Accounts Committee, Session 1987/8. *Efficiency of Nationalized Industries: References to the Monopolies and Mergers Commission*. Fourth Report, HC 26.

National Audit Office (1983) *Departments of Energy, Trade and Industry and Transport: Monitoring and Control of Nationalized Industries*. HC 553.

GLOSSARY

Cash limit The limit on the amount of cash that can be spent on certain specified services during one financial year.

External financing limit (EFL) A form of cash limit for a national-ized industry used as a means of controlling the amount of finance (grants and borrowing) which an industry can raise in any financial year from external sources. The limit is the difference between an industry's capital requirements and its internally generated funds.

Gearing adjustment Either:
1. that part of the adjustment made to allow for the impact of price changes on the net operating assets (including the depre-ciation, cost of sales, monetary working capital, fixed asset dis-posals, minority interest and extraordinary items adjustments) that may be regarded as associated with items that are financed by net borrowing; or
2. those parts of the total adjustments made to allow for the im-pact of price changes on the net operating assets, including the net surplus on the revaluation of assets arising during the period, that may be regarded as associated with items that are financed by net borrowing.

Self-financing ratio Used to mean, often without specifying which, **either** the proportion of the capital expenditure which is financed internally over a period, **or** the proportion of the funds required for a period which are financed internally.

APPENDIX 7.1   OTHER PUBLIC CORPORATIONS

Audit Commission
Bank of England*
British Broadcasting Corporation*
British Technology Group
Commonwealth Development Corporation
Covent Garden Market Authority
Crown Agents
Crown Agents Holding and Realization Board
Crown Suppliers
Development Board for Rural Wales
English Industrial Estates Corporation
Her Majesty's Stationery Office
Highlands and Islands Development Board
Housing Action Trusts
Independent Television Commission*
Land Authority for Wales
Letchworth Garden City
National Dock Labour Board*
National Health Service Trusts
New Town Development Corporations and the Commission for the
   New Towns*

Northern Ireland Electricity Service
Northern Ireland Housing Executive
Northern Ireland Public Trust Port Authorities
Northern Ireland Transport Holding Company
Oil and Pipelines Agency
Pilotage Commission
Public Trust Ports*
Royal Mint
Scottish Enterprise
Scottish Homes
United Kingdom Atomic Energy Authority
Urban Development Corporations
Welsh Development Agency
The Welsh Fourth Channel Authority

Note: Other than those marked with an asterisk, external finance is included in the planning total. The treatment of those with an asterisk varies – the last *Autumn Statement Statistical Supplement* gives details.

Source: *1991 Autumn Statement Statistical Supplement*. Cm. 1520, p. 52.

8

The National Health Service

Previous chapters have covered central and local government, where fund-raising (e.g. by taxes or borrowing) and expenditure allocation are directly linked to the democratic political process, and also nationalized industries and other public corporations which sell goods and services on a commercial basis and which just happen to be part of the public sector by reason of past political decision to regulate monopoly or control key sectors of the economy. There is a further category of public services which through historical accident or consensus have come to be funded partly or wholly from the public purse, yet which have been allowed a substantial degree of non-political and non-partisan self-governance or autonomy. This category includes public corporations such as the British Broadcasting Corporation (BBC), universities and polytechnics, the Arts Council and the National Health Service (NHS).

Given that the NHS is the largest and most costly of these public services, and given also that it is an excellent example of a complex organization with inherent conflict between professional/service objectives and the overriding requirement to balance the books within funding primarily from central government allocations, this chapter will explain in some detail the organizational, financial and accounting arrangements for the management of the NHS.

Implementation of the 'NHS Reforms' set out in the *White Paper*, *Working for Patients* (1989), has resulted in drastic changes to the organizational and financial arrangements for the NHS since the last edition of this book. Accounting procedures have altered less, except for capital accounting, but there has been increased priority and pressure to improve NHS costing and budgeting quickly, together with supporting computerized management information systems covering procurement, asset stocks, workload and resource use. Some of the changes are being phased-in only gradually over a transitional period of several years, but this chapter will naturally concentrate upon the intended new arrangements and systems.

STRUCTURE, FUNCTIONS AND POLICY-MAKING

National and regional organizations

Nearly all UK hospitals were nationalized in 1948, within the NHS. Hospital doctors and other staff became employees of the NHS, although not civil servants. Family doctors (GPs), dentists, opticians and pharmacists did not agree to become NHS employees, but their work was brought within the NHS by putting them under contract to treat NHS patients under conditions and funding arrangements supervised by the NHS. Community health care and ambulance services remained under the control of local government until the more or less simultaneous reorganizations of local government and the NHS in 1974, at which time these services were transferred to the NHS to be administered and funded on the same basis as the hospital services.

Originally there was a separate ministry for health, but for some twenty years until 1988 a combined ministry, the Department of Health and Social Security (DHSS), supervised policy and funding for both health affairs and social security. The objective was to achieve greater integration – or certainly coordination – in policy and service delivery for these two important areas of public service. But it is not obvious that much progress towards the objective was achieved, and in the summer of 1988 it was announced that there would now be a separate Department of Health (DH), headed by a Secretary of State for Health (Fig. 8.1).

Figure 8.1 illustrates additionally the relationship of the other principal organizational components of the NHS in England. The Welsh, Scottish and Northern Ireland Offices effectively provide the same higher level functions down to and including the role of regional health authorities (RHAs) in England. In Scotland and Northern Ireland the equivalent of district health authorities (DHAs) are known as health boards, and in Northern Ireland these include the administration of social services. In practice the organizational, financial and accounting arrangements for the NHS are closely similar throughout the UK, but strictly speaking the description which follows in this chapter is precise only for England unless otherwise clarified.

The Secretary of State for Health is advised in policy-making and performance review by his civil servants in the Department of Health, and by the Policy Board which provides a kind of umbilicus between the political and managerial levels of hierarchy in the NHS. The NHS Management Executive and its staff have the role of promoting the implementation of policy and the improvement of management performance and cost-effectiveness within the NHS. England is divided into fourteen regional health authorities (RHAs) whose role includes

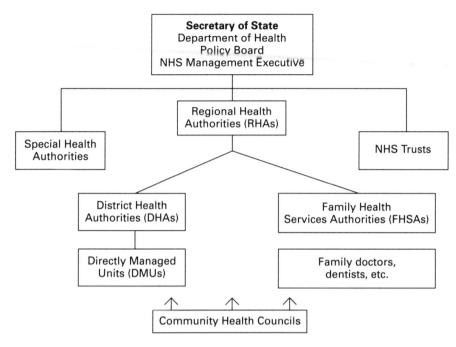

Fig. 8.1 NHS organization structure in England.

planning (including capital planning and the oversight of major projects), financial resource allocation between member district health authorities (i.e. the DHAs), and the monitoring of the performance of the districts. RHAs also provide some common services for their districts, often for reasons of likely economies of scale or policy control, such as blood donor services, medical teaching, manpower planning, and some centralized design, supplies and purchasing support services. There has been challenge to the need for RHAs, or certainly to their scale and costliness in the roles of planning and monitoring services managed operationally by DHAs and the new NHS Trusts, and there has been speculation that RHAs might be abolished, or at least that more of their functions and resources might be redistributed to the DHAs and Trusts.

Special health authorities include the Health Education Authority and a few postgraduate teaching hospitals not integrated into operational DHAs. All England is divided geographically among some 180 DHAs, with populations ranging from about one hundred thousand to about a million. A typical district will have a population of over a quarter of a million, some 4000 employees, and an annual budget exceeding £60 million. DHAs are comprised of a part-time chairperson, up to five executives of the authority including the chief executive and the finance director, and up to five non-executive members mainly drawn from a business background but including one university representative if the authority is a Teaching District linked to a university medical or dental school. The authority is expected to behave in a similar manner to a company board of directors, and, since in the new era in the NHS competition is of the essence in the new 'internal market' (see below), much of the authority's business is considered confidential and is conducted in private.

DHAs are responsible for the provision and monitoring of NHS local community care and hospital services, including emergency services. Their staffs are all NHS employees. In contrast, family doctors (i.e. GPs, or general practitioners), dentists, opticians, etc. are self-employed professionals who contract to provide services of agreed standard for NHS patients. These family practitioners are coordinated by, and have their financial claims on NHS funds supervised by, local Family Health Services Authorities (FHSAs, see Fig. 8.1), accountable to RHAs. FHSAs have their own NHS financial arrangements and systems, but the family practitioners are of course small-scale enterprises using their own diverse financial systems. This chapter will concentrate on the more complex and standardized financial problems and systems of the RHAs, DHAs and their directly managed units, and new NHS Trusts.

NHS Trusts and DHA Directly Managed Units are discussed further below. Community Health Councils are independent local bodies whose role is to monitor the performance of the NHS at local level, and to advise on needs and proposed developments.

District organization and directly managed units

The previous section summarized the formal hierarchy of authority and resources flow downwards from Secretary of State to the DHA, with a matching flow of accountability upwards. We now turn to the operational management arrangements within the DHA. Prior to 1984, health districts (and also the RHAs and the former area health authorities phased out in 1982) were managed by a team of co-equal chief officers who reached decisions on a 'consensus management' basis without benefit of a permanent chairman or chief executive. The Griffiths Report (1983) to the Secretary of State of the (then) DHSS stated in effect that consensus management was a nonsense and that there must be one single individual at each level of organizational management who could and would be held responsible for performance – for success or failure. There should be a general manager in charge at each level, from the new NHS management board recommended by Griffiths, down through the RHAs and the DHAs to the new unit management structures established after 1982.

DHAs normally have at least two Directly Managed Units (DMUs),

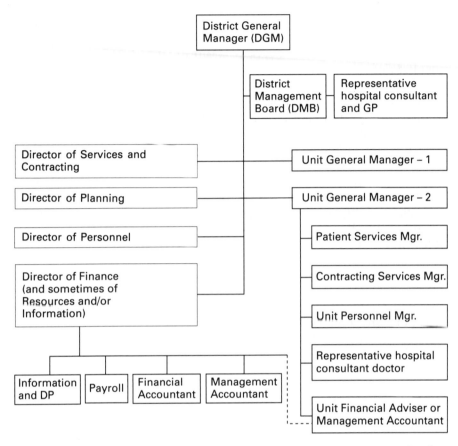

Fig. 8.2 Management structure of a district health authority in England.

one for 'acute' hospital services and one for community care. Larger DHAs may have several units (e.g. for the main district general hospital (DGH), for other smaller or cottage hospitals, for mental illness and mental handicap, and for geriatric and other community care services). District general managers (DGMs) are responsible primarily for the overall planning, coordination, resource distribution and performance of the DHA's total programme, while unit general managers (UGMs) are responsible for the operational management and efficiency of the manpower and financial resources allocated to their units.

Within each DHA there is considerable local discretion regarding how the DGM organizes his internal management structure. Figure 8.2 illustrates just one of the possible variations of such structure. The DGM is supported by a district management board (DMB), which in the example includes one representative of each of the district's hospital consultants (i.e. senior doctors), and of GPs practising within the district. These medical professionals are not under the direct managerial control of the DGM. In contrast, the directors of particular managerial support services listed on the left-hand side of Fig. 8.2, and the unit general managers (UGMs) on the right-hand side, are members of the DMB but also under the control of, or managerially accountable to, the DGM.

One exception to this, however, is that the Director of Finance, by whatever title he is called (and his title used to be 'Treasurer'), still retains separate, personal autonomy and accountability in respect of ensuring the financial probity and financial viability of the DHA's affairs. Normally he will be supported in this role by his DGM, but should the DGM be unhelpful or apparently complicit in any financial impropriety, including wilful overspending of total budgets, then it is the right and duty of the Director of Finance to go direct to the Chairperson of the DHA, or perhaps even to the RHA, to report his concern and request support.

Similarly, any accountant appointed as a Unit Financial Adviser, although ordinarily and managerially accountable to his UGM, should remain accountable to the District Director of Finance for his professional standards and performance, including the right and duty to report any financial malpractice, including wilful overspending, observed within the unit.

NHS Trusts and their organization

The White Paper, *Working for Patients* (Department of Health, 1989), led on to the National Health Service and Community Care Act 1990 to authorize proposed reforms, including the creation of NHS Trusts. NHS Trusts are formed by transferring the assets and management responsibility of DHA Directly Managed Units into a new corporate status, largely independent although ultimately accountable to the Secretary of State (i.e. accountable directly as distinct from via the hierarchy of DHA and RHA). The Trusts must earn their income from service contracting (see below) and other approved sources such as private health care, sale of assets, receipt of gifts, etc. Each Trust, unlike a DMU, has its own chairman and Board of Directors. Beneath Board level, the management structure of a Trust can be very similar to a DMU, although probably more orientated to commercial market objectives and constraints. Trusts have wider financial powers (see below) than DMUs or even than DHAs and RHAs, but in return for this they are expected to break even, taking one year with another, and failure to be financially viable (or to properly carry out contracted service obligations to the NHS) could lead to the dissolution or winding-up of a Trust by the Secretary of State.

FINANCING AND RESOURCE ALLOCATION

The scale of the NHS

The NHS rivals Education as the UK's most costly public service. It takes up 15% of total public spending, or if we delete Social Security expenditure which is mainly 'transfer payments' for pensions and welfare income redistribution, then the cost of the NHS exceeds 22% of total public service expenditure. The cost of the NHS in England now exceeds £22 billion per annum, or over £600 per adult each year, increasing at an annual rate currently of about 8% compound (of which some 7% reflects inflation and 1% real growth). About 70% of NHS cash spending is on pay, and the NHS nationally provides employment for about one million workers (including in this the staffs of Family Health Practitioners).

Funding the NHS centrally

While the NHS locally may be able to obtain modest amounts of funds from donations, voluntary fund-raising, and charges for private patients and for services to the private sector (e.g. diagnostic back-up services for private hospitals), in practice nearly the whole of NHS funds are provided by the government, following Cabinet agreement on total public spending and the relative resource needs of the numerous branches of the public sector. The decision on the total funding allocation to the NHS is independent of how much is raised in income from prescription charges and other fees, or from that small portion of National Insurance charges that is notionally designated as a National Health Insurance charge. Strictly, these apparently health-related sources of income have no more direct impact on determining total expenditure on the NHS than do vehicle and petrol taxes on the level of highway construction and maintenance. Currently about 3% of total NHS expenditure is met by income from health-service charges and some 11% is provided by notional health insurance levied with National Insurance contributions. The remaining 86% of expenditure is provided from the general pool of government taxation revenues.

It appears that the funding of the NHS has been the most successfully protected from economic crises, with almost continuous growth in real terms, even though at rates varying through time, of all the major public services. Indeed this is only rational, since health care for the sick is perhaps the least postponable of services. And as the environment has improved (better education, water, sewerage, control of pollution, and improved housing and health care for at least the large majority of the population) people live longer. Thus the numbers of the elderly increase, and the increase of those over 75 years of age is especially prominent. But the longer people live, the more prone they are to diseases which are not immediately life-threatening but are debilitating, crippling or otherwise destructive of the quality of life. About half the total resources of the NHS are expended on persons aged 65 or over, and it is estimated that the rising population of the elderly requires expansion of NHS resources by about 1% per year just to cope with this demographic change in the population.

But there are also other pressures for sharing in any growth moneys the NHS may secure. Technological progress in curative medicine is costly: new 'wonder drugs' are typically expensive, as are many of the newer surgical techniques, including not just the well-publicized heart and kidney transplants but also the more numerous and much-needed interventions such as artificial joints for those crippled by arthritis but otherwise in good health and able to look after themselves.

Funding allocations to regions and districts (WCF)

Until the Crossman formula of 1970 and its first major reorganization in 1974, the NHS simply grew organically and incrementally. That is, generally speaking, it grew on an unplanned basis, roughly proportional in each locality to its pre-existing size, and with little coherent guidance for equalizing the scale and accessibility of health-care resources across the regions. Historically the poorer and industrial parts of the country had fewer beds, doctors and support resources, and this historical pattern was little altered in the first quarter-century of the NHS. But the matter caused increasing dissatisfaction, culminating in 'equal access to health care' as a main objective of the 1974 reorganization, and in the establishment of the Resource Allocation Working Party (RAWP). RAWP (DHSS, 1976) proposed that health-care funds should be allocated to the regions of England according to equitable criteria of need, as measured by objective formulae (and similar proposals were brought forward separately for Wales, Scotland and Northern Ireland). Accordingly, it became accepted that the practical policy was to progress to RAWP equalization of resources regionally by increasing the funding allocations of the best-provided regions only slowly, while using the bulk of the annual growth in funding to accelerate the expansion of health-care resources in the under-provided regions at a faster rate. At the time (in the mid-1970s) it was hoped that resource equalization might be achieved nationally by 1990 or even earlier. But as economic depression settled on Britain, and the annual rate of growth in real terms of NHS funding was cut back, the horizon date for expected equalization receded.

The RAWP formula approach, used between 1977 and 1990, was based on the populations served by each RHA, weighted for the age, sex and marital status composition in each region. RHAs then applied similar formulae to redistribute allocations to their DHAs, but taking account of the populations currently served and not just the populations resident within each district's geographical boundaries. The latest approach, the Weighted Capitation Formula (WCF) was launched in 1990 and is to replace the RAWP allocations over a transitional period originally targeted to end in 1993, but which could take longer.

The weighting factor in WCF is primarily based on the age structure of the resident population. For example, the reported capitation funding weights for 1990/91 (HFMA, 1990) were expected to range from a low of £89.27 per head for the 15–44 age group, up to £1452.35 per head for the 85+ age group. Added to the weighted resident population allocations, where appropriate, are allowances for a London Weighting, a Thames Region allowance, and a market forces adjustment for authorities competing for staff in job markets with above-average pay levels.

The distinctive feature of the new WCF funding is the emphasis upon each RHA and DHA being financially responsible for, as well as funded for, the health-care cost of each and every member of the resident population. That is, patients treated outside their district of residence, as is commonplace especially in London and other large conurbations where health district boundaries are close together, will in future have to be paid for by their DHA of residence, through pre-arranged service contracts, or, if the treatment is not planned and negotiated in advance, then by 'extra-contractual referrals' (ECRs). This new approach raises difficult problems for health authorities in respect of identifying which patients fall into which category, determining relevant costs and charges, and setting up billing systems and ensuring cash collection between health authorities. Also, with ECRs, there is the problem of forecasting the scale of these, and what reserves DHAs must hold back from contracting to their own local services, in order to afford the ECR transfer payments to other health authorities.

Not all RHA funds are reallocated to DHAs. RHAs must retain funds for their own administrative costs, and for regional service programmes such as blood collection and treatment. Also, the authorized allocations of GP Fundholders located in each district must be deducted from the relevant DHA's allocation, as these are a first charge on district funding directly administered by the RHAs. RHAs also have to provide funding for regional clinical specialties, medical and nursing education and training, and the extra costs of teaching hospitals as defined by the Service Increment for Teaching and Research (SIFTR).

Revenue and capital funds allocations

Like most services directly funded and controlled by central government, the NHS has been administered under the Cash Limits system (Treasury, 1976) although certain Family Health expenditures are not cash limited owing to contractual commitments to reimburse practitioners for medical, dental and pharmaceutical, etc. services. Similarly, there has been the usual rigid separation of revenue funding from capital funding, reflecting this separation in parliamentary votes. However, very limited powers of virement (i.e. funds transfer between budget categories) have been allowed between revenue and capital, and the NHS has usually been allowed to carry forward up to 1% of total unspent revenue and capital allocations to the following year. Virement and carry-forward facilities, even though small in total amount, provide health authorities with a valued element of flexibility in expenditure planning, given that with general acknowledgement that there is unmet need for health care it is widely felt within the NHS that to underspend available funding is fully as reprehensible as to overspend.

Capital funding has been kept separate from revenue funding in the NHS and other public services partly for reasons of parliamentary and macroeconomic policy control, and partly because previously capital has been distributed as a 'free good' – that is, without any requirement of repayment of principal, or of interest or depreciation charges on either the monetary or real value of capital assets in use. However, with the introduction of both interest and depreciation charges in future, it is hoped that local decision-markers in the NHS will be able to make informed decisions on the best mix of funds use as between revenue and capital commitments Thereafter it may become feasible to allow all NHS funding (other than funds specifically ear-marked, or top-sliced, for specific policy commitments such as GP Fundholder budgets) to be distributed using the WCF, with decisions on the split of use between revenue and capital being made locally but in consultation with RHAs.

Purchasers and providers

There are well-publicized waiting lists for many non-life-threatening medical and especially surgical treatments, and there is yet further health care which would be supplied and appreciated if funding were available. So health-care delivery in the UK (and also to a greater or lesser degree in almost all other countries) involves processes of rationing and prioritizing treatments. It was deemed this was a role to be undertaken by the local DHA, which anyway has past experience of resource rationing through the control of the funding of new de-

velopments, and of the staffing of senior posts. The DHA was to take
on the role of purchaser of health care on behalf of its resident population. However the government additionally wished to test whether
family doctors (GPs) themselves could serve as effective purchasers of
care by becoming Fundholders with a budget to purchase approved
hospital diagnostic and treatment services for their own patients. GP
practices with at least 7000 patients on their lists have been allowed,
and indeed encouraged, to become Fundholders, and they have been
given expense money for the administration of this new role. Thus
we have a new system in which there are two classes of purchaser
arranging health care on behalf of the resident population of a district, GP Fundholders for a proportion (perhaps 10%, but likely to
rise) of spending, and DHAs for the balance.

Health-care purchasers contract to buy services from the health-
care providers. The providers are the organizational units which actually provide treatment and support services. The major providers are
hospitals, but also they include community care services, ambulance
services, etc. These providers can be organized as directly managed
units (DMUs), or as NHS Trusts (see below). For anything approach-
ing a 'perfect market' one of the conditions is that buyers and sellers
should be independent of each other (otherwise we are forced back
into 'transfer pricing' as distinct from 'market pricing'). However,
DMUs as providers are in fact administratively accountable to DHAs,
the major purchasers in the new internal market in NHS care. This
problem could be one of the main arguments leading the government to the creation of NHS Trusts, as these are administratively
independent of their DHAs and account only directly to the Secretary
of State.

Contracting for care services

The NHS has always had contracts for the bulk or regular supply of
various inputs, such as supplies, fuel, agency staff, support services
shared with other authorities, etc. During the past ten years or so
some support services, formerly provided in-house by NHS staff, have
been put out to competitive contract, especially in the areas of laundry,
cleaning and catering. But what is now beginning is of a different order
of magnitude and significance – the contracting of total medical care.

Health-care providers will offer to supply care at specified prices,
especially seeking new business outside their own district boundaries
if they have surplus capacity available or in prospect for particular
specialties (i.e. areas of clinical specialization, such as obstetrics
or orthopaedics) or support services such as radiology. Purchasers,
whether DHAs or GP Fundholders, must assess and specify the services
needed for their residents/patients. DHAs must distinguish between

'Core Services' for which patients must have guaranteed local access (e.g. Accident and Emergency services), and 'Non-core Services' where there is the feasibility of delay and/or travel for treatment outside the district. For Core Services, purchasers and providers must reach a bargained local contract, whereas for Non-core Services purchasers are free to 'shop around' for best value-for-money contracts. Contracts are expected increasingly to specify standards of service or quality, and waiting times or promptness of service, not just price. There are three types of contract, as follows:

1. **Block contracts** in which the provider receives a predetermined annual sum paid monthly in instalments in return for residents' access to a defined range of services, as needful;
2. **Cost and volume contracts** in which the provider is paid an agreed sum in return for treating a specified number of cases of a particular type. There can additionally be a variable cost component for each case treated between a specified minimum and maximum volume;
3. **Cost per case contracts** in which the provider is paid a unit price for each individual patient treated.

The above contracts should cover the large majority of treatments, on a planned basis. But there can also be extra-contractual referrals (ECRs), which arise either as an emergency when a resident is in a different locality, or as a non-emergency when a patient is sent somewhere unplanned, on referral by a GP or hospital consultant. Purchasers must pay for emergency treatments, but for the non-emergency referral the provider is required to obtain advance approval from the purchaser if reimbursement is to be claimed. ECRs introduce financial uncertainty for both purchasers and providers, and adequate reserves must be maintained especially during the transitional period of the introduction of the new internal market system. For stability during this transitional period, most contracts are expected to be of the block type, to be followed later by the increasing use of cost and volume contracts where price competition and incentives to efficiency are expected to strengthen.

In general, the prices set and agreed for the new contracts are expected by the DH to be based on full costs (inclusive of depreciation and interest capital charges). Marginal-cost-plus pricing is to be used only where there is short-term spare capacity, and there should be no planned cross-subsidization between services. Market forces are expected to operate not initially by forcing down the prices of local cost-based contracts, but by the fact or threat of diversion of contracts to lower-cost providers forcing higher-cost providers to improve cost efficiency or else cease supplying some Non-core Services. The new system of capital charges, and the systems and problems of costing in the NHS, are discussed in later sections of this chapter.

NHS TRUSTS AND GP FUNDHOLDERS

The new NHS 'internal market' could have been launched without the additional complications of simultaneously starting the NHS Trusts and GP Fundholder budgets. DHAs would have operated as purchasers from providers comprising their own DMUs, the DMUs of other DHAs, and, if offering better value, private health-care suppliers. However, the lack of independence between the paymaster DHAs, and their administratively subordinate DMUs, would have greatly reduced the potential competitiveness of the internal market. Thus the logic of converting DMUs into Trusts independent of their local DHAs and accountable only directly to the Secretary of State for Health. Ideally to create a level playing field for competition and market forces, all DMU providers should have been converted into Trusts simultaneously. However, this was not practicable because there were not sufficient senior managers in the NHS trained in commercial management, and because the management information and costing systems needed as bases for accurate pricing, workload monitoring, and services billing, were not yet widely available throughout NHS DMUs. So Trusts have had to be established only when adequate management structures and information and control systems have become available. Even so, many of the first (1991) wave of Trusts have experienced widely publicized financial and managerial problems. By the time this new edition is published there could be over 300 NHS Trusts, representing about half the service delivery of the NHS.

NHS Trusts

NHS Trusts are largely autonomous financial and managerial entities linked by accountability ultimately to the Secretary of State, but not linked otherwise to the NHS except through contracts. At the time of the *White Paper* (1989) the new Trusts were expected to be mainly based, at least in the first instance, on major acute hospitals. However they can be comprised of just ambulance services, particular community care units, or indeed the total combined former DMU services of a DHA. Trusts have their own boards of directors, chief executives and finance directors. They have wide powers, more similar to those of public corporations than to the remainder of the NHS or most other services administered by central government. Subject to certain regulations and limits, these powers include freedom to:

1. acquire, own and dispose of assets;
2. submit cases for capital development to the NHS Management

Executive (thus bypassing district and regional capital planning and allocation procedures);
3. borrow, both for capital developments and for working capital;
4. employ staff directly, and set their own terms and conditions of employment;
5. advertise their services (within approved guidelines) and actively seek new business, including private health-care business.

Trusts are established as self-contained financial entities with the opening value of net assets transferred to the Trust being balanced by an originating capital debt (owed to the Exchequer) comprising two elements. The first is interest bearing debt (IBD) which has defined interest and repayment terms. The second is public dividend capital (PDC), a form of public equity capital also used sparingly in some nationalized industries, and on which dividends may in future become payable to the government if and when the Trust Board and the Secretary of State deem this commercially prudent. It is understood that for most Trusts so far created, the originating capital structure ratio between IBD and PDC has been 50–50. This ratio will change through time in accord with each Trust's performance in respect of earning surpluses or deficits, relative to its capital growth through capital borrowing.

Like public corporations, each NHS Trust will be assigned annually an external financing limit (EFL), which effectively is a cash limit. The total for all Trusts' EFLs will be determined in the annual Public Expenditure Survey, and each Trust's share in that will be determine in negotiation with the NHS Management Executive after productio of a detailed business plan. EFLs could be 'negative', involving Trusts in repaying debt instead of raising capital for new development or modernization. Trusts are expected to earn a real pre-interest return of 6% on average net assets, a target consistent with the guidelines on capital charges for DMUs to be included in NHS pricing for the internal market. The Secretary of State can dissolve or wind up a Trust for significant failure to remain within EFLs or to achieve the financial target return on assets.

The annual accounts of the Trusts will be broadly consistent with the Companies Acts' requirements, and will show a 'true and fair view' of the Trust's affairs. In these matters, as in the form of capital structure, depreciation accounting and financial targeting, one can perceive similarities to the financial and accounting arrangements for regional water authorities prior to their privatization.

GP Fundholders

Some health economists and health policy thinkers have argued in recent years that the most efficient and equitable system of resources funding (and rationing) in health care would be for family doctors (GPs), who know individual patients best and have a role as the patients' advocates and gatekeepers into the maze of NHS hospital and community services, to hold most NHS funding (aside from that for Accident and Emergency, and public health and shared support services) for use to purchase health care for their patients. In the 1990s reforms the government has not gone that far, but it has launched an initiative to encourage initially the larger practices to take on a limited fund-holding or budget-holding role. The size of GP practice participating is of some importance, since the start-up and running costs of the accounting and administrative systems and computing needed for each fund-holding practice are substantial.

GP Fundholders must make their case for budget funds to their RHA, who, if they approve, will allocate the GP funds and deduct the total from the residual funds to be allocated to DHAs. Unlike traditional GP spending, which is monitored but largely not cash limited, the new fund-holding budgets are from cash-limited resources and could constitute a stage of progression towards cash limiting all NHS medical spending. The new fund-holder budgets are divided into three parts, to cover approved additional costs of their own practice staff to provide services which otherwise would have to be 'bought in' from other providers; to cover drugs prescribed by the practice; and to recover the cost of purchasing approved hospital services. The latter is the most significant of the GP budget innovations, since it puts the GP in place of the DHA as the primary purchaser to negotiate prices and service, for those services allowable under the scheme. Those services comprise specified types of elective surgery referrals and out-patient attendances, and certain hospital support service referrals such as radiology and pathology, etc. At least during the introductory, experimental stages of this new scheme, fundholders will be allowed to 'vire', or transfer, money from one of the the three types of spending, or budget heads, to another, and to carry forward savings from one year to another. Savings can then be spent on further services or practice improvement, but cannot be paid out as profits to the GPs themselves.

ACCOUNTABILITY

Accountability is a vexing problem for the NHS. In commercial businesses, the enterprise must in particular give satisfaction to, and/ or account to, both the customer and the shareholders. The NHS has no shareholders and no profit motive, just the government as proprietor and source of funding in the public interest. The NHS has few customers, defined as consumers paying personally and directly for what they receive. The NHS is largely a monopoly supplier of a public good. Patients have only a limited choice of the service they receive, they lack the skill to evaluate much of the quality of that service, and at the time of greatest medical need patients are often in no mental state to 'shop around' or to assess the technical efficiency or value for money of the care they receive. Moreover within the NHS there is potential conflict in that the leading role in health care delivery is taken by doctors and other professionals whose objectives and codes of ethics and behaviour are not always fully compatible with the search for efficiency and value for money carried forward by NHS managers and accountants to meet government policy and directives.

National accountability

The government, through the DH, receives a large number and variety of statutory and other reports on financial and other resource use in the NHS. Many of these reports are not made public (or only published after a long delay in processing financial and statistical information), but instead are used internally in the DH for monitoring performance and the degree of achievement of centrally determined objectives and policies. Arguably the greatest power of the DH over accountability lies in the appointment of regional top management, and the chairpersons of health authorities and Trusts, increasingly on performance-related short-term contracts.

Parliament obtains accountability from the NHS in respect of the evidence of compliance with the votes of parliamentary funding. Also, the accounting officer of the DH is required from time to time to appear before the Public Accounts Committee to answer questions on the performance of the NHS, especially on matters arising from the reports of the National Audit Office. Reports from the Audit Commission are noted as well (see Chapter 9 for discussion of audit arrangements for the NHS). There is also a parliamentary select committee, the Health Committee, with powers to select topics for enquiry, invite witnesses and obtain evidence, and publish its findings in reports to Parliament.

Local accountability

Managerial accountability of Directly Managed Units (e.g. major hospitals) has been strengthened by the sequence of reforms since the Griffiths Report (1983), and the *White Paper* (1989). But, arguably, accountability to the local community in which health authorities and their hospitals operate has been reduced in recent years. The access of Community Health Councils and the press to NHS meetings, staff and information appears to have been reduced, as NHS districts and units have been required to act in a more competitive, commercial manner so that much information has come to be treated as confidential. Health authorities, and NHS Trusts, produce annual reports, but it may be that, as with the annual reports of business firms, these are mainly written as public relations exercises and may be far from objective reports on the progress and problems of the organizations reporting. Recent organizational changes in the NHS appear to have centralized policy-making and control more fully than in the past, while at the same time giving local management greater discretion in the day-to-day implementation of national policies on resource use and service development.

FINANCIAL ACCOUNTING AND REPORTING

Financial accounting

Health authorities receive cash-limited allocations of revenue funding and, separately, cash spend authority for approved capital projects. FHSAs additionally process various contractual family health expenditures which are closely monitored, but not cash limited. This section will concentrate on DHAs, as they have particular interest because of the new role of health-care purchaser assigned to them, and the need to segregate expenses and disbursements arising from this role, from expenditure on their own service activities and general administration.

The first priority in NHS financial accounting needs to be cash (or, cash flow) accounting, combined with good cash management. Cash flow forecasts must be sent to the DH weekly. Cash is obtained by requisition from the DH for payment into the authority's bank account, or into a Paymaster General's account used especially for transfer payments between authorities. Cash balances in bank accounts must be kept to a working minimum and not allowed into overdraft. Borrowing from banks or other sources of working capital is not allowed for health authorities, although this and other financial restrictions have been waived in the case of the new NHS Trusts. Given that some 75% of NHS revenue cash flow is expended on pay, and that most trade suppliers' accounts are fairly regular and predictable, the main source of uncertainty in cash management within cash limits arises currently as regards the balance between extra-contractual referrals (ECRs) charges payable to providers outside the DHA, and ECR income earned by the district's DMUs from purchasers outside the district. In future the level of uncertainty may increase if service agreements between purchasers and providers make greater use of flexible cost and volume contracts in place of block contracts – or if the DH should decide to insist that health authorities must accept all ECRs made on clinical judgement.

NHS financial accounts are nowadays almost fully computerized, including supporting feeder systems for payroll, creditors and debtors, etc. Financial Directions are issued by the Secretary of State for Health setting out in general terms the responsibilities for financial accounting and control. These are then interpreted in more detail in locally prepared Standing Financial Instructions. The accounts must be kept as specified in the *NHS Manual for Accounts* issued by the DH and supplemented by occasional revisions and other directives on financial management.

Financial reporting

The financial year for the NHS runs from 1 April, and annual accounts must be completed by 30 June in the following year. The accounts must be certified by the Director of Finance and submitted to the health authority. They have little role in local accountability, but rather exist mainly for accountability to the DH and Parliament. In practice they are consolidated accounts. Entity accounts are prepared for the DMUs or service providers, and these are combined with the central accounts of the DHA into a consolidated DHA financial report. RHAs repeat this process at a higher level of aggregation and submit to the DH. The main function of these accounts appears to be for a general financial performance review, the state of solvency of each DHA having been largely established much earlier by the DH monitoring of cash drawings and forecasts. The accounts of authorities are subject to audit by the Audit Commission or an approved private sector accountancy firm.

The annual accounts of a DHA comprise an Income and Expenditure Account for its revenue funds, a Balance Sheet, and a Sources and Application of Funds Statement which serves to reconcile the under/overspending against cash limits, with the net surplus/deficit reported in the Income and Expenditure Account. Unlike the balance sheet, the other two accounts do not include fixed asset depreciation, indexation or revaluation. That is, these accounts do not include all the elements of full accrual accounting, although this may come about in future to reflect in accounts the effects of the new capital charging on revenue funds income. The accounts must be accompanied by a statement of accounting practice and will normally have extensive supporting notes, including such matters as segmental disclosure of financial information on DMUs, purchaser/provider balances with other DHAs and with NHS Trusts, capital/fixed asset changes and commitments, administrative expense, contingent liabilities, etc.

NHS Trusts, unlike the DHAs, are expected to be on a full accrual basis inclusive of depreciation. Actual interest payments on originating capital debt and subsequent borrowing, and public dividend capital (PDC) dividends, if any, will also be included. Whereas DHAs must balance out to their cash limit drawings, taking one year with another, NHS Trusts are allowed, and expected, to operate so as to achieve a revenue surplus for reinvestment in the service and income-earning programmes of the Trust.

CAPITAL

Like other central government services, the NHS has always obtained its capital as a separate allocation from revenue funding. The NHS has not been allowed to borrow capital. The capital has been supplied on parliamentary vote, as a 'free good', without any interest charge, depreciation charge or repayment of principal. However, it had long been argued that receiving capital as a free good could lead to excessive use or waste of capital on individual projects, even though the great age of much of the stock of NHS buildings and plant makes it obvious that overall the NHS probably needs greater capital investment to improve operational efficiency as well as the environment of care for patients. Development of capital accounting and/or charging has been recommended at least since the financial study for the Royal Commission on the NHS (1978), and since the Association of Health Service Treasurers' Report (1984) which recommended the creation of asset registers for all NHS fixed assets, plus trials of alternative methods of depreciation accounting. The Ceri Davies Report (1983) identified surplus land and underutilized building space within the NHS, and all these and other studies strengthened the argument that depreciation charges together with interest charges would be a desirable discipline to encourage the more efficient use of capital, and the disposal of surplus land and buildings.

Capital charging

The NHS's system for charging for the use of capital assets came into operation in April 1991. This initiative was partly to encourage greater efficiency and accountability in the use of the NHS estate, whose gross value at the higher of market value or replacement cost could be upwards of £40 billion, and partly to provide relevant capital use costs for inclusion in the pricing of hospital and other NHS services, to ensure fair competition in internal market trading within the NHS and also between the NHS and the private sector.

To support the new NHS capital charging system a comprehensive asset register and depreciation accounting system is being introduced. All fixed assets (except land) costing over £1000 (including groups of lesser assets individually in excess of £250) will be depreciated on a straight line basis. Land and buildings are to be valued every three years by the District Valuer, with valuations updated every quarter by index adjustments. All other assets are to be valued at current cost, normally defined as depreciated replacement cost. Depreciable lives will be determined by the DH for standard categories of assets, ranging initially from seven years for vehicles, to eighty years for permanent buildings. This sounds precise, but it leaves considerable room for argument over the determination of the remaining useful life of old buildings and plant, remembering that many NHS buildings have already been in use for well over eighty years.

All assets are to be valued and depreciated for the purpose of balance sheet disclosure for DMUs, DHAs and RHAs, and NHS Trusts. The depreciation charge for each full year shall be based on the average value of fixed assets during the year, defined as the average of the value of assets at the beginning of each quarter. Although the calculations can easily be handled by computer, this somewhat complicated calculation of depreciation can be seen as lending a spurious precision to what is inevitably an exercise in informed approximation. Just to add to the complication, whereas the depreciation charges are levied on the average of quarterly values, the new interest charges for capital in use are to be levied on the opening quarterly values.

The annual interest rate to be charged on the current value of NHS assets is 6%. Some NHS authorities hold much more land than others, and land in prosperous city and urban centres obviously has a higher current value for a given area. Land does not attract a depreciation charge but it does attract an interest charge. It follows that the combined total of depreciation and interest charges can vary significantly between authorities with similar total asset valuations. Also this combined total can vary widely between two DMUs with similar workload capacity and revenue funding, if the ages and values of buildings (and land) are markedly different, or if their locations are in radically different areas of market value. Thus, in particular it is expected that the capital charges for DMU (and Trust) hospitals in London will be relatively very high and make it more difficult for them to price their services competitively in the new internal market.

Above we have considered how the new NHS depreciation and interest charges are to be defined and calculated. The first use for this information is in the traditional role of performance monitoring within each organization, and for performance comparisons between organizations, especially between comparable DMUs, or between DMUs and rival NHS Trusts. The second, more innovative, and more influential use for this information will be within the NHS revenue

funding system. The intention is that DHAs should be liable to their
RHAs, as a first charge against revenue funds, for the total sum of
their depreciation charges and their interest charges. The RHAs will
aggregate and pool all the depreciation and interest charges relating
to their DHAs, and they will then redistribute this pool of revenue
fund clawback, in accordance with the new WCF revenue funding
method based on resident population in each DHA (and which provides
the funds for DHAs to carry out their purchaser roles).

It has been estimated that total capital charges (i.e. the combined
depreciation plus interest charges) will be about £7 billion nationally,
or about 20% of total revenue cash funding voted by Parliament. For
illustration, assume an RHA with £1000 million of revenue funding
for hospital and community services, and with an average capital
stock generating capital charges of £200 million per year. Let us then
take the cases of two of the region's DHAs, X and Y. The calculations
below show how their total revenue funding can be affected by differing levels of value of capital stock.

	DHA X	DHA Y
	£m	£m
Capital allocation	6	35
Revenue allocation (WCF)	90	110
Less capital charges	(24)	(18)
Plus RHA reallocation of its capital charges income (WCF)	18	22
Adjusted revenue allocation	84	114

Capital allocations are based on priority for planned developments.
DHA X has a low capital allocation yet high capital charges, suggesting it may recently have completed major hospital spending. DHA Y
has a high capital allocation and relatively low capital charges, suggesting it has old hospital stock but major investment is in progress
to replace this. After adjusting for both the capital charges owing
to the RHA, and the subsequent redistribution of the RHA's capital
charges income back to purchaser DHAs on the weighted capitation
formula (WCF), it will be seen that the relative revenue funding position of DHA Y has been impoved relative to DHA X. This effect could
be seen as an encouragement to minimize the capital stock. But of
course there are other pressures to upgrade capital stock, not least for
making a good impression in the internal market. Eventually the
quality and value, and capital charges, of capital stock may come to
be more or less equalized across all DHAs and their DMUs. Once this
point is approached it may become feasible for all RHA funding to be

allocated in one single allocation, combining both revenue and capital on a WCF basis of distribution.

Capital charging and NHS Trusts

The third use for capital charging information is in pricing within the internal market, it being the intention that both DMUs and NHS Trusts, in their provider roles, should set prices fairly, on the same basis of full cost recovery, where 'full cost' is defined in the economist's sense to include both capital recovery through depreciation and a social-cost or opportunity-cost rate of return on capital. However, the actual mechanics of the capital charging system will work differently for NHS Trusts, from that described above for DMUs and their DHAs and RHAs.

First, the depreciation charges for Trusts will not be 'payable' to RHAs for pooling and redistribution. Instead, that part of the trading cash flow of Trusts represented by depreciation charges will be retained within the Trusts for future capital renewal. Second, the interest charges for Trusts' assets will not be payable to RHAs, but will be payable to the Secretary of State in respect of the interest bearing debt (IBD) of the Trust, or to any other lenders providing borrowed capital. Overall, the Trusts are expected to earn at least 6% on the current value of all their net assets, and after the interest payments and any public dividends which may in future be called for, any residual trading surpluses may be retained for future capital development of the Trusts. In contrast, DMUs and DHAs are not allowed to retain or reinvest any trading surpluses which cannot be spent on services before the end of the current financial year, except for up to 1% of cash allocation carry forward at district or regional level.

Capital appraisal

Capital appraisal, or investment appraisal, has for some years been known in the NHS as 'option appraisal'. This alternative title is meant to emphasize that in an organization with limited capital resources and a wide choice of potential investment in improved hospitals and support facilities, capital decisions are seldom based on assessing the merits of one investment proposal on its own, but rather involve a selection from alternative uses of capital where the decision criteria include subjective criteria of need and quality of benefit, not to mention political considerations. The biggest capital investments of the NHS are in new hospitals. New hospitals typically provide space and facilities for the latest laboratory and other technical support services, so that generally they lead to higher cost per patient treated, or at least to higher total costs, than for the hospitals they replace.

Thus, discounted cash flow calculations on the consequences of erecting a new hospital will seldom show a positive net present value (NPV). However, comparisons of the forecast costs of alternative hospital designs for the same service delivery can show net savings between designs, and the NPV of this can be calculated to set alongside the subjective or qualitative decision criteria affecting choice between the alternative designs. Each option should be fully explored and documented for all quantifiable and non-quantifiable decision factors. This form of capital appraisal can have more in common with the economist's cost/benefit analysis than with the private sector investment appraisal model seeking to maximize future profitability through selection of the alternative with the highest NPV.

Under the recent reforms the NHS is being encouraged to manage its resources more competitively and efficiently, in the internal market. Such market competition implies the possibility that some hospitals may thrive and expand, while others may shrink or shut down. Thus some DMUs, or more especially some NHS Trusts, may use capital appraisal to test the financial implications of building larger new hospitals in search of attracting greater numbers of patients from the NHS or as private patients. This approaches to the private sector use of capital appraisal, but only time will tell whether or not the market in health care is sufficiently mobile and elastic as to make such developments feasible in service terms, and financially successful in generating surpluses for reinvestment in improved health care.

Turning to smaller capital outlays, some of these will be decided on service grounds and professional judgement, with little scope for formal capital appraisal. One example would be a decision to purchase a new, unique but expensive piece of clinical scanning equipment (where often the follow-on revenue running costs may be more critical than the original capital outlay). But in other cases, a more conventional capital appraisal may be used; for example in choosing between alternative heating system boilers and boiler fuels (assuming equally acceptable environmental impacts between the choice of systems).

BUDGETING, COSTING AND PRICING

Financial control in a business is probably best achieved by monitoring revenues achieved, combined with measuring and controlling the cost of resources consumed in producing and supplying the specific goods and services generating individual revenues. Until recently, public services have not been run as 'businesses' with their revenue dependent on measured outputs or market values. Thus financial control has concentrated on monitoring and controlling inputs for their own sake, regardless of the outputs achieved. Given the traditional system of parliamentary control based on cash expenditure rather than the cost of resource consumption, financial control in the NHS and similar public services has concentrated on the control of cash flow, purchasing procedures, and the accountability of budget holders for current expenditure on resource inputs.

In studying the evolution of financial control in the NHS, two fundamental conditions must be borne in mind. First, effective budgetary control systems must mirror the organizational structure and accountability framework for the time being in use in the organization. Second, for budgetary control to be effective it is essential that the costs or expenditure reported against budgets must be highly accurate and quickly available for discussion and management action, or else the whole budgetary exercise will lose credibility and authority. Broadly, the NHS has met the first of these two conditions, but following the recent change of emphasis from controlling cash expenditure inputs to costing and pricing the value of resource inputs used in producing 'marketable' service outputs, the NHS's systems have not yet adapted effectively to fulfilling the second condition.

Functional budgeting

Budgeting and budgetary control in the NHS has been based on what is termed 'functional budgeting'. The term derives from the 'functional' form of organization adopted by the NHS at the time of the 1974 reorganization, which laid great stress on the organization and management of the service by functions, i.e. disciplines of professional specialization. Prior to 1974, budgets and accounts had been mainly on a subjective basis for an entire hospital or other organizational unit. After 1974 the subjective data had to be recast across a matrix to relate to the authority and accountability of individual senior managers of functions for the resources they authorized to be used across the whole of each health district, e.g. the salaries, training costs and certain other expenses of nurses in a district for the accountability of the district nursing officer (Fig. 8.3). Each senior functional officer could in turn delegate specified parts of his or her overall budget to particular managers within the function, while of course still retaining overall responsibility for the budgetary performance of that function as a whole. The strengths and weaknesses of the functional budgeting system were explored in some depth in Research Paper No. 2 for the Royal Commission on the NHS (1978).

Unit and general management budgeting

The 1982 reorganization of the NHS abolished area health authorities, raised district health authorities in status, and required that

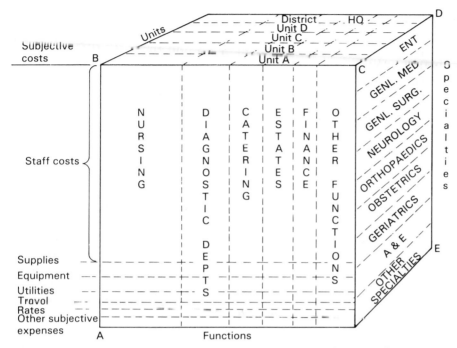

Fig. 8.3 NHS budgets subdivided by subjective costs, functional management, management units and specialties (or clinicians). (Source: J. Perrin (1988) *Resource Management in the NHS*, Chapman & Hall, London, p. 36.)

within DHAs there should be delegated 'units' of management in order to bring management authority and accountability to a lower organizational level nearer to where operational work is carried out. Typically the new units (now known as DMUs) were based on major acute hospitals (DGHs), on groups of smaller hospitals, on mental handicap or mental illness services, and on other community health care services. The existing functional budgets then had to be subdivided and reallocated between the new units within each district. This appeared to create some degree of potential conflict between functional officers at district level and functional officers in the units with regards to the determination and control of budgets for particular resources (e.g. the appointment and location of nursing staff).

Then came the Griffiths Inquiry Report (1983), whose major recommendation was that the functional/professional consensus/team management approach in the NHS was inefficient and should be replaced by chief executives (to be known as 'general managers') at every level, from the national Management Board through RHAs and DHAs down to the new units of management. At the local level this altered the main debate concerning budgetary allocations and control from a 'horizontal' dialogue between district and unit heads of individual functions (i.e. professions or services), to a 'vertical' dia-

logue between the new general managers in the districts and their units. Of course the new general managers received advice from their respective functional department heads, but the nature of the budget bargaining process was changed to a more 'businesslike' arrangement in which overall workload targets and performance were central.

Prior to 1974 the standard system of budgeting had been based on a 'line item' or 'subjective' classification of the types of goods and services (including staff pay) acquired for an entire district or other major organizational component. The 1982 reorganization retained the above budgetary system, simply subdividing the subjective budgets among smaller organizational units (see Fig. 8.3). Even the post-1983 appointment of general managers did not alter the budgets, although it did often alter role relationships and the channels of communication and decision over the setting of budgets and review of budgetary performance. Thus the standard budget system in the NHS continued to be on a line item/subjective basis, although subdivided by units and increasingly controlled on an integrated basis by unit general management. Here 'integrated basis' means that, through the coordination provided by the general manager, a conscious attempt is made to optimize the size of the various budget headings to match the real (i.e. physical) resource needs of the separate budget departments in order to deliver a balanced programme of care to meet agreed health service objectives.

Budgets as determined above are essentially 'input budgets', as they are primarily linked to claims of need for resources and are not directly linked to targeted or achieved workload outputs or quality of outcomes (i.e. effectiveness). This approach to budgeting in the NHS (and other public services) has given concern to many accountants, economists and other critical commentators.

Specialty costing

The service outputs of the NHS (and especially of NHS acute hospitals) can be studied and costed at different levels of disaggregation. At the broadest level we can cost and budget for the work and output of individual specialties (such as general surgery or obstetrics). Some specialties are subdivided between 'firms' (i.e. teams) of consultant doctors working together. Or cost analysis can be taken down to the level of the individual consultant doctor, the ultimate decision-maker determining who is admitted for treatment, the mode of treatment, and how available resources shall be used or consumed in providing treatment. But of course specialties, firms and individual consultants are only front-line providers or channels of outputs. The actual outputs are the patients treated and discharged. But the cost and budget consequences of the work of individual consultants, firms or specialties can be taken as relevant surrogates for the treatment of reasonably similar groupings or aggregates of service outputs (see Fig. 8.3).

The (Körner) Steering Group on Health Services Information was established about 1980 under joint DHSS and NHS sponsorship to make recommendations on how to improve information for management control in the NHS. This covered information on activity and workload, manpower and its utilization, and finance. In the Sixth Report (1984), the Körner Steering Group recommended that the NHS should adopt 'specialty costing' as part of its financial management information system, both for local management and planning use, and for reporting and performance review at RHA and national levels.

Accurate specialty costing requires the tracing of all direct costs incurred by the consultant members of a specialty, as well as all indirect costs incurred by or attributable to the specialty and the patients it has treated. While direct costs can be traced and validated fairly easily, many indirect costs (e.g. the expense of X-rays, laboratory tests, therapy staff assistance and even the appropriate proportion of nursing pay costs) are much harder to trace, record and validate or audit with a high degree of accuracy.

Clinicians in planning and budgeting

A distinctive feature of financial control in the NHS is the limited role played by its 'production managers'. These are the clinical consultants, and although a few of them double as department managers (e.g. for diagnostic and medical services), the majority of them who treat patients directly and who determine the workload or throughput of the hospitals, do not yet hold budgets for the expenditure they cause. This situation has arisen from the historical background of the development of the role and status of consultants, relative to the hospital management structure. It is defended on the doctrine of clinical autonomy whereby the consultant is personally responsible for the care of patients, so that he argues that he must have the right to call out whatever **available** treatment (i.e. resources) he feels necessary. This doctrine is not in dispute at the level of care for the **individual** patient, but as the growth of the NHS has slowed down and additionally has become constrained at the margin on a cash-limit basis of firm control against any expenditure beyond original authorizations, a growing number of clinicians have come to realize that in order to obtain the best outcome for all patients it is indeed necessary to pay heed to the costs of resources, the comparative costs and benefits of alternative modes of patient management, and the trade-offs of benefit at the margin from using scarce resources in different combinations.

The most interesting initiative to involve clinicians has been the set of projects initiated by CASPE (Clinical Accountability, Service Planning and Evaluation) (see Wickings, 1983). With varying detail, these projects tested ways in which to involve clinicians – and sometimes nurses and other resource providers as well – in consultation on choices for the best uses of scarce resources which can be varied in amount by careful planning, but are restricted in their total cost by the cash-limit system. This will often involve making clinicians budget holders, although this is not an essential requirement, and a variety of responsibility-sharing arrangements is possible. Where clinicians do become budget holders, it is essential to segregate the variable costs of services which they can control from the fixed and indirect costs that remain under the decision-making and control of function (and unit) budget holders.

An example of the kind of monthly budgetary-control report which can be used in clinical management budgeting is reproduced in Table 8.1. Current-month and cumulative year-to-date expenditure is shown, together with budgeted amounts and variances. The report, which is simulated and does not itemize as many categories of cost as may in practice come to be used regularly in clinical budgets, begins with two sections detailing costs directly controlled by the head of the surgical team. The next section lists budgetary costs influenced by the team (i.e. costs of resources administered by nurses and other department heads, but which are dependent on the admission and treatment policies of clinical consultants). These include both the variable costs of wards and clinics, i.e. the consumables, and also the service department overheads which are fixed costs in the short term but may be altered by policy decisions on the form and volume of treatment over the longer term. The final two sections show the share of general overheads (over which the consultant has no direct influence) apportioned, plus a set of memorandum statistics which comprise selected indicators of both the surgical team's workload or throughput, and its volume consumption of key resources controllable by the team's decisions.

Resource management

'Resource management' is the name given to a new generation of projects to involve doctors and nurses in using financial and other management information to help achieve more efficient and effective use of resources (Perrin, 1988). This initiative was announced in the DHSS's HN(86)34 (1986), which in effect admitted that attempts to interest clinicians in management budgeting to date had not been very successful. This was probably partly because clinical management budgeting had come to be seen as primarily a cost control tool mainly of benefit to financial and general management, and partly because of the serious delays in getting resource use information systems computerized, so as to be prompt and accurate in their reporting of data doctors could see to be meaningful to improving the management of their own work-loads.

The management budgeting approach was largely a top–down system in practice, creating resentment among health care professions not accustomed to close managerial monitoring or discipline. The new approach is bottom–up, involving finding out what information doctors and nurses think would be helpful, and then developing data capture and information analysis systems to meet these interests. Trial projects have included work on clinical budgeting, on nursing cost and management information systems, and on case-mix costing, i.e. the costing of the treatment of individual patients, or of patients classified by similar diagnostic conditions and likely treatment costs (e.g. patient diagnosis related groups (DRGs) – see Perrin (1988)).

Even before the results of the initial trials of the resource management approach had been completed or evaluated, the government determined to give it a high priority in NHS managerial reforms and in the allocation of financial support for improved management information systems in the NHS. Under the label of the 'Resource Management Initiative' (RMI) new management information projects were planned and launched. Meanwhile, the experience of the first six trial sites was being monitored by researchers from Brunel University. Their final report (Packwood et al., 1991) concluded that even after four years of development of the resource management approach at the trial sites, it was still not possible to confirm major success in improving the quality of local resource use and control. However, it was felt that the experience of being involved in the resource management *process* had led to positive changes in attitudes to the organization of work and use of resources. Against this must be set the very high cost of the infrastructure of computer systems which have been introduced to support RMI.

The measurement and reporting, let alone the control, of costs in the NHS is a complex matter. The product output of treated patients is clinically classifiable within a range of some 10 000 conditions (i.e. products). The ideal is to be able to predict and monitor the cost of treatment of individual patients, but the feasibility of this is for the long term. The approach is called 'case mix costing' and appears to be of great interest to many NHS doctors, nurses and other professionals. The first need in moving towards accurate case mix costing is to have much more accurate recording, and timely reporting, of the real/physical consumption of resources for each patient. Once real resource consumption is known, costing is relatively easy, as it simply involves using the computer to multiply resource use by agreed input prices, coded both to the individual patients as outputs/products, and

Table 8.1 Budget report for surgical team or specialty

	Current month			Year to date		
	Budget	Actual	Variance	Budget	Actual	Variance
Staff costs controlled by team						
Medical staff costs	10 998	10 697	-301	54 990	53 166	-1024
Other exp controlled by team						
Prescribed drugs	12 499	12 014	-485	62 495	58 712	-3783
Histopathology – consumables	290	248	-42	1450	1193	-257
Radiology – consumables	7697	9016	1319	40 837	44 808	3971
Operating theatre consumables	7283	7892	609	36 415	38 878	2463
Total costs controlled by team	38 767	39 867	1100	197 187	196 757	570
Costs influenced by team						
Ward – consumables	4166	5152	986	20 830	22 584	1754
Outpatient – consumables	83	149	66	415	495	80
Ward – overheads	11 572	10 983	-589	57 860	58 592	732
Outpatient – overheads	41	193	152	205	452	247
Pharmacy – overheads	1565	1782	217	7825	8571	746
Histopathology – overheads	833	814	-19	4165	4046	-119
Operating theatre – overheads	8208	7932	-276	41 040	40 643	-397
ECG – overheads	4107	4182	75	20 535	21 916	1381
Physiotherapy – hydrotherapy	15 485	15 654	169	77 425	75 296	-2129
Total costs influenced by team	46 060	46 841	781	230 300	232 595	2295

General services overheads

Unit administration	2499	−238	12 495	11 236	−1259
Catering	973	55	4865	5386	521
Domestic	1219	−402	6095	3932	−2163
Linen/laundry	832	114	4160	4701	541
Estate management	7499	−746	37 495	35 388	−2107
Total general serv. overheads	13 022	−1217	65 110	60 643	−4467
Total costs for team	97 849	664	491 597	489 995	−1602

Memorandum statistics

Inpatients – days	857	21	4285	4382	97
Outpatients – attendances	148	45	740	849	109
Histopathology – tests	499	−203	2495	2650	155
Radiology – tests	473	209	2801	3690	889
Operating theatre – hours	599	35	2995	3286	291

Preliminary draft report, with simulated figures, from the CASPE Project at Lewisham and N. Southwark Health Authority, by permission.

to the budget holders accountable for the consumption of resources/
inputs. It has been estimated that at least 80% of the cost of IT (i.e.
the computerized information systems) in the NHS relates to tracking
the use of real resources, or other clinical information needs, and
only 20% or less of the IT cost relates directly to the accounting and
financial control processing and use of the management information
provided.

Once accurate historical and predictive information for the costing
of individual patients is available, this can of course be aggregated by
individual consultant doctor, by diagnostic group of patients, by firm
or specialty, or by ward or hospital, as needed for financial planning,
control, and output pricing. But the case mix costing and pricing of
the care of individual patients, generated routinely from IT systems
as distinct from expert estimates made on the back of an envelope,
is some years away.

Meanwhile, for the introduction of the internal market, the standard system of pricing for contracts appears to be based on specialty
costing, although with some attempt to subdivide specialties into major
diagnostic or treatment categories for greater sensitivity in analysis
and pricing. For most NHS treatments only a small fraction of the
total costs consists of drugs, surgical appliances and supplies directly
traceable to the individual patient. A high proportion of NHS costs
are fixed costs, although many of these may be directly allocable to
specific wards or personnel treating identifiable patients or providing
support activities (e.g. X-rays). Nevertheless, at the present state of
the art of cost tracing and charging in the NHS, only a small proportion of cost is chargeable to specialties with a high degree of accuracy, and capable of being confirmed as accurate by audit. The large
balance of indirect and overhead costs has to be charged/apportioned
by judgement. Judgement can differ between individuals, and it can
vary widely from one DMU/Trust to another for both rational and
irrational causes. It follows that, until workload and resource-use
measurement reporting systems are considerably improved, locally
calculated costs of treatment for individual specialties, let alone for
any further disaggregation to diagnostic groups or individual patients,
must be highly suspect as to their accuracy, and thus as to their
reliability and relevance for internal market pricing. Until these costing
problems are overcome, it may be the best solution, howevermuch
second-best, for internal market pricing to be based mainly on DH
national average specialty costs, subject to any market bargaining
discounts negotiated thereon.

SUMMARY

NHS accounting and finance is in a state of change. The government
objective is for rapid change, to bring most aspects of commercial

accounting into use in the NHS to facilitate service pricing, resources control, and performance accountability in the new internal market which differentiates the separate roles of purchasers and providers of health care. The most radical accountancy innovation is the introduction of capital asset accounting and depreciation on an index-linked current cost replacement/market value basis. The most radical policy innovations are the creation of NHS Trusts and GP Fundholding budgets. A general election will be held before this new edition is published. If the present government is re-elected, the recent reforms seem likely to be pressed forward with renewed vigour. And there is little doubt that management information computerization and more refined cost and budgetary systems will continue to develop and evolve, indefinitely and expensively.

FURTHER READING

The effects of the recent NHS reforms on accounting and finance in the NHS are covered concisely in the *Introductory Guide to NHS Finance* (HFM/CIPFA, 1991), while NHS management accounting is treated in some depth in *Resource Management in the NHS* (Perrin, 1988). Updated technical information on NHS accounting and finance is available from volume 30 of CIPFA's *Financial Information Service*. News coverage of the latest developments is best obtained from the weekly *Public Finance and Accountancy* and *Health Service Journal*. There are occasional articles on health services financial topics in academic accounting journals, especially *Financial Accountability and Management* and *Public Money and Management*.

9

External audit

This chapter discusses the external audit of public sector bodies, its nature and its objectives. Comparisons will be made with the audit of companies and other organizations in the private sector. There will be discussion of recent developments in public sector audit and of the differing views which have emerged about its proper scope and organization. There will be no attempt to give instruction in detailed audit techniques: for that a specialized professional training is necessary.

INTRODUCTION

It has already been shown that the public sector in the UK comprises a variety of organizations, but the main divisions of the sector into central government, local authorities and nationalized industries and other public corporations will be followed in examining the role of audit. Before examining the three main areas, it is necessary to be clear about the essential nature of an external audit. What is it? What is it for?

The clues to the answers to these questions lie in the words 'external' and 'independent'. In the UK public sector, an external audit is intended first to provide an assurance as to the reliability of the published accounts of the audited body. Second, it is intended to provide a further assurance as to the regularity of the underlying transactions. Third, in the central and local government sectors but not the nationalized industries, it aims to provide an assessment of the efficiency and effectiveness with which the body performs its functions. The auditor provides these assurances and assessments from the standpoint of someone outside the body in question and independent of it. The auditor's examinations and reports are expected to be honest, impartial, dispassionate, indeed fearless, as well, it is to be hoped, as expert and thorough. The independence of the external auditor is crucial if his/her reports are to have credibility and authority. How such independence may be secured is discussed below.

This brief definition of external audit leads immediately to two further questions. First, to whom are these assurances about financial or other matters, provided by this independent character, to be addressed? Second, what is the relationship between external and internal auditors? An answer to the second question can conveniently wait. The answer to the first depends on the constitutional position of the audited body: to whom is it answerable for its actions? A government department is answerable through its minister and accounting officer (see below) directly to Parliament. A nationalized industry is answerable to the responsible minister and then to Parliament on its general performance, but not on its day-to-day operations. A local authority is constitutionally independent of Parliament but can do only what Parliament empowers it to do. While Parliament acts on behalf of national electors and taxpayers and is distinct from the Executive – i.e. the central government – local authorities act on behalf of local electors and ratepayers in both a representative and an executive capacity. It follows that the external auditor of a government department reports to Parliament, the auditor of a nationalized industry to the Secretary of State, and the auditor of local authorities to the authority itself. In doing so, however, they always have in mind the interests of the general public, particularly their interests as the providers of the funds to pay for public services, and all these audit reports are normally publicly available.

The public audit services of most advanced countries set out to provide, in very broad terms, a financial audit of accounts and an efficiency or value for money audit of activities. The first of these centres on the adequacy of the systems for controlling the receipt and payment of public funds, the second on the way the resources purchased with those funds – manpower, capital equipment, buildings, supplies and so on – are allocated and utilized.

The term audit is sometimes applied to a different type of external check; for example, a 'social audit', advocated by some people, would attempt to establish how far public institutions, and indeed large private corporations, had contributed to social, community or similar goals. We are not concerned here with these wider remits as such, though social considerations often play a part in public expenditure decisions and must be recognized and allowed for by the auditor. The critical examination of financial and resource management is a convenient general description of much of the auditor's activity.

AUDIT OF CENTRAL GOVERNMENT

THE STATUTORY BASIS

The law which for many years governed the external audit of central government, and still provides the basic authority for some of it, was the Exchequer and Audit Departments Act of 1866, as modified, in significant but not fundamental respects, by the 1921 Act. The 1866 Act brought together, under the newly created office of the Comptroller and Auditor General, the duties formerly discharged separately by the Comptroller General of the Exchequer, whose origins went back for several centuries, and Commissioners of Audit. It was part of the nineteenth-century reforms intended to give Parliament an effective and unified control over the use of public revenues. At that time the largest spenders of those revenues were the Army and the Navy, and what was then called the Office of Works and Public Building. The Act provided for the appointment, by the Crown, of the Comptroller and Auditor General (whose full title is Comptroller General of the Receipt and Issue of Her Majesty's Exchequer and Auditor General of Public Accounts), but it did not give a separate statutory existence to the department, the Exchequer and Audit Department. It provided instead (as amended in 1921) that the C&AG might appoint staff who would assist him in carrying out the statutory responsibilities for the examination, certification and reporting on government departments' accounts[1]. The C&AG thus took personal responsibility for all the work of his officers, and until the 1970s signed personally the audit certificate and report on virtually every account which the department audited. This contrasts with the arrangements in private auditing firms, where each partner manages the audit of his or her own clients' accounts, or in local government where each district or commercial auditor is responsible by law for auditing and reporting on particular local authorities' accounts.

The C&AG has usually been appointed from outside the Department, with a wide experience of public expenditure and finance provided by service as a top departmental official, and has not been a professional auditor or accountant. Appointment of someone with the latter kind of background would be possible, but since public audit is by no means confined to the financial audit of accounts and demands a close knowledge of the operations of Parliament and of the departments of state, it is clearly desirable that the person in charge should be familiar with public finance and with the problems of managing large departments and securing the best use of very large sums of public money.

The independence of the C&AG, and thus of all his staff, is secured by his appointment by the Queen, on the advice of the Prime Minister, by the payment of his salary directly from the Consolidated Fund, not from annual Votes, and by his/her freedom from dismissal

1 Author's note: Most references to the C&AG are in the masculine gender, even where this is not essential for statutory reasons or historical accuracy. I hope that those readers who would prefer 'he/she' throughout will allow their enthusiasm for reiterated expression of a non-sexist policy (a policy I of course support) to be tempered by the virtue of more fluent and readable drafting.

except on a motion passed by both Houses of Parliament. The C&AG does not answer to any minister of the government, and indeed, although he works on behalf of Parliament, makes most of his reports to Parliament, and is now under the National Audit Act 1983 (see below) an officer of the House of Commons; he cannot be instructed by the House, or by any of its Committees, to undertake particular investigations. Thus within the broad statutory framework governing the audit the C&AG decides how to lay out the resources of his staff, how to conduct the audit work, and what reports to make.

The audit of government departments can be divided into two sectors: the financial, more strictly the certification, audit, and the value for money audit. The basis for the certification audit was laid down in the 1866 Act, which established the arrangements by which the executive – the government – should account for the public revenues they raised and the public funds they spent. Much of the Act dealt with accounting procedures and responsibilities, but its main provisions, which still apply, can be simply summarized. Departments were required to prepare annually 'appropriation accounts' showing how the sums voted by Parliament for specific purposes and services had been spent. The C&AG had to examine and certify these accounts and report thereon to Parliament. If the Treasury failed to present to Parliament by the due date any report by the C&AG, then the C&AG was empowered to do so. This power has never had to be invoked.

Moving forward over 50 years, the Exchequer and Audit Departments Act of 1921 modified and updated the 1866 Act in three respects. First the C&AG was allowed to dispense with the 100% audit of transactions which appeared to be required by the original Act, though it must be highly doubtful whether for many years before 1921 anything of this order had been achieved, or even attempted. Instead the C&AG was given discretion to have regard to the departments' own examination in deciding the extent of the check of transactions. Though not specifically mentioned in the Act, the concept of a 'test audit' was thus established. The way in which test audits should be carried out, to give a reasonable degree of assurance about the particular accounting systems to which they are applied, is an important aspect of audit techniques. It has led into the systems-based audit and the use of statistical sampling where large numbers of transactions are involved, and its application is having to be rethought with the rapid extension of computerized accounting systems and auditing software.

Second, the 1921 Act provided for the preparation and audit in suitable cases of trading, manufacturing or production accounts as well as the cash-based appropriation accounts. Trading accounts are prepared on a similar basis to private sector commercial accounts, with balance sheets and sources and application of funds statements, and are fully accrued.

The third innovation in 1921 was to require the C&AG to examine the revenue departments' accounts (Inland Revenue, Customs and Excise) as well as those of the spending departments. But there is an important difference. The C&AG is expected to be satisfied, and to assure Parliament and the public, about the regularity of the appropriation accounts. In the audit of the Revenue Departments, however, the C&AG is required to be satisfied only that the departments have established satisfactory procedures for the assessment and collection of all revenue due. The C&AG is not required to certify that all revenue which should have been collected has been, still less that individual taxpayers have been correctly assessed for tax. That would indeed have been an impossible task. This approach appears to be an early formulation of a 'systems-based audit', antedating by several decades the general adoption of that technique in both commercial and public audit work.

No further change in the law governing the C&AG's work occurred for another 60 years. But it was progressively developed on a non-statutory basis, particularly in the value for money field, with the active encouragement of Parliament through the Public Accounts Committee (see below) and the acquiescence of government departments. In the late 1970s and early 1980s an upsurge of Parliamentary interest in the public audit system coinciding with a new approach by the C&AG to his role and the responsibilities of his department led to a wide ranging debate and to the National Audit Act of 1983. The main strands in that debate are discussed below, but it is convenient to conclude this section with a summary of the main provisions of the 1983 Act.

The Act provided that:

1. The C&AG should continue to be appointed by Her Majesty on a motion for an address by the House of Commons made by the Prime Minister, whose advice now, however, had to be tendered in agreement with the Chairman of the Committee of Public Accounts (PAC), recognizing the close interest of Parliament in the person, as well as the office.

2. The C&AG should be an officer of the House of Commons; but – subject of course to his statutory duties – should have 'complete discretion in the discharge of his functions including in particular whether and how to carry out a '3E's' type examination under the Act' (see 5. and 6. below). In taking such decisions, however, the C&AG was required to 'take into account any proposals made by the Committee of Public Accounts'. So was resolved the argument whether the C&AG should be subject to the directions of the PAC or, as some members of Parliament would have liked, also of other select committees.

3. A Public Accounts Commission should be set up, to include the Leader of the House and the Chairman of the PAC, with the functions of:
    (a) examining and presenting to the House of Commons the financial estimates for the National Audit Office, modified or not, for which purpose the Commission was to have regard to any advice given by the PAC and the Treasury;
    (b) appointing the Accounting Officer for the National Audit Office;
    (c) appointing an auditor for the National Audit Office, who would have power to carry out economy, efficiency and effectiveness examinations of its use of resources.
4. A National Audit Office should be set up, headed by the C&AG and consisting of such staff appointed by him as he considered necessary 'for assisting him in the discharge of his functions'; their remuneration and other conditions of service also to be decided by the C&AG, thus ending the Treasury's powers in these respects.
5. The C&AG should have a discretionary power to carry out examinations of the economy, efficiency and effectiveness with which government departments and other bodies subject to his audit or inspection used their resources, without, however, being entitled to question the merits of their policy **objectives**, and to report to the House the results of such examinations (author's emphasis).
6. The C&AG should have power to carry out 3E's examinations in any body (except the nationalized industries and certain other public authorities) whose members were appointed by the Crown and where there was reasonable cause to believe that more than half its income came from public funds: thus was resolved the argument as to whether the C&AG should have the right 'to follow public money wherever it goes'.

The Act also repealed a provision of the 1866 Act relating to the appropriation accounts, to allow for some flexibility in the year of account, to speed up certification and presentation; and it removed or amended certain powers by which the Treasury could require the C&AG to carry out particular investigations.

THE OBJECTIVES OF THE FINANCIAL AUDIT

The financial audit of government departments is intended to give an assurance that in all material respects:

1. their accounts properly present the transactions to which they relate;
2. they have spent the money voted to them only for the purposes intended by Parliament, as described in the Estimates and Supplementary Estimates presented at the beginning of each financial year and subsequently; and

3. the expenditure conforms to the authority governing it, i.e. has met the requirements of 'regularity'.

In even plainer words, this means that the money provided by Parliament has been spent as intended, that no unlawful, improper or irregular payments have been made, and that the figures are satisfactory.

These simple-sounding objectives conceal some complex problems for the C&AG and his staff. Although the basic form of the appropriation accounts is simple – cash spent in the year compared with cash voted – the figures in the final accounts run into billions of pounds for all the major departments, and they represent and summarize not only very large numbers of transactions but also very complex purchasing, construction, contracting and staffing operations. The building of hospitals, the design and development of advanced military equipment, the installation of large computer systems, the payment of many millions of social security benefits each week, are just a few of these highly diverse activities. It is therefore a major technical audit task to check that the accounting and financial control systems underlying the figures in the account are reliable and efficient. This work is necessarily done on a selective basis and increasingly utilizes techniques, such as statistical sampling and the evaluation and testing of systems, similar to those applied by commercial auditors in the audit of large private sector concerns.

To check that government spending conforms with the specific terms of statutes, for example that financial assistance given by the Department of Industry to private firms is in accordance with the broad conditions laid down in the Industry Act or other governing legislation, does not in practice raise many difficult problems, or usually take much time. But the audit of regularity extends a good way beyond this. Detailed rules and regulations are often drawn up, under the authority of the governing Acts themselves, to set out the exact conditions and criteria which have to be met if people or companies are to be entitled to various types of state payments. The largest, but by no means the only, services of this kind are social security, and agricultural and industrial assistance schemes. Some social security benefits are payable only if the applicant has made sufficient national insurance contributions. To be entitled to unemployment benefit, a person has to be 'genuinely seeking work'. To qualify for a hill farming subsidy, a farmer may have to maintain his sheep for sufficient periods above certain altitudes. To qualify for an industrial grant, a company may have to build a factory within particular areas and equip it for specified industrial purposes. These rules and regulations can be voluminous, complex and open in some cases to arguments about interpretation. They may take the form of 'subordinate legislation', for example a statutory instrument which has to be laid before, and in some cases approved by, Parliament. They may simply be departmental rules, sometimes approved by the Treasury, sometimes not, which the responsible Minister is entitled to lay down by administrative action.

Very large sums of public money are disbursed under systems of this kind. As a matter of just and efficient administration people should get what they are entitled to, and not more. It is the duty of the National Audit Office, as part of their regularity audit, to check that departments are applying such rules correctly. They will do so selectively, and with regard, as in all their work, for the relative importance, or materiality, of the various areas of expenditure. They may find that some rules are prone to cause errors because they are overcomplicated or unclear. They may find that officials have made payments which, through an honest but excessive exercise of their initiative, bend the rules unduly. They may even come to the view that a scheme, let us say for paying farmers to drain or fence certain types of land, is so complex that it takes too much manpower to administer and might with advantage be replaced by a simpler one.

With the exception of the last, all these illustrations relate to the concept of regularity of expenditure. Similar examples can be found in other government programmes, for example the rules governing the distribution of funds to promote the arts, or sport, or research. Such functions as these are often entrusted to special bodies or councils, subject to rules and guidance by their parent departments: the Arts Council under the Department of National Heritage, the Medical Research Council under the Department of Health, and so on. In such cases as these the rules to which they have to work will be relatively simple, unlike those governing social security schemes, which run into many volumes. But they are further aspects of the way in which regularity, in matters of government spending, is defined.

It is to these features of the accounts – accuracy of the figures, legality and regularity of the transactions – that the C&AG's certificate to Parliament exclusively relates. It is sometimes called the 'attest' function of an audit. It gives independent assurance, within approved standards, that the audited body has properly presented its financial transactions in its accounts and has conformed to the rules governing them. In principle this kind of audit can be, and is, applied to a wide range of bodies, from international organizations, such as the Food and Agriculture Organization or the World Health Organization of the United Nations, to the local cricket club, as well as to government departments.

The essential point with which to close this part of the discussion is that the financial or certification audit, constitutionally important as it is, has limited objectives in the assessment of operational efficiency. It is true that the analysis of government activities and expenditure which is a necessary part of a well-conducted financial audit may well lead into wider studies. It is also the case that an evaluation of financial control and information systems is likely to be of value not only for certification purposes but to judge a department's progress in the development of effective internal management systems. But other operational audit techniques, conveniently subsumed in the term 'value for money audit', need to be developed. Before discussing them, it is first necessary to make a brief digression into the field of commercial accounting and audit.

COMMERCIAL AND GOVERNMENT ACCOUNTING

Government spends money and uses large resources of manpower to provide a wide variety of services to the community: defence, health, support for industry and agriculture, social security, and many others. For the most part these services are not paid for directly by those who benefit from them. Some charges, such as those for medical prescriptions, or for use of the Severn bridge or Dartford tunnel, are made; but the former covers only a small part of the cost and most of the services are not provided with a commercial motive – to make a profit.

It is true that a relatively small part of the activities of government departments or closely related bodies is commercial in its nature and aims. The Royal Mint, as well as manufacturing the coin of the realm, which is 'sold' to the Treasury under rather special arrangements, also manufactures and sells coins and medals for overseas customers and is expected to cover its costs and charge market prices for this business. Her Majesty's Stationery Office publishes and sells many official documents and reports, if not at a profit at any rate with the intention of recovering the cost. The national museums run shops for their prints, replicas and so on where they aim to break even or do better. The special accounts for these activities are themselves commercial in style; they present their results in essentially the same way as an industrial or trading company, and they are audited accordingly. But in the scale of government activities as a whole, this kind of activity is relatively small.

Commercial accounts are intended to show the results of trading operations over the year, and the financial state of the business – more specifically its net book value – at the end of each year. To do so, both income and expenditure have to be assessed as accurately as possible, which is a more complex task than simply logging-up cash payments and receipts. Income has to take account of sums due in respect of various activities and attributable to the year in question; expenditure has to include amounts representing the proportion of the firm's assets, stocks and work in progress used up in producing the year's income; provisions against future loss or liabilities have to be assessed, and so on. When to these calculations it is necessary to add an assessment of the effect of inflation on the firm's profit and asset valuations, through the application of current cost accounting, the production and audit of the accounts of any sizeable commercial concern is a considerable exercise, involving acts of judgement as well as of record and classification.

This brief sketch of commercial accounting is intended only as background to two points. First, as mentioned above, there are some government activities which can and should be presented and accounted for in this way. They include not only the production and sale of a range of goods, from coins and medals to prints of medieval manuscripts, but also, for example, the provision of supplies to departments, where it is thought desirable to work out the 'full cost' on some appropriate type of commercial accounting, to assist control and to promote the right decisions. Pressure is also growing for some form of accounts which recognize the consumption of capital where this is an important feature of the use of resources, for example in NHS hospitals. And the establishment of 'executive agencies' within central government will substantially extend the area in which commercial accounting concepts will need to be applied to help judge their performance.

The second point is a wider and crucial one. The making of profit or loss, and the increase or decrease each year in the value of a business, are critical tests of its success or failure. They measure the extent to which it achieves its essential objectives. There may be others. A firm which contributes to social progress or cultural achievement, which makes its staff happy in their work, or sponsors a tennis tournament, may earn applause for doing so. Its far-sighted directors may well judge that there are also likely to be financial benefits. But if it consistently fails in the primary task of profit making, it is unlikely to survive, short of government rescue, for long. None of this applies, clearly, to government departments providing or promoting the large communal services of defence, education, health, law and order, and so on. Their efficiency, their performance, their success has to be judged by quite different tests, and by quite different methods.

VALUE FOR MONEY AUDIT

This is the field in which the public audit services seek to apply the concepts now broadly known as value for money or efficiency auditing. They do not displace the audit of accuracy in accounting or of propriety and regularity of transactions described earlier. They complement and extend it, and require different techniques. Good financial auditors have produced useful value for money reports on a wide range of financial management matters. Such work can also be satisfactorily done by people without professional accountancy or audit training if they have the right aptitudes and approach.

The prime responsibility for achieving value for money or efficiency is the management's and not the public auditor's. Senior civil servants, and ultimately their ministers, are responsible and are held accountable for all their actions in running and managing their departments. But the C&AG and his staff play their same independent role in assessing and where necessary criticizing the performance of the bodies they audit in these respects as they do in what may be described as the more formal financial audit field. They thus promote two distinct objectives: accountability of the executive government to Parliament and, it is hoped, its efficiency and effectiveness.

The terms 'value for money' and 'efficiency audit' are not terms of art, still less precise definitions. Value for money audit was commonly used in the UK as a convenient description of the evolving interests and work of E&AD over many decades, with its origin sometimes pinpointed at the year 1888 when there was an interesting confrontation between the C&AG and the Army Council over a little matter of contracts for Army medal ribbon, from which the former emerged the winner. The argument was whether the C&AG should have extended the examination of Army expenditure beyond the accepted matters of conformity with Parliamentary authorization into the area of economy in contracts. The C&AG owed success largely to the support of the Public Accounts Committee of the House of Commons, established in 1861, whose present role is described below. Over the succeeding century the C&AG developed the application of value for money audit into many aspects of the financial management of government departments, with a marked acceleration in scale and coverage from the early 1950s, as the great post-war surge in government activity and the corresponding expenditure programmes gathered weight.

Traditionally this work focused on 'the elimination of waste and extravagance'. Within recent years the wider role of national audit offices has been more closely analysed and defined in a way which now has widespread international recognition. The General Accounting Office of the USA is usually credited with formulating, and publicizing, the three-fold division into economy, efficiency and effectiveness audit.

In this context economy is taken to mean the achievement of a given result with the least expenditure of money, manpower or other resources, while efficiency imports the idea of converting resources into a desired product in the most advantageous ratio. But this is sometimes a rather subtle distinction, and the more important divide is between the pursuit and audit of economy and efficiency on the one hand and of effectiveness on the other, because the latter brings into account the goals or objectives which the activity in question is intended to meet.

The examination of effectiveness in government and other public sector programmes and policies raises issues which are often intractable and sometimes controversial. The development or purchase of nuclear weapons is intended to contribute to the goal of national security. The extension of comprehensive education is intended to

promote education and social aims. The introduction of family income support was hoped to secure a minimum standard of living for
the families of low-paid workers in employment. Subsidies for defined
forms of industrial investment aimed to encourage the development
of particular parts of the country, and reduce unemployment. The
transformation of the old employment exchanges into job centres and
their siting in the high street had a similar aim. These cases and a
great many more raise the following questions:

1. should the auditor be involved in effectiveness at all?
2. if so, does this not bring the auditor to question policy decisions?
3. has the auditor the necessary skills?

Parliament decided, in the National Audit Act and the Local Government Finance Act 1982, that the audit of both central and local
government should cover effectiveness. In this respect, so far at least
as central government operations are concerned, the United Kingdom
has lined up with the legislatures of the United States, the Nether-
lands and Sweden among others, while the Australians, for example,
have decided otherwise.

The question of the involvement of the external auditor in policy
questions is a sensitive one. It is for those running an organization,
and answerable for its results, to take and defend policy decisions, for
example to develop a new civil aircraft, to build a new comprehensive
school, or to broadcast news in English to various parts of the world.
But the auditor may feel it necessary and justifiable:

1. to question whether the goals which the policy decisions are meant
   to serve have been established;
2. to examine whether managements have themselves established
   adequate procedures and criteria to assess the effectiveness of their
   policies;
3. to quantify the costs of the decisions taken;
4. to report on whether the goals have in fact been achieved;
5. to suggest alternative ways in which the goals might have been
   more effectively met.

This is a formidable list of possibilities. Few national auditors regard the whole lot as within their remit; probably only the General
Accounting Office of the USA covers 5. The Australian and Canadian
Auditors General are required to stop at 3. and do not go on to 4. or
5. All except 5. would be regarded in principle as within the remit of
the C&AG. But he would be circumspect and realistic in deciding
which particular government projects or programmes to examine in
this way. The C&AG would have in mind the degree of authority and
cogency his report was likely to have, and the impact it was likely to
make. The C&AG is not in business to study policy options, nor to
write academic studies. His object, in this part of the value for money

work, is to contribute to more effective decision-taking, and more efficient execution of policies, by reference to past and current experience, problems and mistakes.

Although it is useful to analyse value for money auditing as above, it is as well not to conceptualize too far. In the UK, at any rate, value for money audit has come to describe a wide variety of enquiries into central government operations, including the development and production of military equipment, the building of hospitals, factories and offices, the application of agricultural and industrial assistance, the design and installation of computer systems, charging policies for government services, use and disposal of land and control of civil service manpower. The C&AG's reports have concentrated on financial management in the broadest sense, including the management of contracts. They have also raised matters of organization, and the control of civil service manpower. They have not, however, extended into the field of operational research or work study. Some people find difficulty in accepting that the 'value' in value for money can be judged by an auditor. As in so much intellectual discourse it depends on what is meant by value. In the practice of public audit it is often necessary to stop short of an assessment of ultimate value, and be content with 'intermediate objectives'. But the questions 'what is to be achieved, by when, and at what cost?' are now supposed to be applied to all expenditure programmes, and NAO reports on the financial management initiative (FMI) and on financial reporting to Parliament assessed progress in these areas. To judge and to report whether performance has measured up to plans, budgets and intentions is certainly one main object of value for money audit.

Traditionally, most E&AD value for money reports had concentrated on individual examples of waste, contractual failings, inadequate planning, or other aspects of financial mismanagement. Such examinations were, however, by no means small in scale: the building of the Thames barrier, the refit of a warship, the construction of motorways or hospitals, and many other governmental operations cost many millions of pounds and require expert planning, contracting and financial control. Scope for shortcomings in one or more of the 3 E's was not lacking, either in major projects of this type or in smaller scale activities, ranging from university land holdings to the provision of meteorological information. Value for money audit was therefore nothing new to the C&AG and the E&AD, whose archives are full of such reports dating back many years.

Nevertheless it became clear in the later 1970s that further development of this work was necessary, and this has been achieved. In particular:

1. A much greater degree of 'top–down' planning and supervision was required to ensure that resources were efficiently used and prior-

ities established. Formerly, most value for money reports had emanated from the audit divisions, often though not exclusively as an offshoot of their financial audit work. This approach fostered and rewarded individual initiative, but could not ensure that the most significant areas were covered. A strategic planning system, looking five years ahead, now operates. Senior management is involved in the choice and conduct of all major studies.

2. Wider studies of departmental operations, including their systems for financial control and the provision and use of management information, needed to be made. From the early 1980s studies looked at programmes, schemes, major activities and whole organizations in a much broader way than formerly. Examples include the C&AG's reports on the development of nuclear power, the monitoring and control of nationalized industries, the housing benefit scheme, the control of NHS nursing manpower, and the financial control and accountability of the metropolitan police.

3. Some subjects important for government efficiency and of interest to Parliament could only be effectively studied by investigating the practice of several government departments. Examples have been the organization and use of internal audit, the Rayner scrutiny programmes, financial reporting to Parliament, the financial management initiative, and computer security in government departments.

4. The E&AD needed to extend their links with the departments and bodies they audited, to spread awareness of their own evolving aims, ideas and methods and to make their decisions on what to investigate and how to do so better informed. By long standing tradition, E&AD's relationship with departments had been markedly at arm's length, with the overriding aim of safeguarding the C&AG's independence. This has now changed and the NAO discuss with departments likely choices for studies. There are also regular contacts between the NAO and departmental finance officers.

5. New methods of value for money investigation, sometimes using skills additional to those of financial audit and applied by specially constituted teams, needed to be tried and assessed. These are now part of NAO's standard approach; academics and management consultants take part in VFM investigations.

To effect changes in these directions, to ensure high standards of financial audit, and to deal satisfactorily with staff recruitment, professional training, relations with other public audit bodies at home and abroad and with the private sector, the senior management of E&AD/NAO was expanded and strengthened, a central capability developed, and the methods of work of the whole office reviewed. Explicit auditing standards, covering both the financial and value-for-money work, were adopted and published.

Table 9.1 Main stages of a typical major audit investigation

Survey of main areas of expenditure and risk	1
Selection of area, programme or project for examination	2
Preliminary study to determine scope, objectives, time-scale and staffing of main exercise, and to prepare plans and work allocations	3
Main exercise carried out by auditor or audit team. Progress and results monitored as study proceeds	4
Results reviewed by senior staff; decisions taken on necessary action	5
Correspondence and discussion with audited body, leading up to draft report (if necessary)	6
Report approved by C&AG; sent to Accounting Officer for confirmation of fairness and accuracy	7
Considered by Committee of Public Accounts with evidence from audited bodies	8
Committee report published and presented to Parliament	9
Treasury Minute published in response to criticisms, comments and recommendations made; confirms remedial action taken or proposed	10
Consideration of Treasury Minute by Committee of Public Accounts, with further follow-up and report as necessary	11

The target time-scale for completion of stages 4–7 would normally not exceed 6–9 months, so as to maintain topicality and impact. Later stages might then occupy a further 39 months from the date of the Committee hearing, depending on the scale of the further examination and the nature of the Government's response to the matters raised.

Source: National Audit Office, by permission.

The new look to value for money work which emerged from these developments is well summarized in Table 9.1, an extract from the booklet published by the NAO in 1983 explaining the C&AG's role and the responsibilities of the Office.

It is worth considering how value for money audit relates to the Rayner studies mentioned in Chapter 4, to assignments undertaken by management consultants, and to the efficiency studies of nationalized industries commissioned by the government from the Monopolies and Mergers Commission or private accounting/consultancy firms. There are some similarities:

1. all such examinations proceed by rigorous assembly and analysis of evidence, both from documents and discussion;

2. every attempt is made to reach agreement with the body under
   examination on the factual adequacy and accuracy of material in
   the final report;
3. provisional conclusions are tested by the reactions of the body
   under examination and account taken of objections or counter
   arguments;
4. the objective is a fair, balanced report, making whatever criticisms
   and recommendations for improvement are thought to be justified,
   on the sole responsibility of the examining body.

But there are significant differences, both constitutional and meth-
odological.

1. The external auditor takes his or her own unfettered decisions as
   to when and what to examine and whether a public or other report
   will be made. Consultancies are by invitation of the client, who
   decides – in discussion with the consultant – the scope of the
   enquiry and how it is to be conducted. The report is an internal
   one. Monopolies and Mergers Commission (MMC) enquiries, or
   those undertaken by consultants on the invitation of the central
   government, are external to the body under examination and are
   normally published but are not self-initiated.
2. Major MMC or consultancy efficiency studies have been wide-
   ranging investigations into the operations of public bodies, leading
   to numerous conclusions and recommendations, sometimes dis-
   puted. An internal consultancy report is usually more narrowly
   defined and is to some extent judged by the acceptability of its
   recommendations to the client, who will have spent money on the
   study in an endeavour to improve efficiency and profitability. The
   C&AG's investigations into the efficiency of departments' use of
   resources are designed for further examination by Parliament under
   the arrangements described below. Local authority auditors and
   the Audit Commission have broadly followed the same approach,
   though they stress the comparative performance of local authorities
   and they have nothing comparable to the external influence of the
   Public Accounts Committee to strengthen their impact.
3. The Rayner studies are carried out internally by particular departments, using selected members of their own staff who examine in
   considerable detail a specific aspect of administration or policy,
   questioning both its objectives and its methods. They are supported
   by the small central efficiency unit and enjoy strong ministerial
   backing.

SPECIAL AUDIT FEATURES

There are three important parts of the central government sector
where special audit features apply, namely the National Health Service, the universities, and the new executive agencies.

The National Health Service

The National Health Service (NHS) is under the full control of the Secretary of State for Health and his department, the Department of Health (DH). Audit of the NHS is now shared between the C&AG and the Audit Commission for Local Authorities and the National Health Service in England and Wales. The C&AG is responsible for examining and certifying the summarized health authority accounts, which bring together the operations of all the individual authorities. But the C&AG's staff have full access to the books and records of all the health authorities, as well as those of the DH and the corresponding Scottish and Welsh Departments. The C&AG is therefore in a position to examine and report on all aspects of the financial control and management of the NHS and its constituent authorities. Reports on health service matters have featured largely in the C&AG's annual reports to Parliament. They have dealt for example with community care developments, the use of operating theatres, and the management of the family practitioner service.

It was suggested during the 1980–1 review of the C&AG's role (see below) that it would be desirable to bring the formal departmental auditors into the E&AD under the C&AG's direction, so that there would be a fully integrated audit service for the NHS. The PAC recommended in favour, but the government preferred not to disturb the existing arrangements. In several cases, however, the audit of health authorities had been placed by the DH with private accounting firms as part of the government's policy of increasing their participation in the audit of public services.

The Audit Commission's responsibility, which was conferred by the National Health Service and Community Care Act 1990 with effect from October 1990, is for appointing auditors for the individual health authorities and other bodies within the National Health Service. This work was previously done by 'statutory auditors', who were mainly civil servants of the Department of Health and the Welsh Office, although some were from private accounting firms. Many of the former statutory auditors and staff transferred to the Commission. As in the case of local government the Commission has increased the share of audit appointments given to private firms to 30%. The remaining 70% of appointments are of its own staff.

The legislation transferring the audit function provided for, or enabled, the Commission's approach to local government audit (see below) to be applied to the health authorities also. A new audit code of practice, covering both local authorities and the health service bodies, has been prepared and approved by Parliament. The Commission is also undertaking studies and has published reports on day surgery, pathology, sterile supplies, estate management and energy saving. There are, however, some points of difference between the powers and responsibilities of the Commission and its auditors in the National Health Service compared with local government. The Commission's powers to carry out studies under Section 27 of the Local Government Finance Act 1982 of matters at the interface with central government do not apply in the health service, although in the course of its studies under Section 26(i) the Commission may take into account the implementation by health service bodies of particular statutory provisions or directions or guidance given by the Secretary of State; these powers expressly do not entitle the Commission to question the merits of policy objectives of the Secretary of State.

There are no public rights to ask questions of the auditor or to make objections about the accounts of health bodies. Nor do the auditor's powers to deal with illegality or losses caused by wilful misconduct apply; instead the auditor must report such matters to the Secretary of State.

The universities

Most of the funds provided to the universities, for both capital and current expenditure, come from the Exchequer. They are distributed by the Secretary of State for Education to individual universities on the advice of the Universities Funding Council (formerly the University Grants Commission). The accounts of the universities themselves are audited by commercial auditors and until 1967 the C&AG had no access to their records or responsibility to report on their affairs. This reflected the view, since proved unfounded, that to involve him would be prejudicial to the universities' autonomy and a possible threat to academic freedom. After sustained pressure from the PAC the government agreed in 1967 to allow the C&AG to inspect the universities' books and to report as he saw fit on their financial management. Since then the C&AG has made many such reports, and it has become generally accepted that the provision of large sums of public money justifies this extra measure of public accountability.

It should be noted that an 'inspection audit' of this kind provides the NAO with the necessary information for examining and if necessary reporting on value for money matters affecting an organization, even though the financial audit is carried out by other auditors. The universities are the most important example of an inspection audit but there are many others in the central government area. As already noted, the 1983 Act authorizes the C&AG to conduct inspection audits in certain bodies receiving at least half their income from public funds.

Executive agencies

The establishment of a large number of executive agencies as a feature of the 'Next Steps' arrangements will bring an expansion in the number of commercial-style accounts produced within central government. All agencies will be required to publish annual accounts audited by the C&AG and annual reports which include the accounts, together with sufficient performance information to form the basis for judging whether the agencies have achieved the objectives set for them by the responsible minister. External audit by the NAO will have an important part to play here.

So far as financial audit is concerned, the examination will need to cover such aspects as the agencies' performance against key financial targets required to be reported in the notes to their accounts; to ensure, by analogy with the directors' report for a Companies Act company, that the information in their annual report is consistent with that included in the accounts; and to verify that measures used as the basis for performance-related pay or bonuses or any other significant expenditure are accurate. Should the Citizens' Charter develop in such a way that public sector bodies have to pay redress in the event of their not meeting performance targets, there will also be a role for the external auditor in examining the basis for such payments. Taken individually, these aspects of financial audit are not new or unique, but overall they are likely to represent a significant part of the arrangements for demonstrating the agencies' accountability to Parliament.

There is also the question of the extent to which non-financial performance information should be subject to independent external examination. Such information purports to give government and Parliament a picture of the effectiveness with which agencies have used their resources in pursuit of their goals; and it seems reasonable to expect it to be subject to independent verification to ensure, for example, that the performance measures adopted are relevant and central to their activities, that the information is materially accurate, and that measures are not selected or dropped from year to year depending on the marks scored. This will be a developing area of interest for the NAO as the agencies themselves establish their own style of management.

INTERNAL AND EXTERNAL AUDIT

Most large organizations, in both the public and private sectors, have their own internal audit arrangements. The essential difference between internal and external audit is that the former is part of the management, is organized and directed and reports as senior management decides, whereas the latter is completely independent and, subject to the law, decides these matters for itself. Internal audit is intended to contribute to the probity and efficiency of the enterprise from within; external audit shares this objective, operating from outside, but also serves the further objective of external accountability. The scope of the work of internal audit staff may therefore be wide or narrow, varying from straightforward matters of internal financial control to a remit virtually as wide as that of the C&AG. The staff are nowadays likely to be led by, and to contain a growing proportion of, professionally qualified people. Some concern has been expressed in recent years about the quality of the approach and work of internal audit in both public and private bodies, and both central and local government are taking steps to raise its standards and improve its effectiveness. This is a matter of considerable interest to external auditors; despite the significant constitutional difference in the two roles it is generally accepted that the measure of independence which ought to be given to internal auditors within the public authority or firm should justify external auditors in relying on their work where they are satisfied that it meets the necessary professional standards. Subject to this essential condition an agreed division of labour between internal and external audit is accepted as a sensible and economical arrangement.

REPORTING TO PARLIAMENT: THE ROLE OF THE PUBLIC ACCOUNTS COMMITTEE

External auditors do not address their reports to the bodies they audit, except in the case of local authorities. In the case of companies, auditors reports to the shareholders, not to the directors. In the case of government departments, the C&AG reports to Parliament, not to ministers. The C&AG and his staff may, and often do, bring to the notice of government departments various matters which appear to need action but do not merit a public report. But that is part of the normal constructive relationship which ought to exist between the two organizations.

By long tradition the reports of the C&AG are considered by the Committee of Public Accounts (PAC) of the House of Commons. The Committee's terms of reference empower them to examine any of the accounts which are laid before Parliament. It should be noted that this gives the Committee a considerably wider remit than that of the C&AG. For example, all the annual reports and accounts of the nationalized industries and other public corporations are laid before Parliament, and could therefore be examined by the PAC, even though the C&AG is not the auditor of most of them. In practice, an understanding was reached that the PAC would leave the examination of the nationalized industries to the former Select Committee on Nationalized Industries – not so far (1992) replaced by any one comparable select committee.

The PAC does not nowadays spend much time on matters of financial irregularity or constitutional impropriety. There are not many of them, and most which do occur are not of sufficient seriousness to warrant intervention by the Committee. Serious fraud cases, fortunately rare in central government administration, certainly engage their attention, as might a failure by a department to secure Parliamentary authority for expenditure. But most of the Committee's work is based on the C&AG's value-for-money reports on financial management, and in deciding which matters merit a report the C&AG has much in mind the likely interest of the subject to the Committee and the prospect of useful recommendations for improvement arising from their enquiries.

NAO staff have full access, not only to the accounts of departments but also to all papers and documents relevant to the departments' administration that may reasonably be required for the purposes of a value-for-money audit. They can thus form their own independent judgement of the merits or shortcomings of departmental action; they are not dependent on government officials to produce their version of events. In the preparation of draft reports care is taken to establish a solid basis of fact upon which the C&AG can take a decision whether to report or not. If the C&AG does decide to report the departmental accounting officer concerned is given an opportunity to comment on the report whose accuracy as to fact is thereafter seldom challenged.

The method of the PAC's own examination is also of special significance. By long tradition, when they decide to take evidence on matters raised in the C&AG's reports they summon the accounting officer, who is not a finance officer, however senior, but the permanent secretary or other official in charge of the whole department. He or she may be and usually is supported by senior colleagues, but he or she is the official witness. The duty of answering to the PAC for the regular and economical administration of the department is a duty which is taken very seriously. Though arduous and sometimes gruelling, the Committee's examination of these senior witnesses sets out to be fair and constructive. The Committee makes its own report to the House on the basis of its examination of the accounting officer and any other witnesses outside the department it may decide to call. It includes criticisms if thought justified, and any necessary recommendations for change or improvements. It may even, on rare occasions, commend good performance.

The next step is for the department to consider the Committee's report and to prepare a reply. It is unusual for the Committee's recommendations to be rejected, but by no means unheard of. The replies of all departments on whose activities the PAC has reported are agreed with the Treasury, and submitted as a Treasury minute to the House of Commons. This is in effect the response of the government to the PAC. A debate is arranged on the PAC's reports, and in the succeeding session of Parliament it is normal for the accounting officers to be examined further on any points in the Treasury minute on which the PAC remains unsatisfied.

This is an effective and well-tried system of accountability. The C&AG works closely with the PAC, though without being subject to their directions, and they with him. The Treasury is always represented at PAC hearings, and though they themselves are sometimes in the dock as well as the witness box their officials also seek to cooperate as far as possible with the Committee. The effect of the system is not confined to the particular matters on which the C&AG reports. The probability that any serious failure of financial control or inefficiency in administration will lead to a report by the C&AG and to a PAC investigation exercises a sharpening effect throughout departmental hierarchies.

Other select committees engaged in monitoring government departments have from time to time cast envious eyes on the strong support provide by the C&AG to the PAC. In a recent (1990) wide-ranging examination of the working of the select committee system the Procedure Committee expressed:

> considerable sympathy for the proposals made by the Chairman of the Defence Committee, namely that in a few carefully chosen cases where the interest of a particular departmentally-related committee is obvious, and with the agreement of all the parties involved, an NAO report would be taken up by the committee instead of the PAC and that the staff of the NAO should be available if necessary to help with such an enquiry.

In their response to this report the government saw no objection in principle to this proposal, on the understanding (*inter alia*) that there should be no changes in the C&AG's statutory remit and that therefore he should have complete discretion in settling the programme of work subject to consultation with the PAC. The C&AG will no doubt acquiesce in devising acceptable arrangements to extend his cooperation 'in a limited and carefully structured way'; but he, and the PAC, willl have as their primary objective the preservation of their long standing and beneficial 'special relationship'.

PROPOSALS FOR CHANGE

The current system of public audit described above has emerged in the last few years as a result of very rapid change. So far as the E&AD/NAO was concerned the initiative for this came from within, but there was also an upsurge of Parliamentary interest in the public audit, and no less than three select committees of Parliament enquired into it and made recommendations for change: the former Expenditure Committee, the Procedure Committee and the PAC itself. The PAC's review of the role of the C&AG in the 1980–1 session of Parliament was the first of its kind since the C&AG and his department had been established well over a century ago. It was itself preceded by the government's decision, stimulated by the increased Parliamentary interest in matters of financial control and accountability, and perhaps by the C&AG's own views, to review the C&AG's role.

In 1980 the government issued a consultative Green Paper. It summarized the C&AG's existing role, supported the development of a systems-based financial and regularity audit, and encouraged the extension of value for money work while stopping short of involvement in the merits of particular policy objectives, but it provisionally opposed any significant extension of his range of activities to cover other parts of the public sector, as had been suggested by the C&AG and generally supported by the other select committees.

Criticism of the existing audit system had concentrated on these points:

1. Compared with other advanced national audit offices, E&AD did too much financial and regularity audit and not enough efficiency and effectiveness audit.
2. The C&AG and the PAC examined past transactions instead of considering current policy options.
3. The C&AG and his staff should be officers of Parliament, subject to directions from the House of Commons.
4. The range of the C&AG's rights of access needed to be extended so that the use of public funds by all bodies receiving them could be examined, and should include access to books and records of the nationalized industries and other public corporations.
5. The C&AG needed to take over responsibility for the local authority audit service in order to improve accountability to Parliament in respect of the very large central government subventions to local authorities through the rate support and other grants.

These criticisms and suggestions are fully explored in the government's *Green Paper* (Cmnd. 7845, March 1980), the PAC's first special report in session 1980–1 on the role of the C&AG (HC 115–1), and the government's response to that report giving their conclusions (Cmnd. 8323). A considerable volume of evidence, both written and oral, was given to the PAC by several interested bodies and persons, and published by the PAC in their report. A guide to these reports and evidence is included in the bibliography. They provide, for the first time in over a hundred years, a source of authoritative material and argument on the subject of the National Audit Office. A summary of the main issues follows.

Criticism 1. that the C&AG's work was largely restricted to financial and regularity audit was misconceived. The C&AG, the government and the PAC continued to put much importance on the need for a sound financial and regularity audit supporting the certification of government accounts; but the criticism appeared to ignore the large volume and wide scope of his reports directed to value for money matters, extending over several past decades.

There is not much more substance to the 'stable door' criticism (2). It is of the essence of an audit that it investigates what has happened or is happening, and seeks to draw useful conclusions and recommendations for change from past experience, and no doubt in many cases past mistakes. In this sense it is concerned with the working out of existing decisions or policies, particularly their financial and economic consequences. It is not primarily concerned with suggesting alternatives, though in some cases this may be a clear implication of audit findings. In short, from an audit of past and present practice one hopes to secure future improvement.

The proposal that the C&AG and staff should be House of Commons staff, subject to Parliamentary direction, was rejected. Its constitutional attraction was apparent, since the C&AG reports to Parliament and works in many ways 'on their behalf'. It was opposed by the C&AG and the professional accountancy institutions, and was turned down by the government. The main argument was that the C&AG should have full independence, within the statutory remit, to decide enquiries and dispose resources as he thought best. The C&AG stressed in his evidence that in so doing the wishes and suggestions of the PAC would be given full weight, and this was reflected in the 1983 Act.

The view that the national auditor should have powers to follow public money – or as the Procedure Committee more narrowly defined it, 'money provided by Parliament' – wherever it went, also has constitutional appeal. Money voted by Parliament finds its way through many different types of grant and assistance to individuals and companies. It had to be asked how practicable and acceptable it would have been to expect the audit staff to have rights of access to all their books and records. The issue has been resolved in the 1983 Act as described above.

The arguments for and against giving the C&AG access to the books and records of some or all of the nationalized industries and public corporations so that he could report on their operations are fully discussed in the evidence submitted to the PAC in the course of their review. The essential arguments in favour were:

1. the industries' assets were acquired from public funds or on Exchequer credit and many of them have a monopolistic position conferred by Parliament;
2. examinations and reports by the C&AG would fill an important gap in the accountability of the industries;
3. they would check on and stimulate their efficiency.

The arguments against were as follows:

1. The industries operated under statutory provisions, reported to Parliament and the public through their annual reports and accounts, and readily responded to requests to give written or oral evidence to select committees of Parliament.
2. The responsible ministers had certain statutory powers of control, most significantly in relation to investment programmes, and had in practice influenced other policies, particularly on prices and major plant closures. Ministers had to answer for these actions to Parliament.
3. The government had indicated that it proposed to extend the use of enquiries by the Monopolies and Mergers Commission to provide an external check on efficiency, so that a further incursion by the C&AG was unnecessary. (This was subsequently carried out in the Competition Act 1980.)
4. The need to justify decisions to the C&AG's staff would inhibit speed and enterprise in decision-taking, responding to external audit enquiries would be expensive in staff time and money, and there would be difficulties about the confidentiality of some information, particularly where commercial partners were involved.

The sponsor departments added:

5. that if the C&AG were to be given access to the records of the industries with a view to reporting on value for money matters, the responsible departments would also need to seek more information to establish satisfactorily their own positions.

The C&AG argued that 1. and 2. did not adequately meet the point about a gap in accountability. There was no effective substitute, from this point of view, for free access by his staff and his right to report to Parliament, independently of both ministers and the industries, as he saw fit. As regards 3. the Monopolies and Mergers Commission had no such independent role; they would operate in this field only when so instructed by the government. On 4. the E&AD had long experience of handling confidential matters; and a body subject to C&AG's audit should continue to take whatever decisions they thought right – they did not have to be justified to the C&AG.

The PAC reported in favour of giving the C&AG this extended remit. The government disagreed. In the debate on the National Audit Bill the advocates of change failed to carry the day, so that the nationalized industries and the local authorities remained outside the C&AG's purview.

The extent of the government's privatization programme in recent years means that the C&AG's lack of audit access to nationalized industries is no longer a significant issue of Parliamentary accountability. It has also led to a new direction to his work in this area. The NAO have examined each of the privatizations with the object of establishing whether fair prices were secured for the public assets sold; and the Office has a continuing role in relation to the regulatory bodies set up to oversee the activities of those privatized concerns which are in effect providing a monopoly or near-monopoly service. The C&AG did not need any additional legislative authority to audit the accounts of OFTEL, OFGAS, OFWAT, and OFFER since they are non-ministerial public bodies with their own appropriation accounts. Consequently he examines their accounts in accordance with the 1866 and 1921 Acts; and he can under the 1983 National Audit Act examine the economy, efficiency, and effectiveness with which they have carried out their important functions. Since the regulatory bodies and their expenditure are small by public sector standards, this is likely to be the main focus of the C&AG's scrutiny.

It may be suggested that the 1983 Act was of limited significance. So far as the scope of the C&AG's audit within the public sector is concerned, this is true. But the Act gave statutory recognition to important changes in the approach and standing of the C&AG and his department. The C&AG's complete independence of any constraint, actual or potential, by the executive government was assured by the substitution of direct Parliamentary controls on his budget for those of the Treasury. The C&AG's establishment as an officer of Parliament, and the provision giving Parliament, through the chairman of the PAC, a statutory voice in the C&AG's appointment neatly recognized his close relationship with Parliament without subordinating to MPs his judgement in discharging his statutory duties and the use of his resources. The C&AG's long standing commitment to value-for-money audit as a major part of his activities was endorsed and the 3E's given statutory status. Moreover, as explained below, the C&AG had already, in the Local government Finance Act 1982, been given a role in the examination of relationships between central and local government, and certain rights in relation to the Audit Commission for Local Authorities to assist him to discharge it. The change of name, from Exchequer and Audit Department, with its undertones of archaism and a Treasury connection, to National Audit Office was more than symbolic of the ending of a long historical phase. It expressed a new outlook and a new approach.

AUDIT OF LOCAL AUTHORITIES

ENGLAND AND WALES

For 140 years, the external audit of local authorities was undertaken primarily by the District Audit Service, succeeded in 1983 by the Audit Commission for Local Authorities in England and Wales. In 1990 the Commission took over responsibility for the audit of health authorities and other bodies in the National Health Service and was renamed the Audit Commission for Local Authorities and the National Health Service in England and Wales.

The district audit system dated from the Poor Law Amendment Act of 1844, which created the office of district auditor to examine the accounts of the local bodies that administered poor law relief. During the succeeding half century, the duties of district auditors were gradually extended to cover the accounts of highway, public health and education bodies, as local administration itself was expanded under Acts of Parliament into these wider fields. By the end of the century, the accounts of most of the local authorities in England and Wales were audited by district auditors.

District auditors were independent statutory officers who took independent personal authority for the audit of the accounts of all the local authorities in their district. In addition to the normal duties of auditors, they had quasi-judicial powers to deal with illegality and losses caused by fraud and other wilful misconduct. On these matters, they were answerable to the courts. But while district auditors and their staff were formally civil servants, by reason of their statutory office and long tradition they were not subject to control or direction by the minister in the execution of their duties. Staff numbers apart, which was a subject of contention, they were treated as an independent professional service.

In addition to the district auditors themselves, the service also included the important post of Chief Inspector of Audit, with a small central staff reporting directly to him. Since district auditors had full personal and professional responsibility for their audit work, the Chief Inspector had no power to direct them. But the responsibility to ensure that proper standards were being maintained gave the Chief Inspector of Audit considerable influence as the *de facto* head of the service.

Prior to 1974, the accounts of most local authorities were compulsorily subject to audit by the district auditor. But for boroughs and county boroughs, this was the position for only some of their accounts. For the remainder, they could choose either the district auditor or a professional accounting firm. From 1 April 1974, when provincial local government reorganization took effect, all the new local authorities were given the right to choose their auditors; they could have either the district auditor or an 'approved auditor', i.e. a firm whose appointment had to be approved by the Secretary of State. In practice, most authorities, about 90%, chose the district auditor at that time. There were some differences in powers between district auditors and firms. In particular, the illegality and wilful misconduct powers were reserved to district audit. But otherwise the emphasis was on achieving common standards, working to the same code of audit practice, and reimbursement through the same scale of audit fees charged to the local authorities.

In the late 1970s, central government, in particular the Treasury, were taking an increased interest in the audit and accountability of local authorities as one aspect of central/local government financial relations and the drive for greater efficiency and cost consciousness in public bodies. In 1976, the Layfield Committee on Local Government Finance (Report, Cmnd. 6453) recommended the appointment of 'an independent official with a similar status to that of the Comptroller and Auditor General' to head an expanded and strengthened local audit service, whose functions would include:

1. the assignment of auditors to each authority, who would no longer have any choice in the matter;
2. the making of regular reports on 'issues of general interest or public concern', which should be made available to the public.

The Committee also recommended the establishment of a 'higher institution' to which the head of audit's reports would be submitted: either a Parliamentary committee with terms of reference similar to those of the Public Accounts Committee, or a body with representation drawn largely from local government. While this particular concept was challenged as constitutionally faulty, the Committee's analysis of the need to strengthen local authority audit was sound. But the proposals were not immediately followed up. Instead, the Secretary of State for the Environment set up an Advisory Committee on Local Government Audit (in England and Wales), headed by an independent chairman and including other independent members as well as experienced councillors and the C&AG. The Committee, which was advised by the Chief Inspector, was intended to give greater weight to the work of the local government audit service and to propose ways in which it could be usefully developed.

At the same time, the C&AG had himself been considering the local authority audit arrangements in relation to his own responsibilities and future role. He put forward a proposal to merge the E&AD and the local government audit service, arguing that:

1. the nature and objectives of the work of the two services were basically similar;

2. local government provides important services, such as education, housing and personal social services, under statutory arrangements and guidance from central government, and for which the taxpayer provides over half the funds;
3. Parliament therefore has a major interest in the arrangements whereby central government departments influence and, to some extent, control these expenditures;
4. bringing together the two audit services under one head would be the best way of achieving an integrated examination of the provision and control of services, respecting the right of individual local authorities to remain free of accountability to Parliament.

In opposition to those views, the local authority associations and other local authority interests argued that the proposal would lead to an unjustified and unconstitutional incursion of central government and Parliament into the affairs of local authorities, who were solely responsible to their own electors.

After some two years of debate, the government decided 'that the interests of all parties concerned, including local electorates, will best be served by the establishment of an Audit Commission for Local Authorities in England and Wales' (Cmnd. 8323, paragraph 16). They attached particular importance to the value for money content of local authority audit, and agreed that it was desirable for cooperation on technical matters to be developed between the District Audit Service and the Exchequer and Audit Department (now the National Audit Office).

The establishment of the new Audit Commission was provided for in the Local Government Finance Act 1982. Its provisions cover the following main points:

1. Members of the Commission are appointed by the Secretary of State, who has power to give the Commission directions, but not directions relating to particular audits.
2. The Commissioners appoint their own staff subject only to approval by the Secretary of State of the appointment of the Commission's chief officer, the Controller of Audit.
3. The Commissioners appoint auditors to local authorities, either from their own staff or from professionally qualified firms.
4. The Commission prescribes scales of fees for audits.
5. The Commission is required to produce an audit code of practice, embodying what appears to them to be the best professional practice with respect to standards, procedures and techniques. This code requires Parliamentary approval every five years.
6. Auditors have comparable responsibilities as formerly with regard to financial and regularity audit and as to illegality or wilful misconduct, and in addition must give an opinion on the accounts.
7. Auditors are required to satisfy themselves that proper arrange-

ments are being made by the audited body 'for securing economy, efficiency and effectiveness in its use of resources'.

8. Auditors are required to consider whether there is any matter which, in the public interest, should be reported to the body concerned so that it may be considered by the body, or brought to the attention of the public.

9. 'Any person interested' may inspect the accounts and related documents, and a local government elector may question the auditor or object in respect of matters of illegality, wilful misconduct, or failure to secure value for money.

In addition, the Commission was given important new duties to carry out studies of local government activities and to publish reports on how local authorities might secure improved economy, efficiency and effectiveness in the provision of services. A further duty requires the Commission to carry out other studies (Section 27 studies) into the effects on local government of the actions of central government, through legislation or ministerial directions. These studies at the interface of central and local government are an obvious area for cooperation with the NAO. Copies of these Section 27 reports are required to be sent to the C&AG, who in turn is required to report to the House of Commons on any matter arising out of the Commission's studies which he considers ought to be drawn to the attention of that House. For this purpose, the C&AG may need to be provided by the Commission with any information obtained in the preparation of the report, other than information in respect of any particular authority.

The main aims of these important statutory changes in audit arrangements for local authorities were to increase the weight and effectiveness of the audit, particularly in the pursuit of value for money, to establish its independence of the government more clearly, and to involve private auditing firms in the work to a substantially greater extent. The power of the Secretary of State to give the Commission directives may be thought to conflict with its independence. It is justified by the government on the grounds that Parliament, which provides substantial funds to local authorities and regulates their activities, would expect the government to have such a power in reserve. In practice, no directions have been issued in the first nine years of the Commission.

The Commission started operations in April 1983. Its first Chairman was an experienced businessman and among its other 15 members were senior local councillors and former officers and independent businessmen and academics. With the assumption of responsibility for health service audits its membership was increased to include members of health authorities, a general manager, a senior nurse, and a general practitioner. Its staff was recruited from the District

Audit Service, other public bodies and the private sector. The first Controller and his successor were both experienced management consultants and had worked in the public sector.

This new body, launched at a time of exceptional tension between central government and local authorities in constitutional, political and financial relationships, faced three main tasks:

1. to establish itself as competent, fair and forceful, and independent of both central and local government;
2. to create an effective and unified approach to wide-ranging audit operations in a large number of disparate authorities;
3. to establish cooperation between its own operational staff and the substantially increased numbers of commercial accountants who had entered an unfamiliar field.

This was a formidable programme. Immediately, the Commission had to appoint auditors for the 456 major authorities. In the first year, 70% of the audits were awarded to the directly employed District Audit Service and 30% to major commercial firms, a proportionate distribution which left the private sector somewhat short of the share which the government had envisaged but which was a matter for the Commission's judgement. The Commission announced that any changes in the proportionate allocation of audits should be based on performance. In recent years it has rotated a substantial number of appointments between the District Audit Service and the firms, and between firms. But the overall effect has been to maintain the 70/30 allocation.

The Commission also set out to establish both a professional and philosophical framework within which its audits would be directed and supervised. Elements in this framework were country-wide comparative analyses of local authority functions, staffing patterns and expenditure programmes, suggested principles of organization, accountability and motivation of staff, and comprehensive guides for the conduct of both the regularity audit and value for money studies.

In producing and disseminating this substantial collection of material, the Commission was at pains to stress its intentions to help local authorities to help themselves, to improve their use of resources and to disprove the view that it had been established as an instrument of central government to help curb and cut local expenditure. It was not their role to determine local government policy, nor to set spending levels or service priorities. But it could consider the consequences of policies being pursued by authorities and comment on their financial and other effects.

The Code of Local Government Audit Practice, prepared following consultation with the local authority associations and the professional accountancy bodies and approved by Parliament, sets out in some detail how the audit is to be conducted. Within these guidelines, the auditor is expected to do his job independently of both the Commission and the local authority. The Code covers both the regularity audit and the value-for-money work or 3E's audit. It remains a primary objective to check that public money is spent only as authorized by law, to expose improper or fraudulent practices and to ensure that the financial statements give an accurate and complete picture of an authority's expenditure, revenue and financial position. In these respects, the auditor is required to apply best professional practice in terms of standards, procedures and techniques.

The importance of sound financial accounting systems for efficiency, clarity and public accountability should not be underrated. Linked, as they should be, with the production of financial management information for councillors and staff, they provide an essential basis for policy decisions, monitoring of service operations and day-to-day control. But emphasis has increasingly been laid on the adequacy of council management structures, the machinery for taking and implementing policy decisions, and the effective use by local authorities of the very large sums of public money and skilled manpower for which they are responsible – in other words, on value for money in its widest definition.

For many years, a value for money audit had been applied to the affairs of local authorities, although its extent had been limited by the available staff resources. The Commission has vigorously developed this work through central studies using teams drawn from the particular specialism under investigation and consultancy experts as well as auditors. Many areas of local government have been examined; and reports published on primary, secondary, and further education, care of the elderly and mentally handicapped, housing, homelessness, police, probation, property management, vehicle fleet management and maintenance, refuse collection, energy conservation, purchasing, cash flow management, rent arrears and other topics. It has also published a series of management papers on issues facing local authorities in the organization and management of their affairs, and a series of occasional papers on topical matters, such as the community charge, compulsory competitive tendering, and information technology. In addition the Commission has published reports of Section 27 studies into the grant distribution system, capital controls, community care, and urban regeneration.

In developing this work the Commission has linked the study processes with the auditor's value for money responsibilities. As well as the reports, the studies generate audit guides which, after training, the auditors use in examining the various activities of individual authorities. This linkage has proved to be highly effective. Auditors are enabled to identify issues for local consideration and these are taken up with the individual authorities. Increasingly in recent years the emphasis has been on the effectiveness of services rather than on savings. Nevertheless, the Commission has reported that at March 1991 authorities have implemented recommendations giving better value for money to the extent of over £600 million a year.

The broad ambit of the local government audit service is thus nowadays similar to that of the National Audit Office, though the structure of local authority accounts and the system of reporting show important differences from those applicable to central government. Five points require specific mention.

1. The right of members of the public, as local government electors, to inspect, question and object to the accounts and to inspect the auditor's report. Any objection is heard by the auditor and if he upholds it, he may take action as in 2. and 3. below. There are no such rights in respect of the accounts of central government.

2. If it appears to the auditor that any item of account is contrary to law, he may apply to the court for a declaration accordingly, except where the item is sanctioned by the Secretary of State. If the court makes that declaration, it may order any person, councillor or official, who is responsible for incurring or authorizing the unlawful expenditure, to repay it in whole or in part. Where the amount exceeds £2000 and the person responsible is a councillor, there is provision for the court to disqualify him/her from local government office.

3. Where money has not been brought to account or loss has been incurred through wilful misconduct, the auditor must certify the amount as being due from that person and, subject to right of appeal to the courts by the person(s) affected by the auditor's certificate, the amount then becomes recoverable. Disqualification from membership again ensues in the case of a wilful misconduct certificate where the amount involved is over £2000 and the person involved is a member.

4. A local elector may make an objection on any matter about which he/she considers the auditor should make a report in the public interest. In these cases, the final decision is taken by the auditor, as he is the only arbiter of whether or not such a report should be made.

5. Local government auditors have been given powers of early intervention where a local authority has taken a decision which would involve unlawful expenditure or a course of conduct which would lead to unlawful loss. The Local Government Act 1988 enables the auditor to issue a prohibition order which, subject to a right of appeal to the courts, precludes an authority from implementing such a decision. The Act also empowers the auditor to apply to the courts for judicial review of an authority's decision. The purpose of these additional powers is to enable auditors to take early action on issues which could be substantial, either in amount or principle, rather than have them dealt with after the event by action as in 2. or 3. above.

The Audit Commission has set out to combine strong 'top–down' direction and assistance for its auditors with a recognition of their full independence in forming their opinions and framing their reports. It has adopted a much more public style than the District Audit Service, which like the former Exchequer and Audit Department operated in a low key with the minimum of publicity. It has sought to involve the local authorities in its broad objectives and has largely overcome the initial suspicion of local authorities about its creation and, particularly, about value for money studies. It is a safe prediction that an extended 3E's audit of publicly accountable non-commercial bodies is here to stay.

SCOTLAND

Prior to the Local Government (Scotland) Act 1973, which reorganized the pattern of Scottish local government, Scottish local councils and associated public bodies were audited individually by private accounting firms, appointed by the Secretary of State. The 1973 Act provided for the creation of an independent Commission for Local Authority Accounts in Scotland, consisting of not more than 12 or less than 9 members, appointed by the Secretary of State for Scotland after consultation with local authority associations and other appropriate organizations.

The Commission's main duties are:

1. to secure the audit of the local authority accounts by appointing 'such officers and agents as they may determine to carry out the audits';
2. to consider all audit reports and to investigate all matters raised therein;
3. to make recommendations accordingly to the Secretary of State;
4. to advise the Secretary of State on any matter relating to the accounting of local authorities which he may refer to them for advice;
5. to appoint a Controller of Audit.

In the Local Government Act 1988 the Commission and the auditors were given statutory value for money responsibilities. These are similar to the responsibilities of the Audit Commission for England and Wales except that there is no provision for studies at the interface of central and local government. There are two other significant differences between the two Commissions. The Accounts Commission does not have the 'prohibition powers' which the Audit Commission has; and, as yet, it has not been given responsibility for the audit of the NHS in Scotland albeit the statutory powers to enable this to happen are in place and simply require to be triggered by the Secretary of State.

The Controller of Audit, who is responsible for coordinating, guiding and supervising the overall audit arrangements, has statutory status and reporting powers. He is **required** to make to the Commission such reports as they may require with respect to local authority accounts. He may make a report to the commission on any matters arising out of the accounts so that they may be considered by the local authority or brought to the attention of the public. And he is **required** to report to the Commission on various types of illegality, improper accounting, failure to account, or loss caused by negligence or misconduct.

The other main feature of the Scottish local government audit arrangements was the appointment by the Commission, on the advice of the Controller, of their own permanent audit staff who now share with private accounting firms, in roughly equal proportion, responsibility for the individual audits. In this respect, therefore, the arrangements for local authority audit in Scotland are now similar to those in England and Wales, although they have developed by different routes. But the Controller of Audit has a more independent position in Scotland, standing, as it were, between the individual auditors and the Commission rather than acting simply as the Commission's chief executive. Thus individual audit reports, whether they take the form of formal qualification, a report to members or a report to officers, have to be copied to the Controller, who himself decides whether a statutory report should be made to the Commission.

As in England and Wales, the development of value for money examinations has promoted closer working relationships between the auditor and the local authority. The auditor is also perceived to have a significant role in an advisory capacity when dealing with certain managerial and procedural issues, for example in the setting up of direct service organizations and ensuring that the authority does not knowingly engage in anti-competitive practices in its handling of tenders.

SUMMARY

This chapter has explained the nature, purposes and methods of the external audit of the various parts of the public sector. It has described the constitution and responsibilities of the Comptroller and Auditor General and the National Audit Office, the Audit Commission and the Scottish Accounts Commission, and the way in which the first, but not the other two, work closely with the Public Accounts Committee of Parliament. It has stressed the important part which is played by '3E's' audit – economy, efficiency and effectiveness – in the public sector in addition to the financial audit, thus differentiating the public from the private sector in this respect.

FURTHER READING

There are few books on the audit of either central or local government. There is, however, an extensive range of reports by the C&AG
and the Public Accounts Committee, covering many subjects and il-
lustrating the way the National Audit Office discharges its remit. The
NAO (Buckingham Palace Road, London, SW1 9SP) would recommend particular reports, to illustrate general or specific interests.

During 1980–1 an extensive and authoritative discussion on the
role of the C&AG and related topics, covering central government,
local authorities and nationalized industries, took place. This began
with the issue of a government Green Paper, *The Role of the Comptroller and Auditor General* (Cmnd. 7845) in March 1980 and led to a
major report by the PAC in February 1981, *First Special Report from
the Committee of Public Accounts, Session 1980–81*. The government's
response to this report was published in July 1981 (Cmnd. 8323).

On local government audit the Local Government Finance Act 1982
and the Audit Commission Code of Practice (HMSO) give the statutory framework. The Audit Commission issues an *Annual Report and
Accounts* (HMSO) and like the NAO has produced a wide range of
reports on specific subjects. A detailed list is available from the Commission (1 Vincent Square, London SW1P 2PN).

10

An overview

This book is neither a primer on bookkeeping for the public sector nor a detailed treatise containing all the statutory and other professional requirements expected of financial officers in any particular branch of the public sector. The former is dealt with in other books with a different kind of purpose, the latter is beyond the capability of any single book. The aim here is to stimulate a greater interchange of ideas and skills, not only among current practitioners in the public sector but also among the students who will be their heirs.

The non-commercial part of the public sector used to be an island – indeed a group of separate islands – of distinctive financial and accounting practice. To some extent that has been changing. But there remains a need for the development of more effective dialogue between the public and private sectors in this field. Both sectors have much to learn from each other.

This final chapter steps aside from the discussion of financial practice in the individual branches of the public sector discussed earlier, and seeks to deal with some matters of general relevance.

FINANCIAL CONTROL

Many of the issues in the field of financial control are common to all types of organization, public or private, profit-seeking or charitable, those producing, transporting or retailing goods, providing personal services or promoting sport or the arts. Such issues include the matching of expenditure and revenue over an appropriate time span, deciding on objectives and priorities, establishing information and control systems, and monitoring results.

In the remaining nationalized industries the techniques of control are essentially the same as those applied in private industry, though sometimes interventions by the government have introduced non-commercial factors and complicated the process. Output is conditioned by demand in the contemporary market and pricing situation. In contrast, in parts of the non-commercial public sector, demand for services, if not unlimited, is not for the most part constrained by people having to pay for what they use or consume. The professionals in charge, and the ministers ultimately answerable to Parliament and the public, are naturally prone to believe that the resources allocated to them by the mechanisms described earlier are in varying degree inadequate to meet 'needs', or even to discharge the broad statutory objectives governing their activities. In a commercial organization a manager may be given a specific workload to complete and be expected to do so at minimum cost. This can also apply in the provision of the more routine of public services, but in other cases the idea of providing anything less than the best possible level of services is unattractive. It is presumed that cost minimization conflicts with this goal. But it is more difficult to monitor and control the best possible level of services for a given expenditure than it is to monitor and control the minimization of cost for the completion of an assigned volume of tasks. The use of performance indicators and other techniques to promote the best use of available resources, though greatly extended in recent years and applied with increasing sensitivity, has yet to attain full acceptance. Some public services, particularly in the NHS and local authority sectors, have traditionally been dominated by the professional rather than the managerial ethos – a problem also responsible for some notable failures in the business world – with the presumption that only some form of peer review, if that, can provide an appropriate evaluation of performance.

These attitudes were fostered during a long period of sustained growth in the public services in the post-war period. With pressure on public spending it is now widely accepted that efficiency must be improved to maintain existing services, and to provide resources to develop new services of high priority. Thus the problem for the budgetary control process is not only that of containing expenditure within prescribed limits, but also of finding activities of low benefit relative to cost on which savings can be made and diverted to activities with high benefit relative to cost. All this involves difficult judgements, and finance staffs on their own clearly cannot achieve it. Rather their task is to help create a climate of opinion favouring efficiency and the continuing attempt to maximize the benefit achieved from a given input of resources. They must also supply relevant and timely information on costs and resource uses to assist the identification of opportunities for efficiency improvements and for savings. Finally, it may be necessary to build incentives into the system, so that managers who take action to improve efficiency or make savings can obtain recognition or indeed the opportunity to use some part of the savings they have achieved on other activities under their control. This may require a change of attitude all round, with finance staff pressing for close personal interaction with other managers and professions to help maximize their contribution to the organization.

In central government operations the problem is less that of welding professional and financial managers into a cohesive team than of giving those in charge sufficient delegated authority, within a framework of policy, to match their personal responsibilities for the efficient delivery of services. The 'Next Steps' initiative will potentially be a major development in this direction.

MEASURES OF PERFORMANCE

Measuring the resources put into a non-profit-making public sector organization is easier than measuring how effectively those resources are used. Attention has been increasingly given across the whole of the public sector to the provision of non-financial performance indicators to assess how well an organization has performed, and whether the trends are going the right way. For nationalized industries, these measures have been part of the financial control framework since 1978. For local authorities and health authorities, a mass of indicators is available to enable comparisons to be made across the country. In central government, performance indicators now feature in all the main published documents. Persistent examination of the objectives of public service programmes and more refined analysis of what they produce is showing that an assessment of effectiveness is not exclusively dependent on the availability of markets.

Performance indicators are undoubtedly a useful addition to the methodology of control. But they need to be used with care. Some of the lessons that have been learned in recent years from their application are set out below, but it is worth noting that the vast majority of these points can be used to advantage by private sector organizations.

Thus in devising the measures, professionals and administrators should be jointly involved, so that those who use them will feel ownership of them. Enough measures should be devised to give a well-rounded picture of performance, but not so few that action is distorted to meet the targets. In this context it may be necessary to build in counters to an excessive concentration on a short-term focus. Measures should not be used only because the measurement process is easier and in particular, adequate weight needs to be given to quality, which is almost always difficult to measure. For those activities where proxies are essential, they should be used with caution. The measures must take account of the nature of accountability in the public sector and allow for the extraneous and uncontrollable factors which may influence recorded performance.

Examples of the importance of these principles are available in all parts of the public sector. To take just three of the principles, on the need for care with proxies, waiting lists or numbers of patients treated per day, is not necessarily a good indication of the quality of health care. Nor is a reduction in the number of social workers per head of population an indication of improved productivity. On taking an appropriate number of indicators, while the Health Service has been criticized as having too many indicators, the story of the Kent policeman boosting the clear-up rate by encouraging those convicted of one crime to admit to others they did not commit shows the problem of concentrating on too few. As a final example, on the importance of taking account of extraneous factors, financially-related measures in generating nuclear power may be affected far more by the weather and by government regulation than by any action taken by the organization. Similarly local authority success in dealing with homelessness may depend largely on action taken by other local authorities and the social and economic policies of central government.

In implementing measures, great care needs to be taken to allow time for those who operate within them to develop an understanding of how they work and what they can do, as well as ironing out any snags. The measures must also be used in conjunction with other performance measurement systems, not in isolation, so that they are fully integrated in the decision-making processes.

In using the measures effectively, managers have to understand that the results are guidance to action, not definitive answers to what must be done, and that interpretation is the key to action. For example, the Audit Commission, in its reports, very often provides the spectrum of performance across a number of public bodies. This provides the basis for asking questions for those whose performance is well out of line with comparable authorities without an apparent reason. (The warning issued annually in the publication of university management statistics and performance indicators by the Committee of Vice Chancellors and Principals – 'Uncritical use of these indicators may seriously damage the health of your University' – should be applied to any public sector body.) The questioning may or may not then provide a satisfactory explanation. The element of follow up and the nature of that follow up is in any case crucial to the successful operation of a performance measurement system. An absence of feedback will mean that the system will soon atrophy and only negative feedback will result in game playing by those whose performance is being measured. Nor should the importance of user-friendly information be ignored. Many systems have been shown to be less effective than was hoped because the information is simply not understood by those who receive it. Finally, those using performance measures need to recognize that there are often complex interactions between measures, and that trade-offs will occur. If an increase in productivity can only be achieved by a reduction in quality, the trade-off between the conflicting objectives must be established and agreed.

ACCOUNTING PRINCIPLES AND PRACTICES

The private sector has relatively homogeneous objectives and a common statutory framework of accountability. Thus there can be generally accepted accounting principles which cover most aspects of individual organizations' accounts, however great their variety. But in the four main branches of the public sector – central government, the NHS, local government and the public corporations – there is great diversity of operational objectives, organizational structure and financial management. This is necessarily reflected in their accounting and reporting systems. Uniformity, either within the public sector or between the public and private sectors, is not therefore to be expected. No accounting principle or system has any inherent validity. It derives its value from its contribution to the efficient performance and presentation of the activities to which it relates. That is not to question the need for the distillation of accounting principles of wide application in business or elsewhere, and for them to be actively promulgated by the professional bodies or other authorities. Nor is it suggested that the public sector need pay no attention to them, still less that its own systems are incapable of improvement.

The nature of the various accounting systems in the public sector has been explained in preceding chapters. Some salient points which have emerged in recent discussions are worth noting.

The nationalized industries, and other public corporations which operate in the market, can be quickly disposed of in this context. With important qualifications deriving from public policy and their statutory positions their accounting and reporting systems are fully commercial in nature, they are all audited by private accounting firms and they subscribe to professional standards and guidelines. The same applies (apart from audit) to government operations with a substantial commercial element constituted as trading funds, or if not formally so constituted, of a similar character.

No such conformity or set of standards applies to the other components of the public sector. Central government has not adopted the accounting principles and practices prescribed by the accountancy profession, at least in its external reporting. Its formal financial accounts have been developed over 100 years and more, primarily to give parliamentary and public assurance that public money has been allocated and spent as intended, and with probity. The cash basis of appropriation accounts serves these purposes well, though it has been argued earlier that it also has wider justification.

In many respects there has been a marked improvement in the clarity of financial reporting in recent years. The arrival of departmental reports to replace the *Public Expenditure White Paper* has made for much greater accessibility for non-specialists and the Annual Reports of Agencies will increasingly provide additional information for a wider readership. Their arrival will leave some unanswered questions on the relationship between documents. Thus even though both 'traditional' reports to Parliament – the Estimates and Appropriation Accounts – have been based on the specific functions for which departments are responsible, their form has remained largely unchanged and it is not clear what role the Estimates will play as parliamentary attention is increasingly turned to the departmental reports. Nor indeed what the relationship between Agency reports and departmental reports will be.

There are also issues on the development and use of management information systems for internal departmental planning and control. It is accepted that the formal annual accounts should, as far as practicable, link with departmental organization and responsibilities. But civil servants as line managers cannot work successfully without a properly devised system of management accounting and control which provides information on which decisions can be taken, in far more detail and much more promptly than on the basis of the annual accounts. The financial management initiative (FMI) is in part directed towards this requirement, and here there is considerable scope for the contribution of professional accountants. The most effective accounting and control arrangements for internal use may combine elements from both commercial and non-commercial systems. A cash system can be converted, if it serves a useful purpose to do so, to a partial accrual system, to give a more accurate idea of 'true' costs or expenditure during a given period and an estimate of future liabilities, without necessarily bringing in depreciation of capital assets, e.g. office buildings. The way in which separate activities are differentiated for budgetary purposes, or overhead and other costs are attributed to individual services under the control of one undersecretary, are examples of the kind of analysis where the skills and experience of professional accountants are likely to make an impact. There are many more possible developments in the field of management information, at whatever level of information technology the problems are being addressed. It is in these areas, whose significance has only in recent years been adequately recognized, that Whitehall has previously failed to apply sufficient professional accounting expertise. In the broader field of public expenditure control, in its macroeconomic and financial context, financial administrators with wide experience of government operations and finance should be well equipped to take decisions and provide ministers with the necessary advice. The wide-ranging reforms of the Exchequer and Audit Department/National Audit Office over the last ten years or so, affecting all aspects of the structure and work of that specialized professional body, were initiated and carried through by C&AGs with that background, and the process is continuing.

EXTERNAL REPORTING

Improving the basis of accounting is one element in improving public sector external financial reporting, but not the only one. Within the public sector there have been criticisms both of the form and content of external reports and also of the systems by which they are generated and used. This topic runs deep into the whole question of accountability in the public sector.

Accountability is of course the basis on which public sector external reports are produced. Yet there are a number of uncertainties and ambiguities after the need for accountability has been established. For example, external reports are certainly used as public relations documents throughout the public sector. This is entirely understandable bearing in mind that public sector bodies are bound to be involved in lobbying for resources and for policies, and that an external financial report is a useful vehicle for such activity. But there must then be an implicit conflict between the idea that a document is designed to give an account of stewardship of public funds and the idea that it is a vehicle for political pressure. This does not mean that there is cheating on the figures themselves, but it is likely that the dual roles will give rise to a conflict about the way the facts are presented and interpreted. Such a conflict is of course not peculiar to the public sector.

Public sector external reports are also often used for reference purposes, as a means of communicating to staff and, in the case of central government, some of the documents are even used as the basis of internal control. But there is a problem throughout the public sector in deciding who exactly the potential readers are and what they require. The constitutional position of elected bodies is usually clear enough, but many elected members of such bodies, including many members of Parliament, are not financially trained. A further conflict therefore often arises in external reporting about the level at which external reports should be pitched. On the one hand there are some elected representatives who are highly trained financially and expert in the field. On the other hand there are those (usually the majority) who are interested laymen and women without financial knowledge. The problem of addressing both audiences is solved in some cases by providing more than one document, in others by providing information aimed at different types of reader in the same document. But often both sets of readers are left unsatisfied because the same document is aimed at the wrong level for each audience. A further difficulty in resolving this problem is that there is usually no easy way of finding what users want and how their information needs can best be met.

Taking various parts of the public sector in turn, there are those who have said that local government suffers from a surfeit of accountability. Certainly the multiplicity of documents provides a benchmark against which other parts of the public sector can be compared. First there are the **Financial Accounts**, which are more often now prepared in line with generally accepted accounting principles and standards. Then there is the mandatory, increasingly comprehensible and in some cases first-class **Annual Report**, which includes performance indicators. Then there is the **Ratepayers' Leaflet**, published before the financial year, which gives key aspects of the budget. During the course of the year, reports on the progress of local authority spending are typically presented in open committee. Finally, before the audit is completed, 'interested persons' may inspect the detailed accounts and put questions to the auditor.

The National Health Service is organizationally similar in one main respect to local authorities in that it has a large number of diverse units, each with a specific controlling body which has a measure of discretion as to how its allocated resources for capital and current expenditure are to be applied. There are also major differences. The NHS is operationally unified and responsible to the Secretary of State, and unlike local authorities it has no significant autonomous source of finance. Its accounting practices are changing radically, especially for capital, but it is not clear how this will be reflected in more informative public reporting.

The position of central government ought to be much simpler, since Parliament is the main 'customer' for the financial information, with the Press, pressure groups and other interested parties interpreting the information for the general public. The sheer volume of information with which they are briefed is certainly impressive, and indeed growing. In the 22 years up to 1990 in which the *Public Expenditure White Paper* (*PEWP*) was produced, it went from 14 pages to over 800 of an equivalent size. In 1991 when the departmental reports replaced the *PEWP*, the number of pages more than doubled from the 1990 figure. Indeed a particular problem for central government is that there is a stream of requests for additional information but not for reductions. There is a tendency for the documents to get bigger, thus erecting another barrier in the way of understanding as the documents become forbiddingly large. And despite the volume of information, the problem of satisfying even the parliamentary audience is similar to that for other parts of the public sector. As already noted, MPs are no more homogenous than any other user group with varying levels of knowledge, interest and attention span. The 'secondary' audiences are similarly diverse, with information used by experts and those just interested in finding out what is going on in Defence or Transport policy.

Finally the position of the nationalized industries is probably the simplest of all the public sector bodies. This is because both the industries and the government have been keen for many years to try and ensure that the industries are as close as possible to private sector practice. Their annual reports are generally of high quality by the standards of either the public or the private sectors and in most cases much more informative. Yet they too suffer from the ambiguities discussed at the beginning of this section.

AUDIT

The professional skills and techniques of the auditor of financial statements and accounts are broadly similar and transferable between the public and private sectors, and between profit-making and non-profit-making organizations. Many non-commercial public sector bodies, including the universities, an increasing proportion of local authorities and several health authorities, are now audited by private sector firms. But there are also important differences. For profit-making organizations the dominant objectives of the audit must be to validate the fairness of the profit figure, and the truth and fairness of the valuations in the balance sheet. This assists owners and lenders, as well as their professional advisers, to assess the value, prospects and risk of their debt or investment. But the non-trading parts of the public sector do not use their assets to produce goods or services for sale, and do not therefore generate profits from their activities. Instead, typically, they expend all their allocated funds on providing services. It is a reasonable concern of Parliament and the public that public expenditure should be made only for duly authorized purposes and should conform to high standards of probity. It follows that public audit must pay careful attention to those requirements.

Beyond this, however, there is growing parliamentary and public concern to make the best use of resources which are scarce in relation to needs by improving efficiency or productivity. In recent years this has provided increased emphasis on the value for money dimension of public sector auditing. Private sector audits do not include this value for money dimension since a simpler criterion of success in meeting commercial objectives is readily available and the statutory framework within which private sector audit is conducted has, accordingly, more limited responsibilities. Private sector auditing firms normally concentrate their evaluations of efficiency in their management consultancy departments, which operate not as auditors but at the invitation of clients. But where the firms are appointed as auditors to public authorities, they are having to extend their activities into the value for money field as an integral part of the audit operation.

SUMMARY

In general, nationalized industries and most other public sector trading organizations follow 'best commercial practice' accounting, financial control and audit procedures – focused on the accurate estimation of profit or loss. But in the non-trading public services quite different accounting systems have developed, perhaps most notably in local government, and usually with particular concern for accountability for cash income and expenditure. Research and debate continues regarding how far local government and other public services such as the NHS should move to full accrual accounting, inclusive of depreciation accounting, on a basis of external reporting and disclosure more comparable to the private sector.

Given the absence of the profit motive and measure for non-trading public services, audit has developed strong emphasis on methods of measuring and reporting performance in 'value for money terms'. This has necessitated closer study of the multiple service objectives of most non-trading organizations, and a great many performance measures have been developed for managerial review and future target-setting, as well as for reference in audit and for parliamentary scrutiny.

Much of the work of non-trading public services has to be tailored to the particular needs of individual clients, patients, students, etc. so that the output or 'product' is non-standard and it has been difficult to introduce conventional management accounting information systems. However, there is progress in developing these, and in linking them to wider performance measures and reviews, and to better systems of budgetary allocation and control. Given cash-limited resource allocations for many public services, good management planning and control by budget is especially important.

Effective financial control in the public sector can be achieved only by accountants working closely with other professions, general managers, planners, economists, senior hospital doctors, etc. Thus wide understanding and good communication skills are needed. Unlike the private sector, specialization or demarcation boundaries between finance/financial accounting and management accounting/financial control are minimal, and effective chief financial officers in the public sector will often have obtained training and experience in both of these key professional areas, and often in internal audit and management information/computer systems as well.

Study questions

CHAPTER 1

1 Historically, public sector accounting and external reporting have developed many practices and conventions which are quite different from the private sector. Why do you think this has happened, and what arguments might be used to explain or defend such differences?

2 Even within the public sector there is great diversity in financial accounting and reporting practice, although also there is increasing pressure for uniformity of practice. What arguments may be advanced for and against uniformity?

3 One argument for diversity between public and private sector financial accounting and reporting is that the 'user groups' for their published financial information are different. Explain this claim and give arguments for and against its validity.

4 Figure 1.1 subdivides public expenditure in four different ways. Why is this important as an alternative to a conventional private sector business analysis directly comparing total costs and expenses against income?

5 Obtain a copy of the annual financial report and accounts for one or more public bodies and study these and make a list of any differences in respect of layout, disclosure, reference to SSAPs, accounting practices, type and detail of information included, etc. as compared to the typical or standard financial accounting model for private companies (as set out in good financial accounting textbooks). N.B.: accounts of nationalized industries, local authorities, health authorities, and some other public corporations such as the BBC (i.e. look for the *BBC Handbook*) may be found in your college library, or try the local public library, or failing these sources your own local authority or health authority may be willing to give you copies of their reports.

6 In the public sector, compared to the private sector, there is much more frequent reference to the concept of 'accountability' for financial performance and use of resources. Define 'accountability' in

the context of accounting and finance, and suggest possible reasons for its apparently greater importance in the public sector.

CHAPTER 2

1 'Public sector financial reports are really just public relations documents.' Discuss.
2 Evaluate the financial report of your own local authority.
3 'Public sector financial reports are neither better nor worse than those prepared for the private sector.' Discuss.
4 Explain how you might find out about users and potential users of the financial report of a public sector organization.
5 Explain to what degree you think public sector financial reports provide good measurement and disclosure of public sector performance and accountability.
6 Can you suggest reasons why some public sector organizations still do not use full accrual accounting, in the manner required under 'best commercial practice' accounting in the private sector and indeed in many public corporations?
7 Can there be uniformity in public sector financial reporting which mirrors that adopted in the private sector? Explain (ACCA, *Public Sector Financial Management*, June 1991).
8 Discuss the relevance of UK accounting standards for the financial reports of public sector organizations (CIMA, *Financial Accounting*, stage 2, Nov. 1988).
9 Outline the respective roles of the Accounting Standards Committee (ASC) and the Public Sector Liaison Group (PSLG). Making use of appropriate examples, discuss the relevance of the various formats of the ASC pronouncements to public sector organizations (CIPFA, *Public Sector Accounting*, Dec. 1989).
10 Compare and contrast the methods of accounting for the use of fixed assets in the private and public sector. Discuss the recent developments in this area in both sectors (CIPFA, *Accounting Theory and Practice*, Dec. 1990).

CHAPTER 3

1 'Unlike with financial accounting and external reporting, management accounting in the public sector is not distinctively different from the private sector.' Discuss.
2 What is the difference between economy, efficiency and effectiveness; and how might our awareness of these three different types of concern and measurement affect the design of cost and management information systems in the public sector?

3 VFM, or value for money, has become a major influence on public sector management, and on public sector audit. Discuss the management accounting problems in measuring and reporting VFM, given the wider concern for 'effectiveness and quality of outcomes'.

4 Describe and evaluate the cost and management accounting information systems in one institution or branch of the public sector with which you are familiar.

5 What do you understand by the term zero-base budgeting? Why do you believe this technique has failed so far to gain wide acceptance in the UK? (ACCA, *Public Sector Financial Management*, June 1988).

6 What rationale lies behind the government's policy on investment appraisal of promoting the use of the net present value (NPV) approach to discounted cash flows? (ACCA, *Public Sector Financial Management*, Dec. 1989).

7 What do you understand by the term planning, programming budgeting system? Why do you believe this technique has failed to gain widespread acceptance in the UK? (ACCA, *Public Sector Financial Management*, Dec. 1989).

8 Three essential steps in programme analysis are identifying relevant objectives, criteria by which to evaluate the effectiveness of alternatives, and the population or client groups which will be affected by the alternatives.
Discuss the importance and interdependence of these elements of programme analysis (ACCA, *Public Sector Financial Management*, June 1990).

9 'While the limitations of investment appraisal in the public sector are obvious enough, having to set out the calculations can be a valuable discipline in its own right, often uncovering possibilities.' Do you agree with this statement? Why or why not? (ACCA, *Public Sector Financial Management*, Dec. 1990).

10 The absence of the profit measure in Not for Profit (NFP) organizations causes problems for the measurement of their efficiency and effectiveness.

You are required to explain:

1. why the absence of the profit measure should be a cause of the problems referred to;
2. how these problems extend to activities within business entities which have a profit motive. Support your answer with examples.
(CIMA, abridged, *Control and Audit*, stage 4, Nov. 1989.)

CHAPTER 4

1 Examine the problems that the absence of a profit motive poses for management control of an organization in the public sector

(Chartered Association of Certified Accountants, *UK Public Sector Financial Management*, 1986).

2 Assess the effectiveness of the mechanisms for scrutinizing the actions and decisions of the Executive. Assess the means whereby Parliament might influence the Executive (CIPFA, *Policy Making in the Public Sector*, 1988).

3 The Appropriation Accounts of government departments show cash spent on heads and subheads compared with cash voted by Parliament. What additional types of accounts would you expect a department to maintain (a) for its own use; (b) for public information?

4 What do you understand by a management accounting system in central government?

5 The government uses the Public Expenditure Survey Committee process in planning and controlling public expenditure. Discuss the usefulness and importance of this process to the government (CIPFA, Nov. 1980).

6 In recent *White Papers* increasing emphasis has been placed on the role of output and performance measures as a means of demonstrating and securing better value for money in the public sector. What reasons do you believe lie behind this trend, what types of measure are used and why? (ACCA, June 1989).

7 Central government exercises control over the financing of the public sector. Explain the reasons for this control and the methods by which it is exercised using as examples at least two areas of the public sector (CIPFA, *Public Sector Accounting*, 1990).

8 In 1982, the UK Government published a *White Paper*, *Efficiency and Effectiveness in the Civil Service*, which introduced the Financial Management Initiative (FMI).

    You are required to describe:

    1. the aims of the Financial Management Initiative;
    2. the procedures by which it was to be implemented;
    3. the bodies responsible for assisting and monitoring progress.
    (CIMA, abridged, *Management Accounting/Financial Management*, stage 4, May 1990.)

9 'Central government does not need to control local government expenditure'. Discuss (CIPFA, *Public Finance*, 1988).

10 Explain the relationship between parliamentary control of expenditure and cash limits.

CHAPTER 5

1 What are the criteria by which to judge a locally based tax? Using these criteria, compare and contrast the community charge, domestic rates and the proposed council tax.

2 Is there a case for the return of national non-domestic rates to local government control?

3 To what extent can local authorities determine the standard of local services and is there a case for more local autonomy?

4 Describe the external controls on local authority capital expenditure and the advantages and disadvantages in the context of the control of public expenditure.

5 Why have 'capping' powers been introduced and is there a case for their abolition?

6 1. Analyse the nature of the current relationships between central government and local government in England and Wales, and highlight any significant differences between policies for different services.

   2. What implications might be projected for future central and local government relationships and structures? (CIPFA, PE2, *Policy Making in the Public Sector*, 1988).

7 'Central government does not need to control local government expenditure'. Discuss (CIPFA, PE2, *Public Finance*, 1988).

8 What factors influence the relationship of central government with local government? Outline areas where recent changes in legislation will affect the relationship, and consider the consequences of these changes. Support your answers with examples (CIPFA, PE2, *Policy Making in the Public Sector*, 1989).

9 The concept of 'The Enabling Council' implies a fundamental change in the nature of local government. Management styles will also change.

   Discuss the managerial implications of the move towards 'the enabling council', tracing recent developments as described by Bains and Widdicombe and assessing the need for further changes (CIPFA, PE2, *Policy Making in the Public Sector*, 1990).

10 Comment on recent reforms in local government finance in the context of the Layfield Committee's recommendations.

11 Central government can impose a variety of constraints on local authority spending. How might these constraints best be classified? Explain. (ACCA, *Public Sector Financial Management*, Dec. 1990.)

CHAPTER 6

1 'All of the problems of local authority accounting could be overcome if local authorities were required to comply fully with the accounting requirements of the Companies Act 1985.' Discuss.

2 Are accounting standards developed primarily for commercial organizations equally relevant to local authorities? Discuss.

3 Discuss the significance of the *Code of Practice on Local Authority Accounts*, outlining its objectives and main provisions.

4 'Comparability is an essential part of accountability.' Discuss this statement in the context of local authority accounting.

5 The Layfield Committee suggested that there is a need for a different form of capital accounting to provide information on the cost of using the assets of local authorities. Why has this suggestion been made? (ACCA, Level 2, *UK Public Sector Financial Management*, June 1989).

6 'CIPFA's proposals for a new system of capital accounting by local authorities are irrelevant, as they will not produce any practical benefits for local authorities.' Discuss the implications of this statement.

7 What are the principal objectives of a local authority's annual report and accounts, and how can these best be met?

8 'Nobody reads local authorities' published reports and accounts, so why bother about the quality of financial information contained within them?' Discuss.

9 A district council has a department which is responsible for the collection and disposal of all household waste from the premises in the area. The productivity of this department has been compared unfavourably with that of outside contractors, and the council is under pressure to reduce its expenditure. It is the council's policy to keep as many of its services as possible under its own control.

   You are required to list, and explain briefly, all the factors which should be reviewed to improve the department's performance. (CIMA, *Management*, stage 2, May 1990.)

10 What is the rationale for, and what are the practical implications of, the current trend within local authorities towards devolved systems of budgeting and financial management?

11 What are the objectives of a local authority's annual budget development process, and how does the annual budget relate to longer term financial planning?

12 'The lesson of PPBS, MINIS, and ZBB is that it is foolish to try to turn a subtle, time consuming, complex and multi-faceted decision making process into a pretty rigid, mechanistic format with a tight timescale' (P. Morgan, *PFA*, Feb. 1985).

   Considerable criticism has been levelled at the alternative budgeting models to the traditional 'incremental' approach to budgeting.

   You are required to:

   1. examine the theoretical purposes and functions of budgets within the public sector and discuss the role which budgets **traditionally** perform in the public sector;
   2. appraise the usefulness of zero-based budgeting in the light of

the above statement and compare and contrast ZBB with the incremental approach.
(CIPFA, *Auditing and Control*, Dec. 1989.)

CHAPTER 7

1 How would policy making in a public corporation be changed if equity capital were introduced? (CIPFA, *Policy Making in the Public Sector*).
2 Under the 1978 *White Paper*, nationalized industries like gas and electricity were asked to aim for a required return on their investment programme. Examine the rationale (CIPFA, *Public Finance*).
3 Explain the strong opposition of nationalized industries to the use of EFLs as the most important element in financial control by government.
4 'It is unrealistic to have multiple targets for nationalized industries of the kind set out in the 1978 *White Paper*. They are difficult to calculate, impossible to reconcile and not understood by managers.' Discuss.
5 'Cash flow is the key to nationalized industries' performance, since the calculation of profit and loss is too subjective.' Discuss.
6 'Historic cost figures are misleading but current cost figures are wrong.' Discuss this statement in relation to one particular nationalized industry or nationalized industries as a whole.
7 Discuss the case for setting accounting standards for nationalized industries in a different way to those for the private sector.
8 'The accounts of nationalized industries are just like those of private sector organizations except that the government is the sole shareholder.' Discuss.
9 In relation to the financial management of nationalized industries in the UK, you are required to explain:

   1. what types of objectives are set for an industry and how they are established;
   2. how approval is given to investment plans and on what basis investments are appraised;
   3. how financial targets are set;
   4. what sales pricing principles will be applied;
   5. what is the meaning of 'external financing limits';
   6. how results are monitored and performance is scrutinized.
   (CIMA, *Management Accounting/Financial Management*, stage 4, Nov. 1989.)

10 Six main measures have been used at various times by government to monitor the performance of nationalized industries. They are:

1. return on net assets;
2. profit margin;
3. return on equity;
4. (for loss making industries) operating within a given level of grant or minimizing losses;
5. self-financing ratio;
6. operating within the cash limit.

Write notes on the appropriateness of any FOUR of these measures. (ACCA, *Public Sector Financial Management*, June 1989.)
11 Examine the significance of the conflicts in the policy processes of public corporations or nationalized industries (CIPFA, *Policy Making in the Public Sector*).

CHAPTER 8

1 Which main interest groups are concerned with the accountability of the National Health Service? Discuss whether the needs of these groups are met in terms of the financial information made available to them (ACCA, *Public Sector Financial Management*, June 1991).
2 'Explain the main points of SSAP2, Disclosure of Accounting Policies; in particular the four fundamental accounting concepts. Discuss its application...' to the NHS (CIPFA, *Public Sector Accounting*, Nov. 1981).
3 The Griffiths Inquiry of 1983 and more recent government initiatives in Resource Management have sought to involve doctors, nurses and other health-care professional staff more actively in the use of costing, budgeting and other performance-related monitoring and control systems. What are the difficulties, and the potential benefits, in seeking to involve such professional staff in the financial information and control process?
4 HN(86)34 announced a change of policy as to the speed and approach with which management budgeting for clinicians (CMB) should be developed throughout the acute services of the NHS. Instead of priority for CMB, emphasis is to be given to the wider concept of 'resource management'. Why was this change in emphasis necessary? (ACCA, *Public Sector Financial Management*, Dec. 1990).
5 There are three approaches to specialty costing: the 'statistical' approach, the 'sampling' approach, and the 'continuous' approach. Discuss each approach, particularly with respect to the advantages and disadvantages associated with each for monitoring specialty and clinical budgets (ACCA, *Public Sector Financial Management*, Dec. 1989).
6 Evaluate the case for the creation of internal markets in the National Health Service (CIPFA, *Public Finance*, Dec. 1988).

7 'The government is currently encouraging the "privatization" of as many public sector services as possible. Discuss the policy-making implications of privatization . . .' in respect of the management of the NHS (CIPFA, *Policy Making in the Public Sector*, Nov. 1981).

8 In the NHS internal market the DH requires that prices should be set so as not to cross-subsidize between services. Contract prices must be justifiable on the evidence of relevant costs. Discuss the problems which arise in meeting the above requirements, given the NHS's complexity of inputs, services and outputs, and its cost and management accounting systems.

9 Briefly explain the new NHS capital accounting and charging systems (for directly managed services as distinct from NHS Trusts), and discuss how far the new systems are compatible with full commercial accrual accounting for capital, depreciation and capital maintenance.

10 A public health clinic is the subject of a scheme to measure its efficiency and effectiveness. Among a number of factors, the 'quality of care provided' has been included as an aspect of the clinic's service to be measured. Three features of 'quality of care provided' have been listed:

1. clinic's adherence to appointment times;
2. patients' ability to contact the clinic and make appointments without difficulty;
3. the provision of a comprehensive patient health monitoring programme.

You are required to:

1. suggest a set of quantitative measures which can be used to identify the effective level of achievement of each of the features listed;
2. indicate how these measures could be combined into a single 'quality of care' measure.

(CIMA, Abridged, *Management Accounting/Control and Audit*, stage 4, Nov. 1989.)

11 J. Cloth,
Treasurer,
Clarkshire District Health Authority
Red Square
Clarkshire

Dear Jim
As you know, following my defeat at the General Election, the Secretary of State for Health has approved my appointment as a member of the Clarkshire District Health Authority. I must confess to knowing little about the workings of the NHS, having spe-

cialized in Energy matters in the House of Commons, so I was wondering it you could clarify a few matters regarding NHS finance for me:

First of all can you explain what this Revenue Support Grant that funds the NHS is all about? Also I'm not sure how the debt charges are calculated for Capital financing.

However, my main interest at the moment is to look to the future and in particular the reforms that appeared in the *White Paper, Working for Patients*. A few matters are of particular concern.

1. Many of my former constituents are very worried about hospitals and GPs being privatized. If they all 'opt out' will ordinary people be able to get treatment and will they have to pay?
2. I've heard that in future money will be allocated specifically for each person in the Health Authority area. How much will everyone get? and will they be free to spend it on private health care?

I hope you can clear up these matters for me and look forward to receiving your reply.

Yours sincerely

IMA Twitt

Required:

As finance trainee you have been asked to draft a suitable reply to this letter.
(CIPFA, abridged, *Public Sector Accounting*, Dec. 1989.)

CHAPTER 9

1 Outline the concept of public accountability in the public sector. Select two parts of the public sector and assess the extent to which formal accountability mechanisms are effective (CIPFA, *Policy Making in the Public Sector*, 1989).
2 The National Audit Act 1983 established the National Audit Office which took on new responsibilities in the field of value for money. How does the NAO discharge its VFM responsibilities? (ACCA, *UK Public Sector Financial Management*, 1991).
3 What are the main similarities and differences between external audit in the public and private sector? What special experience would you expect private firms to bring to the audit of public bodies?

4 What is meant by the examination of economy, efficiency and effectiveness in public sector operations?

5 What are the arguments for and against an external value for money audit of nationalized industries and other public corporations of a commercial type? Do these arguments apply equally to such government trading fund bodies as the Stationery Office and the Royal Mint?

6 Outline the role and operations of the Public Accounts Committee of the House of Commons. How would you rate the success of the work of this committee? Why? (ACCA, 1989).

7 Compare internal and external audit in the public sector. Do they require the same skills?

8 The creation of the Audit Commission under the Local Government Finance Act 1982 raised many doubts and criticisms. It was suggested that the Commission would lack independence but have the power to interfere in the management of a local authority's affairs. It was suggested that the Commission would increase audit fees and expand the role of private audit and consultancy firms in the public sector.

   1. By reference to the Commission's audit code of practice and the policies it has adopted discuss whether these criticisms are fair.

   2. How far has the Commission achieved the objectives for which it was established? (CIPFA, *Professional Examination 2*, 1985).

9 As external auditor of a government department you have been critical of the work done by the internal audit section. The chief internal auditor has written a memorandum to you outlining his current priorities which have been agreed with the Principal Finance Officer. He says that these are, in order of importance:

   1. investigation of discovered irregularities;
   2. advice on systems and design of financial stationery;
   3. assistance with the completion of accounting records at outstations;
   4. regularity audit, and specifically compliance with financial regulations;
   5. contract audit;
   6. systems audit;
   7. computer audit;
   8. value for money audit.

You are required to state the issues which you would wish to see included in a management letter to the Principal Finance Officer (abridged from CIPFA, *Auditing and Control*, Dec. 1988).

CHAPTER 10 AND REVISION

Note: In preparing answers to these questions it could prove helpful to refer back to earlier chapters and the publications included in their recommended reading and source citations (see Bibliography).

1 Explain, with reasons, why you think each Accounting Standard (i.e. SSAP) is, or is not, relevant to one branch of the public sector with which you are familiar.
2 Explore the relevance of the capital maintenance concept, and of depreciation accounting, to non-commercial public bodies such as universities, the NHS or the armed forces.
3 At a time when the private sector appears to be minimizing the importance of inflation accounting (e.g. CCA) in published accounts, the government appears to be encouraging public bodies taking up depreciation accounting to base this on current replacement values. How do you explain or justify this apparent paradox?
4 Local government accounting appears to be more distinctively different from the private sector model of 'best commercial practice' than in most other public bodies. How is this explained and justified?
5 What differences would you expect to find in the budget-setting and budgetary-control practices of a public sector trading enterprise as compared to a non-trading public service? Why may such differences exist, and how far and why may they be justifiable in future?
6 'Accountability is unthinkable without good accounting.' Discuss.
7 Value for money auditing appears to receive a much higher allocation of time and status in the public sector than in the private sector. Can this be explained and justified?
8 In recent *White Papers* on public expenditure increasing emphasis has been placed on the role of output and performance measures as a means of demonstrating and securing better value for money in the public sector. What reasons do you believe lie behind this trend, what types of measure are used and why? (ACCA, *Public Sector Financial Management*, June 1989).
9 'In the public sector a quiet revolution has been taking place. In both published accounts and asset management, public bodies are beginning to move ahead of their private sector counterparts' (Noel Hepworth, *Accountancy Age*, 26 Apr. 1990).

   Discuss the above statement with particular reference to recent initiatives in the areas of financial reporting and capital accounting in the public sector (CIPFA, *Public Sector Accounting*, Dec. 1990).

10 1. Why has central government sought to place local authority and health authority activity in a more competitive environment?
   2. Evaluate the effects of this policy, using examples to illustrate your arguments.
   (CIPFA, *Public Finance*, Dec. 1989.)

11 A change in governmental policy in the United Kingdom has meant that, for the first time in their history, schools are to be individually responsible for their own budgets and the use of financial resources.

   Knowing that you are studying for CIMA, a family friend who is a Headteacher of a secondary school which has 1200 boys and girls aged from eleven to sixteen years has sought your advice about the financial information he ought to have to help him to manage his school.

   You are required, in the format of a report, to advise the Headteacher, bearing in mind the following points:

   1. the principles of cost accounting and financial control;
   2. 80–85% of all costs are likely to be the salaries and wages of teachers, support staff and cleaners;
   3. comparisons of costs of activities, it is hoped, will be made in the future against other similar schools;
   4. personal computing facilities will be available.

   Note: This question does not require special knowledge of UK schools but relates to any separately-managed school which has budget responsibility.
   (CIMA, *Cost Accounting*, stage 2, May 1991.)

12 Assess the use of cash limits in controlling the expenditure of public sector organizations. Illustrate your answer with appropriate examples (CIPFA, *Public Sector Accounting*, Dec. 1988).

13 There has been much debate concerning whether the government has achieved its objectives when privatizing state controlled enterprises. Choose one incidence of privatization that has occurred within the last five years and discuss whether these objectives were met on that particular occasion (ACCA, *Public Sector Financial Management*, June 1991).

14 'Accountability' is a recurring theme throughout the public sector. What is it and why does it merit such attention?

   Assess the effectiveness of the formal and informal accountability mechanisms in two areas of the public sector, making comparisons between the two where appropriate (CIPFA, *Policy Making in the Public Sector*, Dec. 1990).

15 Brankstone, the well-known Victorian seaside resort, has decided

to improve its facilities to attract conferences to the town. The main new investment will be the provision of a Conference Centre, exhibition hall and swimming pool in one large complex. The Conference Centre will provide a multi-purpose hall to seat 2000 people and it can be used both for conferences and as a concert hall. While the revenue will not make the complex self-supporting, it is anticipated that the conference trade will supply much needed support for local hoteliers and traders.

As internal auditor of Brankstone Borough Council, the Director of Finance has asked you to maintain an audit involvement throughout the project and during the first three years of the operation of the Centre.

1. What criteria would you use in deciding whether the Conference Centre provides good value for money?
2. What financial management arrangements would you establish to monitor the performance of the Centre?

(Abridged from CIPFA, *Auditing and Control*, Dec. 1989.)

16 A statutory transport authority is committed to the provision of rural passenger transport services in an area between two large cities. It has received applications from operators as follows.

1. A Ltd offers to operate a limited stop service between the two main cities in the authority's area. Buses would be timed at hourly intervals from 6 a.m. until 8 p.m. on condition that the authority would authorize no other operator to service this route or any part of it. A Ltd also requires that district councils would grant the required permissions to allow on-board catering.
2. T Ltd is willing to operate 'social-service' vehicles for disabled passengers and others between the urban areas. Services would operate half-hourly from 5.30 a.m. until 11 p.m. at a cost to the authority of £2000 per week for the service. All fares would go to the authority. It is estimated that total fare income could eventually amount to £1200 per week but would initially be between £400 and £750 per week. Six-months' notice of termination would be required from the authority or the operator, should it be found that some other service is more appropriate to travellers' needs.
3. R Ltd proposes to operate dial-a-bus rural services (a service by which intending passengers can telephone for a bus). Travellers from within the rural area between the two cities would be able to make use of these out-of-town services to and from either centre at reasonable cost. The authority would need to subsidize the cost of this service by regular weekly payments of £1500 and all fare income would be retained by R Ltd.

You are required to:

1. discuss the criteria which should be applied to evaluate the three proposals, taking account of the authority's need to seek out the best value for money;
2. discuss how such an authority can quantify the value of a social service such as a public passenger transport facility to the community;
3. describe and assess other sources of funding that might become available for the successful operation of a rural passenger transport facility other than revenue earned from passenger fares and public funds.

(CIMA, *Management Accounting/Strategic Planning and Marketing*, stage 4, Nov. 1989.)

17 PG is an university. It is a 'not for profit-making' organization.

PG earns its income from charging fees to its students, and these are set by central government.

PG is not the only university in the market, and there are other educational institutions, whose prices are also controlled by the government. These institutions are competing with each other, as they all search for a bigger market share.

You are required to:

1. describe the ways in which PG can compete against the other institutions;
2. describe how PG can establish the extent to which its users are satisfied with its services;
3. describe how PG could measure the effectiveness of its use of resources.

(CIMA, *Management Accounting/Strategic Planning and Marketing*, stage 4, May 1991.)

18 1. Analyse the nature of the current relationships between central government and local government in England and Wales, and highlight any significant differences between policies for different services.
2. What implications might be projected for future central and local government relationships and structures?

(CIPFA, *Policy Making in the Public Sector*, Dec. 1988.)

Bibliography

AAA (American Accounting Association) (1973) Committee on not-for-profit organizations, supplement, *Accounting Review*, 1972–73.

ASC (1976) *The Corporate Report*, Accounting Standards Committee, UK.

Association of Health Services Treasurers (AHST) (1984) *Report of the Capital and Asset Accounting Working Party*, CIPFA, London.

Audit Commission (Annual) Report and Accounts, HMSO, London.

Audit Commission Studies, Reports and Occasional Papers, HMSO.

Audit Commission (1984) *The Impact on Local Authorities' Economy, Efficiency, and Effectiveness of the Block Grant Distribution System*, HMSO, London.

Audit Commission (1988) *Code of Practice*, HMSO, London.

Audit Commission (1990) *Code of Audit Practice for Local Authorities and the National Health Service in England and Wales*, HMSO, London.

Bains Report (1972) *The New Local Authorities: Management and structure*, HMSO, London.

Barlow, J. (1981) The Rationale for the Control of Local Government Expenditure for the Purposes of Macro-economic Management. *Local Government Studies*, May/June 1981, 3–13.

Barnett, J. (1982) *Inside the Treasury*, Andre Deutsch, London.

Beesley, M., Likierman, A. and Bloomfield, S. (1986) *Controlling Public Enterprise in Europe*, Economic Council of Canada, Discussion Paper, No. 302.

Berry, A.J., Capps, T., Cooper, D., Ferguson, P., Hopper, T. and Lowe, E.A. (1985) Management control in an area of the NCB: rationales of accounting practices in a public enterprise. *Accounting, Organisations and Society*, 10(1), 3–28.

Bevan, G., Copeman, H., Perrin, J. and Rosser, R. (1980) *Health Care Priorities and Management*, Croom Helm, London.

Brown, C.V. and Jackson, P. (1986) *Public Sector Economics* (3rd edn), Martin Robertson.

Butt, H. and Palmer, B. (1985) *Value for Money in the Public Sector*, Blackwell, Oxford.

Byatt Report (1986) *Accounting for Economic Costs and Changing Prices* (a report to HM Treasury in 2 Vols), HMSO, London.

Byrne, P. (1990) *Local Government in Britain*, Penguin Books, Harmondsworth.

Caulfield, I. and Schultz, J. (1989) *Planning for Change: Strategic Planning in Local Government*, Longman, London.

CIPFA, *Financial Information Service (FIS), Volume 4, Budgeting*, CIPFA, London. (Updated regularly.)

CIPFA, *Financial Information Service (FIS), Volume 30, Health*, CIPFA, London. (Updated regularly.)

CIPFA (1975) *Local Authority Accounting I – Accounting Principles*, CIPFA, London.

CIPFA (1983) *Capital Accounting in Local Authorities*, CIPFA, London.

CIPFA (1987) *Local Authority Accounting Manual*, CIPFA, London.

CIPFA (1988) *Standard Classification of Income and Expenditure*, CIPFA, London.

CIPFA (1989) *Capital Accounting in Local Authorities: The Way Forward*, CIPFA, London.

CIPFA (1990a) SORP on *The Application of Accounting Standards (SSAPs) to Local Authorities in Great Britain*, CIPFA, London.

CIPFA (1990b) *Capital Accounting in Local Authorities: Final Report*, CIPFA, London.

CIPFA (1990c) *Local Authority Accounting Manual for Scotland*, CIPFA, Edinburgh.

CIPFA (1991a) *Code of Practice on Local Authority Accounting for Great Britain*, CIPFA, London.

CIPFA (1991b) Institute statement on *Accounting for Overheads in Local Authorities*, included in the Management of Overheads in Local Authorities, CIPFA, London.

CIPFA (1991c) *Code of Practice for Compulsory Competition*, CIPFA, London.

CIPFA (1991d) Institute Statement on *Capital Accounting in Local Authorities, Public Finance and Accountancy*, 31 May 1991, pp. 6–7.

CIPFA (1991e) *Councillors' Guide to Local Government Finance*, CIPFA, London.

The Citizen's Charter (1991) *Raising the Standard*, Cmnd. 1599, HMSO, July.

Clarke, M. and Stewart, J. (1990) *General Management in Local Government; Getting the Balance Right*, Longman/Local Government Training Board.

Colville, I. (1989) Scenes from a budget: helping the police with their accounting enquiries. *Financial Accountability and Management*, 5(2), 89–105.

Commission for Local Authority Accounts in Scotland, *Annual Reports*.

Committee on the Management of Local Government (1967) *Report* (Maud Report), HMSO, London.

Davies, C. (1983) *Underused and Surplus Property in the National Health Service*, DHSS, London.

Departmental Committee on Accounts (1907) *Report*.

Department of Health (1989) *Working for Patients*, White Paper on the Health Service for the 1990s, HMSO, London.

DHSS (1976) *Sharing Resources for Health in England*, Report of the Resource Allocation Working Party, HMSO, London.

DHSS (1981) *Care in the Community*, HMSO, London.

DHSS (1982) *Investment Appraisal in the Public Sector*, NH(82)34, DHSS, London.

DHSS (1983) Ceri Davies, Chairman, *Underused and Surplus Property in the NHS*.

DHSS (1985) *Health Services Management Budgeting* (HN(85)3).

DHSS (1986) *Resource Management (Management Budgeting) in Health Authorities* (HN(86)34).

DOE (1977) *Local Government Finance*, Green Paper.

DOE (1981) *Local Authority Annual Reports*, HMSO, London.

DOE (1981) *Alternatives to Domestic Rates*, Cmnd. 8449, HMSO, London.

DOE (1983) *Accounts and Audit Regulations 1983*, SI 1761, HMSO, London.

DOE (1983) *Rates. Proposals for Rate Limitation and Reform of the Rating System*, Cmnd. 9008, HMSO, London.

DOE (1986) *Paying for Local Government*, Cmnd. 9714, HMSO, London.

DOE (1990) *Local Authority Capital Finance*, Circular 11/90, HMSO, London.

DOE (1991a) *A New Tax for Local Government*, Department of the Environment Consultation Paper, April, London.

DOE (1991b) *The Structure of Local Government in England*, Department of the Environment Consultation Paper, April, London.

DOE (1991c) *The Internal Management of Local Authorities in England*, Department of the Environment Consultation Paper, July, London.

Efficiency Unit (1991) *Making the Most of Next Steps*, Report to the Prime Minister, HMSO, London.

Emmanuel, C., Otley, D. and Merchant, K. (1990) *Accounting for Management Control* (2nd edn), Chapman & Hall, London.

FASB (1980) *Objectives of Financial Reporting by Nonbusiness Organizations*, Financial Accounting Standards Board, USA.

Ferguson, K. and Lapsley, I. (1988) Investment Appraisal in the National Health Service. *Financial Accountability and Management*, 4(4), 281–9.

Glynn, J.J. (1985) *Value for Money Auditing in the Public Sector*, Prentice–Hall International in association with ICAEW, London.

Griffiths, R. (1983) *NHS Management Inquiry Report* (i.e. the Griffiths Report), DHSS, London.

Griffiths, R. (1988) *Community Care: Agenda for action*, HMSO, London.

Harrison, A. (1989) *The Control of Public Expenditure 1979–89*, Policy Journals.

Harrison, A. and Gretton, J. (eds) (1987) *Reshaping Central Government*, Policy Journals.

Hatch, J. and Redwood, J. (1981) *Value for Money Audits*, Centre for Policy Studies, London.

Heald, D. and Rose, R. (1987) *The Public Expenditure Process: Learning by doing*, Public Finance Foundation, London.

Health Service and Community Care Act 1990.

Healthcare Financial Management Association (1990) *Health Database 1990: Health Service Trends*, 2 vols. annual, CIPFA/HFMA, London.

Heclo, H. and Wildavsky, A. (1981) *The Private Government of Public Money* (2nd edn), Macmillan Press, London.

Henderson, J. (1984) *Appraising Options*, No. 2, Health Economics Research Unit, University of Aberdeen.

Hennessy, P. (1989) *Whitehall*, Secker and Warburg, London.

Hepworth, N. and Vass, P. (1984) Accounting standards in the public sector, in *Issues in Public Sector Accounting* (eds A. Hopwood and C. Tomkins), Philip Allan, Deddington.

HFM/CIPFA (1991) *Introductory Guide to NHS Finance*, Healthcare Financial Management Association (with CIPFA), London.

Hofstede, G.H. (1968) *The Game of Budget Control*, Tavistock Institute, London.

Hofstede, G. (1981) Management control of public and not-for-profit activities. *Accounting Organizations and Society*, 6(3), 193–211.

Hopwood, A. and C. Tomkins (eds) (1984) *Issues in Public Sector Accounting*, Philip Allan, Deddington.

Jones, R. and M. Pendlebury (1988) *Public Sector Accounting* (2nd edn), Pitman, London.

Kilgour, L. and Lapsley, I. (1988) *Financial Reporting by Local Authorities in Scotland*, Institute of Chartered Accountants of Scotland, Edinburgh, and CIPFA, London.

Korner, E. (see entry under NHS/DHSS Steering Group).

Lapsley, I. (1986a) Investment appraisal in UK non-trading organisations. *Financial Accountability and Management*, 2(2), 135–51.

Lapsley, I. (1986b) Investment appraisal in public service organisations. *Management Accounting*, June 1986, pp. 28–31.

Layfield Committee (1976) *Local Government Finance: Report of the Committee of Enquiry*, Cmnd. 6453, HMSO, London.

Lee, T.A. and Stark, A.W. (1984) A cash flow disclosure of government supported enterprises results. *Journal of Business Finance and Accounting*, Spring.

Levitt, M.S. and Joyce, M.A.S. (1987) *The Growth and Efficiency of Public Spending*, Cambridge University Press, Cambridge.

Likierman, J.A. (1983) Evidence on accusation of manipulating profitability adjustments for inflation by the nationalised industries 1976–81. *Accounting and Business Research*, Winter.

Likierman, A. (1988) *Public Expenditure*, Penguin, Harmondsworth.

Likierman, A. and Vass, P. (1984) *Structure and Form of Government Expenditure Reports – proposals for reform*. Certified Accountants Educational Trust, London.

Local Government Act 1972.

Local Government Act 1988.

Local Government Finance Act 1982.

Local Government Finance Act 1988.

Local Government and Housing Act 1989.

Local Government Planning and Land Act 1980.

NAHAT (1991) *NHS Handbook* (7th edn), Macmillan Press, London.

National Association of Health Authorities (NAHA) (1988) *Funding the NHS: which way forward?* NAHA, Birmingham.

National Audit Office Annual Report. NAO, London.

National Audit Office, *A Framework for Value for Money Audits*. NAO, London.

National Audit Office, *Auditing Standards*. NAO, London.

National Audit Office, *Helping the Nation Spend Wisely*. NAO, London.

National Audit Office, *List of National Audit Office Value for Money Reports*. NAO, London.

National Audit Office (1986) *Financial Reporting to Parliament*, HC 576, HMSO.

NHS/DHSS Steering Group on Health Services Information (Chair, Mrs E. Körner) (1984) *Sixth Report on Financial Information*, HMSO, London.

PAC (1976–7) *Cash Limits*, 3rd Report, HC 274.

PAC (1977–8) *Supply Estimates and Cast Limits*, 4th Report, HC 299.

PAC (1978–9) *Parliamentary Control of Public Expenditure*, 3rd Report, HC 286.

PAC (1978–9) *The Work of the Committee of Public Accounts and the Status and Functions of the Comptroller and Auditor General*, 2nd Special Report, HC 330.

PAC (1979–80) *Parliamentary Control of Public Expenditure*, 13th Report, HC 570.

PAC (1980–1) *Treasury Carry-over of Cash Limits at the End of the Financial Year*, 14th Report, HC 376; 18th Report Session 1981–82, HC 383.

PAC (1981–2) *Publication and Content of Appropriation Accounts*, 8th Report, HC 383.

PAC (1986–7) *Financial Reporting to Parliament*, 8th Report, HC 98.

PAC (1988–9) *Financial Reporting to Parliament*, 18th Report, HC 354.

Packwood, T., Keen, J. and Buxton, M. (1991) *Hospitals in Transition: the resource management experiment*, Open University Press, Milton Keynes.

Perrin, J. (1984) Accounting for public sector assets, in *Issues in Public Sector Accounting* (eds A. Hopwood and C. Tomkins), Philip Allan, Deddington.

Perrin, J. (1988) *Resource Management in the NHS*, Chapman & Hall, London (in association with Health Services Management Centre, Birmingham).

Perrin, J. (1989) Management accounting, in *Public Sector Accounting and Financial Control* (3rd edn), VNR International, London.

Phyrr, P. (1970) Zero-base budgeting. *Harvard Business Review*, 43(12), 111–121.

Pliatzky, L. (1984) *Getting and Spending* (rev. edn), Basil Blackwell, Oxford.

Pliatzky, L. (1985) *Paying and Choosing*, Basil Blackwell, Oxford.

Pollitt, C. (1990) *Managerialism and the Public Services*, Blackwell, Oxford.

Prosser, A. (1986) *Nationalized Industries and Public Control*, Blackwell, Oxford.

Public Finance and Accountancy (1988) *Financial Management Initiative* (ten reprint articles with new foreword by Professor P. Jackson), CIPFA, London.

Public Finance Foundation (1991) *Public Domain* (annual report on the public sector), PFF with KPMG, London.

Royal Commission on Local Government in England, 1966–69 (1969) (the Redcliffe Maud Report), three volumes, Cmnd. 4040, HMSO, London.

Royal Commission on the NHS, Research Paper No. 2 (1978) *Management of Financial Resources in the NHS* (the Perrin Report), HMSO, London.

Royal Commission on the NHS (1979) *Report*, Cmnd. 7615, HMSO, London.

Rutherford, B.A. (1983) *Financial Reporting in the Public Sector*, Butterworths, London.

Scottish Home and Health Department (SHHD) (1986) *Health Building Procurement – Approval in Principle Conduct of Options Appraisals*, DGM (86), SHHD, Edinburgh.

Smith, P. (1990) *The Use of Performance Indicators in the Public Sector*, J.R. Statist. Society, A, 153, Part 1.

Stewart, J. (1983) *Local Government: the Conditions of Local Choice*, George Allen & Unwin, London.

Stewart, J. (1984) *The Politics of Local Government: Implications for Management Development – A Discussion Paper*, Local Government Training Board.

Stoker, G., Wedgwood-Oppenheim, F. and Davies, M. (1988) *The Challenge of Change in Local Government*, INLOGOV, Birmingham.

TCSC (1981) *Efficiency and Effectiveness in the Civil Service*, 3rd Report, Session 1981–2, HC 326.

TCSC (1981) *Budgetary Reform*, 6th Report, Session 1981–2, HC 137.

TCSC (1984) *The Structure and Form of Financial Documents Presented to Parliament*, 2nd Report, Session 1984–5, HC 110.

TCSC (1986) *Financial Reporting to Parliament*, 6th Report, Session 1986–7, HC 614.

TCSC (1988) *Financial Reporting to Parliament*, 6th Report, Session 1987–8, HC

TCSC (1989) *The Presentation of Information on Public Expenditure*, 6th Report, Session 1988–9, HC 217.

TCSC (1991) *The New System of Departmental Reports*, 5th Report, Session 1990–1, HC 2980.

TCSC (1991) *The Next Steps Initiative*, 7th Report, Session 1990–1, HC 496.

Thain, C. and Wright, M. (1990) Conceding Flexibility in Fiscal Management: The Case of Public Spending Year-end Flexibility. *Fiscal Studies*, 11(4).

Tomkins, C.R. (1987) *Achieving Economy and Effectiveness in the Public Sector*, Institute of Chartered Accountants of Scotland, Edinburgh.

HM Treasury (1976) White paper, *Cash Limits on Public Expenditures*, Cmnd. 6440, HMSO, London.

HM Treasury (1978) *The Nationalized Industries*, Cmnd. 7131, HMSO, London.

HM Treasury (1978) *The Test Discount Rate and the Required Rate of Return on Investment*, Treasury Working Paper No. 9.

HM Treasury (1982) *Investment Appraisal in the Public Sector*, HMSO, London.

HM Treasury (1988) *The Financing and Accountability of Next Steps Agencies.*

HM Treasury (1988) *The Management of Public Spending*, 2nd edition.

HM Treasury (1988) *A New Public Expenditure Planning Total*, Cmnd. 441, HMSO, London.

HM Treasury (1988) *Financial Reporting to Parliament*, Cmnd. 375, HMSO, London.

HM Treasury (1989) *The Financing and Accountability of Next Steps Agencies*, Cmnd. 914, HMSO, London.

HM Treasury (1989) *Trading Accounts: A Guide for Government Departments and Non-Departmental Public Bodies.*

HM Treasury (1990) *Central Government Borrowing: A New Presentation*, Treasury Bulletin, Summer.

HM Treasury (1991) *Economic Appraisal in Central government: A Technical Guide for Government Departments.*

Wickings, I., *et al.* (1983) Review of clinical budgeting and costing experiments, *BMJ* 286.

Widdicombe Report (1986) *The Conduct of Local Authority Business*, Cmnd. 9797, HMSO, London.

Wildavsky, A. (1975) *Budgeting: A Comparative Theory of Budgetary Processes*, Little Brown, Boston.

Wright, H.C. (1979) *The ZBB Process: A Practical Guide to Evaluation, Implementation and Use*, Society of Management Accountants of Canada.

Index